Hope That Springs Eternal

by

Esther Recinos

TEACH Services, Inc.
www.TEACHServices.com

**PRINTED IN
THE UNITED STATES OF AMERICA**

World rights reserved. This book or any portion thereof may not be copied or reproduced in any form or manner whatever, except as provided by law, without the written permission of the publisher, except by a reviewer who may quote brief passages in a review.

The author assumes full responsibility for the accuracy of all facts and quotations as cited in this book.

Copyright © 2010 TEACH Services, Inc.
ISBN-13: 978-1-57258-645-1
Library of Congress Control Number: 2010940786

Published by
TEACH Services, Inc.
www.TEACHServices.com

Dedication

I dedicate this book to the memory of my parents:

To Mamma, whose girlhood dream of going to Spanish-speaking countries and speaking Spanish brought all this about. In her humble way, she planted and watered a seed that has grown and borne fruit in the blessing of salvation and a better life to thousands of people.

And to Daddy, who worked so hard to make her dream a reality.

I look forward to the resurrection when they will see with joy the extent of the results of their sacrifice and loving work.

"And I heard a voice from heaven saying unto me, Write, Blessed are the dead which die in the Lord from henceforth: Yea, saith the Spirit, that they may rest from their labours; and their works do follow them" (Rev. 14:13).

Forward

When I was a child, I heard of an American missionary in one of the Spanish–speaking countries who was walking somewhere one day and saw a man riding a horse while his wife trotted along behind him with a load of wood on her back. The missionary, anxious to correct cultural evils, stepped out in front of the horse and its rider and asked the man reprovingly, "Why do you ride a horse while your wife walks along behind, carrying a load of wood?"

The man looked at the missionary and said condescendingly, "Because my wife has no horse!"

Sometimes we wonder why people of other cultures cannot see the obvious, and they sometimes wonder the same about us. I have found that human nature is the same the world over, regardless of custom or culture. It is the Spirit of God in the heart that makes a person kind, considerate, and courageous, and it is the spirit of the evil one that leads human beings, created in the image of God, to be cruel and indifferent to the sufferings or happiness of their fellow men.

I grew up in three countries—the United States, Mexico, and Guatemala—but most of my time was spent in Guatemala. I am very much American, but inside I am also Guatemalan. My husband is Guatemalan, and we have been happily married for nearly twenty years. For most of our married life, we have lived in Guatemala on a coffee farm, but we have also spent a considerable amount of time in the United States. In fact, we have a son who was born in Idaho.

I wrote the following stories of my experiences and those of some of my dear, brave friends in an effort to share with you how the Lord has led and continues to work in one small country called Guatemala. I have also included some stories from Mexico.

The fields in these and other countries are ripe for the harvest. The

Lord is raising up His humble servants to do the job. It is my prayer that the following stories will be a source of inspiration and blessing to you.

Sincerely,

Esther

Esther

Contents

Chapter 1	The Early Days	1
Chapter 2	Of Knocking on Walls and Burning Jails	8
Chapter 3	Eating and Pulling Teeth Under a Parachute	12
Chapter 4	The First Converts	20
Chapter 5	A Tap on the Shoulder	24
Chapter 6	Footprints in the Jungle	29
Chapter 7	Some Adventure and Some Folly	33
Chapter 8	Why Not Stay at a Hotel?	43
Chapter 9	Hot Rice Beverage and Sweet Bread	47
Chapter 10	Ahma Blommer	53
Chapter 11	A Set of Dentures	58
Chapter 12	Eye Infection	61
Chapter 13	Clinic Days	65
Chapter 14	A Hole in the Wall	75
Chapter 15	Little Starving Girls	83
Chapter 16	Man on a White Horse	88
Chapter 17	A New Township	95
Chapter 18	Money to Throw Away	101
Chapter 19	We Want Blood	113
Chapter 20	Ixcán	117
Chapter 21	Because of a Ride	130
Chapter 22	One Tiny Baby	135
Chapter 23	No Laughing Matter	141
Chapter 24	Holdup	145

Chapter 25	Angels	157
Chapter 26	The Blood of Jesus	167
Chapter 27	Santa Ana Invasion	176
Chapter 28	Some Battery Acid and a Prayer	182
Chapter 29	Soloma	185
Chapter 30	Providences	193
Chapter 31	Pastor Rudy	198
Chapter 32	In Perils Oft	204
Chapter 33	Led by the Spirit	210
Chapter 34	Limestone Oven	217
Chapter 35	Guerrilla Invasion	225
Chapter 36	Where Vengeance is a Way of Life	235
Chapter 37	Elena	243
Chapter 38	Some More Miracles	245
Chapter 39	To Raise a Child	255
Chapter 40	The Young Plantation Owner	260
Chapter 41	A Few Questions	270
Chapter 42	The Move Home	280
Epilogue		292

Chapter One

The Early Days

Five miles inside the border of Guatemala, in the department (or state) of Huehuetenango, was once a missionary clinic nicely situated on approximately ten acres of land. It was sandwiched between a beautiful little river and the Pan-American Highway, which for a few years was simply a little, narrow dirt road. Later it was paved and called the U.S. Military Highway.

I remember the place as a little tropical paradise under the brilliant blue sky, warmed by the penetrating rays of the sun and rich with citrus, mango, banana, and papaya trees.

Along the edge of the river, under the huge sabino and pomarrosa trees, was a little trail that was delightfully fun to run up and down in between swims in the slightly deeper parts of the river. During the rainy season months, the river would often come rushing down from the high mountains in a raging, muddy torrent that would sometimes overflow its banks.

Rich with the songs of birds, bright with the colorful butterflies that flitted about, and fragrant with the sweet smell of the honeysuckle bushes that grew along its banks, the little river trail proved to be a great attraction to a little barefoot girl with long blond braids.

The pomarrosa blossoms were white; they looked like long thick hair on little fairy dolls. When the blossoms fell off the trees and the fruit ripened then the fun began. Pomarrosa fruit is white. It is a spongy texture with big black seeds that shake a little in the middle, and the taste is like honeysuckle and rose petals blended together in a lovely fruit. I ate many of them as I played along the riverbanks, running up and down the trail.

During the rainy season my big sister and I loved to watch the storm clouds raise their giant heads into the deep blue sky and begin to rumble a warning of the cloudburst that would soon follow.

The memories of those days are sweet indeed, and we saw many people baptized in "our" river. But now I am getting ahead of my story.

My Adventist heritage goes back at least five generations on my mother's side through my grandmother and my great-grandmother to my great-great-grandmother, Lottie Emerson, a descendent of the royal family of England, whose father (we believe) joined the Advent movement around the year 1844. My grandpa, Sherman Booth, on my mother's side, was a descendent of a Huguenot who escaped to the American colonies.

My dear grandpa, Sherman Booth, was raised a Methodist in Pennsylvania. At age twenty-four he was working in Florida. One day he saw a billboard with pictures of ugly monsters on it and an announcement of sermons to be given on Daniel and Revelation. He determined to go and find out what it was all about. The first sermon "hooked" him, and he was soon baptized.

Shortly after that, he decided that he needed to find a different job. Somehow he found his way to a homestead farm in Saskatchewan, Canada, that was owned by my great-grandfather. I'm sure you've guessed it. He soon fell in love with Mary Etta, the beautiful brunette daughter of his German employer. They were married a few months

The Early Days

Grandpa and Grandma Booth on their wedding day. (Sherman Booth and Mary Etta Henkes). They were married in Saskatchewan, Canada in 1914.

later, but he soon discovered to his sorrow that his lovely Mary Etta had a very sharp tongue. Of course, he had solemnly vowed before God to love and cherish her until death should separate them, and that is exactly what he did. Grandpa died at ninety years of age in Guatemala in 1976, and Grandma lived on for another five years.

After working on the farm, Grandpa found a job teaching in the government schools on the Indian reservations in Nevada and Oregon. My mother, Iris, and her two brothers, Ernest and Elwood, grew up in these states. When his children reached the age of adolescence, Grandpa decided that they should have a Christian education, and he left the security of his job to move to College Place, Washington, so his children could go to school at Walla Walla College. That was a big step during the Depression, but although they saw hard times, the Lord didn't let them down.

Chester Green, father of the author. Graduated from Walla Walla College and married Iris Booth in the 1930s.

My father's ancestors came over on the Mayflower, so all in all, I was taught to appreciate our freedoms and to be thankful that I was born in the "great United States." I was also taught that we have a great responsibility to communicate our light and knowledge to the rest of the world. We are erring human beings who have been entrusted with a message of truth to give to our fellow men.

My father, Chester Green, one of seven children, was born in North Dakota in 1912. The family later took out a homestead in Alberta, Canada, where they lived for about ten years. Then they moved to the vicinity of Coeur D'Alene, Idaho. At the age of twenty-one, my daddy was an honest-hearted atheist. However, one evening he went to an evangelistic meeting being held by a Seventh-day Adventist preacher. That night the preacher spoke about the fascinating prophecies of Daniel, and Daddy's keen, discerning mind was fully convinced.

The Early Days

My daddy promptly began attending the local Adventist church. On the third week the minister said, "All those who want to go to heaven, please stand up."

Daddy looked around and saw several people standing, and he thought, I surely don't want to go to hell! It would be better to go to heaven. I had better stand with the others. So he stood to his feet, and the preacher took them out to the lake and baptized them.

When my daddy was baptized, he still believed in evolution; however, in due time he studied his way to becoming a died-in-the-wool Seventh-day Adventist. Before too long, he decided he needed an education, so he and some of his brothers and his sister enrolled at Walla Walla College. My daddy decided to pursue a theology degree. While attending college, he met and fell in love with my mother. They were married in 1939.

Upon graduating, my daddy was offered one of fourteen internships. Being a kind man, when he saw the bitter disappointment of another young man who did not get an internship, he generously gave him his own. Without an internship, my daddy took a job teaching church school for a very low salary. My parents both taught in the state of Washington for a few years, and it was there that my big sister, Bethel, and older brother, Jordan, were born.

Later my folks took a job teaching at a little missionary school on Lookout Mountain in Tennessee. Those were pioneer days, but now there is a thriving little church and school in that place comprised of the children and grandchildren of the children who my parents and others taught.

When my mother was a girl, she was fascinated with the Spanish language and people. She spent many hours studying Spanish on her own, in addition to her other studies. That is what led to Daddy and Mamma going to Mexico to help with mission work a couple

Iris Booth Green, mother of the author, Esther Recinos., graduated from Walla Walla College, and Married Chester Green in the 1930s

of years before I appeared on the scene. Those were days filled with fun and adventure for my parents and older brother and sister. Paved roads were uncommon in Mexico then—they would not even qualify as such today—and rivers for the most part had to be forded. In some places you could use a railroad trestle to cross the rivers as long as you timed it to cross between trains.

When it was nearly time for me to be born, my folks crossed the border and stayed in St. Helena, California. I was born in the Adventist hospital there. My sister was sixteen, and my brother, thirteen, at the time. My appearance created quite a stir in the family, and I never lacked for lots of attention. .

My first name is Rosalind, given to me by my sister. My second, Eugenia, was given to me by Mamma and was the name of one of the nurses who helped with my delivery. When it came Daddy's turn to give me a name, he said, "I will call her Esther, because perhaps she has 'come to the kingdom for such a time as this.'"

Daddy is asleep in Jesus now, but in that simple Bible name, he gave me a sense of direction and special meaning to my life that I will always cherish.

When it came Jordan's turn to give me a name, he shook his head wisely and said, "She won't want to be bothered with so many names. I won't give her one." And he was absolutely right. I appreciate the name that my borderline genius brother didn't give me as much as the ones the others did give me.

Chapter Two

Of Knocking on Walls and Burning Jails

When I was about one year old, my family moved bag and baggage (although they really didn't have much baggage) to Yerba Buena Mission in Chiapas, Mexico. Yerba Buena is located high up in some very rugged mountains, near a little town called "Pueblo Nuevo," meaning "New Town." The *Chamula* Indians live in those mountains. They wear bright, colorful costumes and speak the *sotzil* dialect.

My first memories are of Yerba Buena, the modest little house we lived in, the Mexican girls who helped care for me sometimes, and our American friends who ran the mission. Maurice Butler was the doctor who ran the clinic, and Ray and Marie Comstock were the founders of Yerba Buena. I will never forget the smell of pine, the abundant Spanish moss, and the grey days. We were about fifty miles from the nearest paved highway, and it took about eight hours to drive that fifty miles of rough road winding through the mountains.

In those days my father made several trips hauling truckloads of equipment from the U.S. to the mission. I wish he were alive to tell about the miracles the Lord performed at the international border crossings for him.

After a time it was necessary for Daddy to go back to the States to work and earn some much needed money. In addition, Bethel and Jordan needed to go to school, so they all left and my mother and I stayed behind.

Our little house was in a rather isolated spot, and Mamma was afraid the natives would come in during the night. There was no glass or screens on the windows, only wooden shutters. You either had to open them or close them, and Mamma decided to close them.

It was the second or third night on our own, and we had gone to bed. The door was bolted shut, and so were the shutters on the windows. Mamma left a kerosene lamp burning low all night. The lamp cast a soft glow on us as we knelt together for prayer. Mamma was holding me in her arms while kneeling on the bed, when suddenly a loud intermittent knocking began to resound all over the adobe walls. Mamma knew that knuckles don't make any sound knocking on adobe walls, and it sounded like someone knocking on hollow wood. The knocking came in a tango rhythm, and she knew it was not human.

She began to pray more fervently, and each time the knocking came, she felt a shielding shelter of protection over our heads. The knocking continued for about twenty minutes, then it grew fainter and fainter until it stopped altogether.

After the knocking stopped, Mamma said, "If the Lord can protect us from the devil who can get past locks and bolts, He can surely protect us from human beings also." And she left the doors and windows open after that so we could have fresh air at night.

Antonio Díaz and his sweet wife María were the first *Chamula* Indians in the area to turn away from devil worship and accept the Advent message. Antonio became a mighty missionary to his own people, and I'm sure his crown will be bright with thousands of stars.

Antonio was alert and intelligent, and he soon invented an alphabet and a way to read and write in the *sotzil* tongue. He then translated the Bible into that dialect, beginning with the New Testament. He would go on foot to the surrounding mountain villages for days at a time to preach to his people.

One day Antonio told María that he must leave again to preach in the mountain villages, and bidding her farewell, he took another young convert with him and started on his journey. After several days of traveling and preaching, they arrived at a village where prejudice against Christianity was strong. The people had been taught to mix shrine worship and burning candles to the saints with devil worship, and they wanted nothing to do with "the new religion."

Upon entering the village, Antonio and his friend were thrown into the jail, and the door was chained shut. A mob stood outside arguing about what to do with the hated preachers.

The jailhouse was a thatched roof hut, and it was government property by law. But the crowd grew bold, and someone shouted, "Burn the heretics!" With that, someone quickly lit a match and set fire to the thatched roof. In moments it went up in a blaze. The mob quickly scattered; no one wanted to be blamed for destroying government property.

Word soon reached María that she was a widow. She grieved for three long, lonely days. Then the door opened and in walked Antonio and his friend.

Turning pale, María whispered, "What happened?"

"Well," answered Antonio, "when the jail began to burn, we couldn't get out, so we began to sing like Paul and Silas. Suddenly the door just swung open, and there was no one outside, so we walked out and came home."

"An angel must have taken the chain off the door and let you out," whispered María reverently.

Of Knocking on Walls and Burning Jails

But the story didn't end there. Within a few years there was a thriving Adventist church in that village, and the man who lit the match to burn the jail down became the head elder.

Chapter Three

Eating and Pulling Teeth Under a Parachute

At the time of my birth, my father met a doctor in California by the name of Harold L. Graves. Dr. Graves expressed a desire to serve the Lord in a foreign mission field.

"I'm tired of just making money," he said. "Here I am one doctor among the many. I want to go to a place where there is no doctor, and no mission work has been started yet."

"Well," said my father, "lets take a trip and go find such a place."

So off they went through Mexico, searching for their mission field. But the price of land wasn't right, and the legalities for a foreigner purchasing property in Mexico made it impossible for them at that time.

At last they found themselves at the Mexican-Guatemalan border at the inland crossing of La Mesilla. "Well," said Daddy after they pondered the situation for a few minutes. "Why not? Maybe the Lord has the right place for you in Guatemala."

So they crossed the border and drove up the dirt road that had just been built the year before. Eight kilometers into Guatemala they found the right place. After negotiating the purchase of the land, they hurried back to the States to arrange the move to Guatemala.

Eating and Pulling Teeth Under a Parachute

Dr. Harold Leland Graves with his wife, Rosalee.

The Graves family included Harold and Rosalee and their three teenage children: John, Dick, and Marilee. Dr. Graves' mother also accompanied them. She was a precious lady who lived to be ninety-seven—she died and was buried in Guatemala, where she rests until the resurrection. I often heard her play the piano, singing beautiful old songs with her cheerful voice.

Upon arriving in Guatemala after a long, grueling trip over Mexico's dirt roads, they set up an old parachute on the land they had purchased. They then built a thatched roof supported by poles. The parachute served as kitchen, clinic, and dental office. They stacked old-fashioned wooden fruit crates on top of each other for shelves for medicine, dental tools, and dishes.

The thatched roof served as sleeping quarters and a shelter for their furniture. Grandma Graves slept in a tent. They lived in this fashion during the dry season.

Hope That Springs Eternal

After setting up shop, they soon discovered that they had inadvertently set up the parachute right over the path where the women of the neighborhood walked down to the river with their clay pots to get water. However, these ladies were not disturbed in the slightest by the parachute or the presence of the Graves family. They walked right through the kitchen with big friendly smiles. As soon as it became apparent that the spoons were disappearing, the parachute was moved away from the path. Many of these women were baptized later, and their children and grandchildren are a large part of the church there today.

It was at this time that we joined the Graves. The year was 1960, and I was two years old. My father and the doctor began building an adobe building to serve as the clinic. They were kindred spirits, and neither one of them thought it was very important whether or not the windows were straight, centered, or balanced. Looking at the overall picture, it was plain to see that there were other things of far greater magnitude to consider. The rainy season was approaching, and the roof was not on yet. Adobes melt when they are rained on, so this was a matter of concern. But they prayed and continued building.

In those days when Guatemala was still truly the "Land of Eternal Spring" and a tropical paradise, the weather followed a precise, uniform pattern. It was possible to predict the beginning of the rainy season to the very day. The natural resources of the country had not yet been exploited, and the jungle covered the mountainsides.

The first rain was expected on May 3, and that day arrived with the roof far from being finished. Dr. Graves and my father continued to work and pray, and the day passed as beautiful and cloudless as the day preceding it. The next day was clear as well, and the next, and the next, and many more, until the roof was finished.

Meanwhile the family had been moving all of their belongings and supplies in as fast as they could. Finally, the last roof tile was in

Eating and Pulling Teeth Under a Parachute

place, and the last of their belongings were inside. That night it rained ten inches, and three bridges were washed out on the road to Huehuetenango, which is the department or state capital, eighty kilometers away. The rainy season had held off for nineteen days!

For a time the people were suspicious of the new American doctor. They had never had a doctor in the area before, and the road was new as well. In fact, a short time before the road was put in, the only people living there who had ever seen an automobile were those who made the three-day journey on horseback to the town of Huehuetenango. The coffee plantation owners transported their harvested coffee by horseback to that little town, which at that time was mostly narrow dirt streets and adobe buildings with tile roofs. The coffee was sold to the representatives of Juan Waelti, an American company, or Intercafé, a German company.

When I was ten years old, Argentina, a fifteen-year-old girl who attended the little missionary school with me that year, told me the following story: "When I was five years old, there was no road here yet; only a trail for horses, mules, and people to walk on.

"One day a *gringo* came as far as Camojá on a motorcycle." (Camojá is pronounced Cah-moe-há. It is a little township about one half kilometer up the road from the clinic, which was in the little neighborhood or township of Valparaíso, a poetic name meaning "Valley of Paradise.")

She continued, "The people of Camojá and Valparaíso ran out of their huts and grabbed onto the motorcycle, forming a line all the way from where the clinic is to Camojá. The people in front were hanging onto the *gringo* and the motorcycle, and all the people all the way through the line were hanging onto the ones in front of them and shouting.

"The people all wanted to see what the motorcycle was, and with

Hope That Springs Eternal

Chester and Iris Green, author's parents. Iris's brother, Ernest Booth was the founder of Linda Vista College in Chiapas, Mexico. Chester and Iris graduated from Walla Walla college.

them all hanging on like that, the *gringo* couldn't go anywhere! After about three hours, the commotion died down enough for him to turn around and go back."

Motorized transportation was definitely a rarity. At the time that the Graves settled in Guatemala, there were a few little rickety buses in the area that transported people to Huehuetenango, which took about three hours one way over eighty kilometers or fifty miles of dirt road. They were old worn out school buses from the United States. With limited access to parts to repair them with, the resourceful Guatemalan folks who ran the bus lines were able to keep them running for quite a number of years.

Dr. Graves had an old car that he used as a little private taxi for about twenty years, transporting people to the Sunday morning market that was held in the little village of La Democracia about five kilome-

Eating and Pulling Teeth Under a Parachute

ters from the clinic going toward Huehuetenango. La Democracia was also the municipality, or county seat.

As I said earlier, the people were reluctant to start coming to the doctor for treatment. They were used to the witch doctors and spirit mediums, and human nature is always slow to accept something new.

One day, however, a fifteen-year-old young man was carried down to the clinic from a new township called "El Chalum," which had very recently been hacked out of the virgin forest in the mountains about eight kilometers away.

He was in critical condition. He could not open his mouth or talk, and it surely seemed that the grim reaper was stalking him. This boy worked on the coffee plantation of a man by the name of Eustaquio Matías Recinos. He was a broadminded, intelligent man who was always open to investigate new things.

When the boy returned home one Sunday from the market in the township of El Injerto with a strange sickness that grew progressively worse by the hour, Eustaquio directed the boy's family to carry him down at once to the American doctor. This they did, and he accompanied them himself to see that the boy was properly cared for.

Upon arriving at the clinic, Dr. Graves thoroughly examined the young man and discovered a small wound between his toes. He concluded that he had stepped on a rusty nail and contracted tetanus.

The doctor's medical supplies were limited, and the nearest drug store was eighty kilometers away in Huehuetenango. It was a six hour round trip, besides time spent waiting for the bus to come by and time spent buying the medicine in town, so Dr. Graves lost no time writing a prescription and sending Eustaquio after the medicine.

Meanwhile, they prayed earnestly for the recovery of the young man. They also sent someone after some pine wood to burn. They then took the charcoal, crushed it into a powder, and added it to a bucket of hot water to soak the boy's foot in. After a few minutes they put his foot into cold water for a few seconds, then back into hot water with the charcoal powder. They kept this up for hours until Eustaquio returned with the medicine. Then the doctor quickly injected it into the boy's foot.

The boy's family was delighted with his rapid recovery, and the news soon spread to all of the townships in the surrounding mountains. Soon the people began flocking to Dr. Graves, whom they called the "*Gringo*," for treatment.

It was not long before the Graves built a Spanish-style adobe house with garden space in the middle and rooms and a corridor all around it. They also built a high adobe wall around approximately two acres of land and put up big gates to keep out prowlers. The wall was protected with white plaster and clay tiles along the top with pieces of broken glass closely cemented all along the wall, thus discouraging anyone from trying to climb over. The gates also had sharp spokes at the top. Crime was practically nonexistent there in those days, but petty thievery and night prowlers were common.

Dr. Graves planted citrus trees of many varieties inside the walls around the house and left a beautiful garden space across the little driveway from the clinic. Eventually he also built a system to generate his own electricity.

The clinic was a two-story adobe building with a mosaic tile floor downstairs and a wooden floor upstairs. The staircase was outside on one end of the building. The upstairs was used for a Dorcas room and bedrooms for people who later came to live there and help the mission project. At one time they boarded students who attended classes at the little mission school, and they stayed upstairs in the clinic. It was all plain and simple, but very lovely.

The various rooms in the downstairs of the clinic were used for treating patients, and one section was used for a dental office. A small fee was charged each patient to help defray expenses, but if the patient could not pay, he or she was treated for free. Sometimes they paid with eggs or corn. Generous friends in the States also donated money and supplies to help support the mission project.

The place was called "Clínica Valparaíso," and eventually a pretty, inviting sign was painted and hung out at the entrance turning off the highway. Beneath the sign was a bench with a little roof over it where people could sit and rest.

Occasionally someone would go down to the little border town of La Mesilla to pick up the mail. It took a letter three months to a year to come from the States, or vice versa. And about half of the mail never arrived. But the letters that did come through were very much appreciated.

Chapter Four

The First Converts

*A*nastacio and Humberto Martínez were brothers who lived in La Democracia. They had an older brother named Pedro and some sisters. They also had many aunties, uncles, and cousins. Their father had died when they were quite young.

When Anastacio was eighteen, a neighbor man hung himself from the rafters of his hut. A few days later Anastacio and another young man were discussing it. "How could he ever do such a thing to himself? What does it feel like to die?" they asked each other.

Soon they agreed to try an experiment, and finding a rope, each boy tied one end around his neck in a slipknot. Then they climbed up into the rafters and dropped down on opposite sides of one beam, both suspended in midair by the same rope. Their weight pulled the rope tight around their necks, and because of the weight of the other boy, neither one could loosen the rope around his own neck.

There they hung, helplessly strangling, when a neighbor happened by, and seeing their predicament, quickly cut the rope with one swing of his machete. The two boys dropped to the ground, and the man launched into a tirade about their youthful folly. But the two young men were so glad to be alive that they were glad to listen respectfully to their rescuer's lecture.

The First Converts

One day the village of La Democracia buzzed with news of an American doctor who had come to live in the township of Valparaíso, five kilometers away. Masonry being the family profession, Anastacio decided to go see if they would hire him to help with their building. Sure enough, they were glad to hire him, so he took a few personal effects and worked and lived at Clínica Valparaíso for a time. Each evening Rosalee would hand him a silver fifty-cent piece. (The coins are now collectors items and worth a lot of money.)

After a short time, Anastacio sent for his younger brother, Humberto, to come and be his assistant. Upon arriving, Humberto found that the American family had a thing called a piano that one of the ladies would play for the family to sing with morning and evening. They also read from the Bible and prayed. That first evening Anastacio whispered to Humberto during the worship hour, "We must kneel when they do."

It was all new and interesting. The Graves were learning Spanish, and the young people of the family learned it much more quickly than their parents.

As time went by, the gospel leaven did its work, and Humberto asked to be baptized. It was a happy day when the pastor came out from Huehuetenango and performed the baptism in the river.

Anastacio liked to drink and go to the "fiestas," so he was a little more slow to make his decision. But before long he also requested baptism.

In the beginning, the Graves selected bright, promising young men from among the converts and paid them a small salary to go out and preach and give Bible studies full time. The salary was equivalent to what they made working on the coffee plantations. The money for their salaries was supplied by friends in the States, and the plan proved to be a great success right from the start. These young lay evangelists were the right-hand helpers of the district pastor, and the work grew from one small church in the department capital of Huehuetenango to many churches and branch Sabbath Schools all over the entire department.

Humberto was one of the young men who went out to "harvest" the fields. He became a much loved and trusted lay evangelist in the area, and eventually he married Barbara Pierson, an American girl who went to Guatemala to help with mission work. They now live in Texas and have two beautiful daughters about twenty and twenty-one at the time of this writing.

Anastacio married a lovely girl by the name of Rosaura from a village called El Tablón, about thirty kilometers from La Democracia and Valparaíso. In those days it was accessible only by foot trails.

Anastacio and Rosaura had a son whom they named Felman, after Luís Felman, a Seventh-day Adventist German immigrant living in Guatemala City at the time. Mr. Felman was a good friend and help to Dr. Graves. He was kidnapped once and held for ransom by the communist guerrillas. Fortunately, he was released, and he started a successful prison ministry in Guatemala City before he died.

Anastacio and Rosaura's second child was a girl whom they called María Magdalena, calling her Magda for short.

Felman later attended our SDA boarding academy in the department of Petén, Guatemala. He then went on to graduate from the university of San Carlos in Guatemala. For lack of funds, he was unable to attend our college in Costa Rica, but he is now working for the Seventh-day Adventist Church. His sister, Magda, graduated with training as a bilingual secretary.

This little family proved to be our most trusted and devoted friends during all those years of happiness and laughter, and the times of perplexity as well.

Those were small beginnings, but the results have been amazing.

At the time of this writing, thirty-four years later, there are now thousands of Seventh-day Adventist Christians in that part of the country, comprising many churches and branch Sabbath school groups. In Guatemala each district pastor has many churches under his care, and the laymen are very active. The pastors and laymen alike are self-sacrificing, humble people whose greatest goal in life is to lead precious souls to Jesus Christ.

And as I said before, this is by no means the end of the story!

Chapter Five

A Tap on the Shoulder

After seeing that the Graves were getting situated, my family went back to the States for a few months. Daddy worked as a logger to earn some much-needed money, and we visited my sister and brother where they were going to school. During the next few years we split our time between Guatemala, Mexico, and the States, spending a few months of the year in each country.

In the process of helping some Mexican orphans, my parents met Lucas and Eva Hernandez, a delightful couple from Pachuca, Hidalgo, which is located about eighty kilometers from Mexico City. Eva's father was the first ordained Seventh-day Adventist minister in Mexico.

Uncle Lucas and Aunt Eva, as I grew up calling them, had both joined the church many years before in their youth. But the anxieties of trying to make a living in a poverty stricken country soon led Lucas to take a job in the silver mine in Pachuca, which required working six days a week including the seventh, called *sábado* in Spanish, which means "Sabbath." Lucas knew it to be the scriptural day of rest, and he was not happy with his job.

Sometimes he would read Genesis 2:1-3: "Thus the heavens and the earth were finished, and all the host of them. And on the seventh day God ended his work which he had made; and he rested on the seventh day from all his work which he had made. And God blessed the seventh day, and sanctified it: because that in it he had rested from all his work which God created and made."

"Jesus kept the Sabbath," he would say to himself while he worked, "but I am not keeping it." The words of Mark 2:28 would ring in his ears where Jesus said, "Therefore the Son of man is Lord also of the sabbath," referring to the seventh-day Sabbath. *The apostles kept the Sabbath, and neither Jesus nor they changed it*, he thought.

Passages of scripture such as the fourth commandment in Exodus 20:8-11 would flash into his mind: "Remember the sabbath day, to keep it holy. Six days shalt thou labour, and do all thy work: But the seventh day is the sabbath of the LORD thy God: in it thou shalt not do any work, thou, nor thy son, nor thy daughter, thy manservant, nor thy maidservant, nor thy cattle, nor thy stranger that is within thy gates: For in six days the LORD made heaven and earth, the sea, and all that in them is, and rested the seventh day: wherefore the LORD blessed the sabbath day, and hallowed it."

Then he would think of the words of Jesus in John 14:15: "If ye love me, keep my commandments." And Matthew 5:17 and 18 says, "Think not that I am come to destroy the law, or the prophets: I am not come to destroy, but to fulfil. For verily I say unto you, Till heaven and earth pass, one jot or one tittle shall in no wise pass from the law, till all be fulfilled."

The voice of the Holy Spirit would whisper to him, "Jesus loves you. He died for you. John 3:16 says, 'For God so loved Lucas that he gave his only begotten Son, that if Lucas believeth in him he shall not perish, but have everlasting life.' Come and work in my vineyard," pleaded the Holy Spirit.

"But how will I earn a living?" countered Lucas.

Back came the answer: "My God shall supply all your need according to his riches in glory by Christ Jesus."

"But how, Lord?" Lucas responded.

The Holy Spirit brought Matthew 6:25-33 to his mind: "Therefore I say unto you, Take no thought for your life, what ye shall eat, or what ye shall drink; nor yet for your body, what ye shall put on. Is not the life more than meat, and the body than raiment? Behold the fowls of the air: for they sow not, neither do they reap, nor gather into barns; yet your heavenly Father feedeth them. Are ye not much better than they? . . . Therefore take no thought, saying, What shall we eat? or, What shall we drink? or, Wherewithall shall we be clothed? (For after all these things do the Gentiles seek:) for your heavenly Father knoweth that ye have need of.all these things. But seek ye first the kingdom of God, and his righteousness; and all these things shall be added unto you."

For thirty-five years Lucas worked in the mine and struggled with his conscience. During that time he built a two-story house on a steep hillside of Pachuca where much of the city was built, with rugged, rocky desert mountains towering just overhead.

Lucas and Eva's home was lovely. In the enclosure behind the house, they had a little bit of ground terraced for a garden, and some for a chicken yard. It was closed in with high walls, with close neighbors on every side. The street leading up to it was very steep and rocky.

My mother and I stayed with them for six months one year, then six months the next year. We always stopped to visit them on our trips to and from Guatemala, and they were always eager to welcome us with cordial, Mexican hospitality. "*Mi casa es su casa,*" meaning, "My house is your house," was a saying I heard often. And they meant it with all their hearts. They would run to meet us with arms wide open when we came, and my parents would visit with them for many hours. They affectionately called my parents "Papá Chester" and "Mamma Iris."

A Tap on the Shoulder

During our first stay of six months, my mother and Uncle Lucas studied the Bible together quite often. One morning at the breakfast table Mamma said to him, "Well, Lucas, when are you going to quit the mine?"

The question hit him like a thunderbolt, but he said nothing. Pretty soon he went out and climbed up to those rocky, forbidding mountain heights and knelt to pray.

"Oh God, what shall I do?" he cried in despair.

Suddenly a hand tapped him on the shoulder, and a voice said, "Mamma Iris is the messenger of the Lord. Obey her!" He quickly looked around, but he saw no one.

He continued to pray for some time. Again the hand tapped him on the shoulder, and again the voice said, "Mamma Iris is the messenger of the Lord. Obey her!" Again he looked around, and again he saw no one.

He continued praying for hours, until his decision was made. Then he went and resigned from his job at the mine. Soon after his resignation, the Mexican government gave him a good-sized tract of land in the Lacandón Indian country in the state of Tabasco. His land was within half a kilometer of the Guatemalan border over by Petén. It was a two-day hike from the end of the road to his land, but he heard God's call to work among the Lacandón Indians.

Aunt Eva stayed on at Pachuca for some time until the house sold. Then she moved to Estación Zapata, a few kilometers from the end of the road. Her health was not good enough to live in the jungle, but she got as close as she could so he could visit her as often as possible. She no longer lives in a two-story house. She lives in a little one-room tin building in the steamy heat of Tabasco.

She is now an old lady nearly blind, but she has raised up a group of believers in that town. She has also suffered persecution. Her life is

Hope That Springs Eternal

hard, but she is cheerful and her faith is strong. My mother sends her one hundred dollars a month from her social security check, and that is what Eva lives on.

Chapter Six

Footprints in the Jungle

*L*ucas worked hard to clear his land and plant crops. He would have liked to have left some of it as virgin jungle, but if he did, the Mexican government would take it back. He had to cultivate it all if he wanted to keep it.

It wasn't easy to clear the land with machete and hoe, so he hired some of the Lacandón Indians to help him. Lucas was a brilliant man who knew something about everything. In the jungle, his knowledge of plants and herbs for first aid came in handy. He was able to help the native Lacandón Indians as well as look after his own health. Not only did he help them physically, but he helped them spiritually. The Indians he hired to help him clear his land were converted before too long.

Lucas always told us miracle stories from his time in the jungle. One story in particular stayed deeply impressed in my mind.

One time Lucas needed to go to town for supplies. That was while Eva was still in Pachuca, and he wanted to make a trip to see her, too. So, early one morning he started off on the by-this-time-familiar trail through the jungle with a hammock and some other necessary things on his back.

He hiked until about noon. Looking around, he was startled to find that he was lost in the jungle. He walked for about an hour searching for the path, but without success. It was so strange to get lost from the trail like this, and he knew that if he did not find it soon, he would be in a serious predicament. Ordinarily he would arrive at the hut about dusk where he usually spent the night during his trips to and from civilization. And to be lost in the jungle at night without protection would be dangerous. There were wild animals and poisonous snakes and insects that would be very hard to contend with in the dark.

But as he had become accustomed to do in all emergencies, he dropped to his knees out there in the jungle and prayed. "Lord, I don't know why I lost the trail, but I sure do need to find it quickly! Otherwise, I will not arrive at the hut before darkness comes. Please help me!"

Just then he heard a voice say, "Go to your right." He looked to the right and saw only a solid wall of jungle.

"Lord," he cried, "are you sure?"

Again the voice repeated, "Go to your right."

"All right, Lord," he said, "I will."

With that he rose from his knees and resolutely began to cut a path through the jungle in the direction that the voice had indicated. It was slow going, and Lucas sweated profusely in the steamy heat of the dense jungle growth. The hours wore away. Finally, after what seemed like an eternity of hacking out a trail with his machete, he suddenly stepped out onto the path he had lost, only much farther ahead of the place where he could definitely remember having last been on the right trail. In fact, he was so much farther ahead that he was almost to the hut where he would sling his hammock from the rafters to sleep in that night before continuing the second half of his journey to the highway the next day.

A few minutes after he had arrived at the hut, a tourist guide with two European couples came to the hut also. Night was just beginning to fall, and they had been hiking hard all day.

"Are we ever glad to find this hut!" They exclaimed when they saw Lucas. "We are so tired and hungry!" After purchasing some food from the residents of the hut, they sat down to eat on the ground near the fire. One of the ladies peered at Lucas curiously through the fast gathering darkness. "Where is your wife?" She asked in heavily accented Spanish.

"My wife is far away near Mexico City," replied Lucas. "I am traveling alone."

"But you have a traveling companion who was hiking with you today," the other lady said in slightly easier to understand Spanish. "We know, because we followed your trail and saw the footprints."

"What footprints?" queried Lucas.

"Yours and those of your traveling companion. We were lost in the jungle, and we found a freshly cut path. We were deliberating about whether or not it would be safe to follow, because it might lead us nowhere, and we needed to find a hut where we could stay for the night before dark. Then we noticed two sets of fresh footprints leading all along the trail, and we concluded that they must belong to a man and his wife. One set was larger, the other smaller, like a man and a woman. We thought surely we would find a hut if we followed the trail, and sure enough, we did. We know that you made the trail, but where is the person that was hiking with you on that trail today? If it had not been for the second set of footprints, we would not have ventured to follow."

"My traveling companion is the angel of God," replied Lucas reverently. "He led me off the path into the jungle and let me think that I was lost in order to lead you to safety. I serve a great God."

"Tell us more about him!" They exclaimed, almost in unison. Lucas shared his faith that night as they all lay in their hammocks. The next morning he offered them some tracts to read that he carried with him to give away to anyone who might be interested in reading religious magazines, and they gladly accepted them.

"You see," said Uncle Lucas when he told the story. "God works in mysterious ways to bring us in contact with the very people who need our Christian witness. Never despair when things go wrong because God has a wise purpose in all He does. We must trust Him at all times, and not worry."

Chapter Seven

Some Adventure and Some Folly

My sister Bethel married Mike Gordon when I was almost five years old. After a Sabbath afternoon fellowship dinner, they stood up and said their wedding vows. This took place in College Place, Washington, in someone's back yard. Shortly thereafter they went to Escondido, California, and worked for my uncle Ernest Booth for several months. He was a biologist who traveled worldwide and published a magazine called *Outdoor Pictures*.

A short time later my mother decided to go there and work for my other uncle, Elwood Booth, in his College Biological Supply Company for a few months. Daddy was away logging, and money was needed.

My two uncles had their homes and businesses on some acreage that they called "The Booth Ranch." Grandpa and Grandma Booth lived there too, and Mamma and I stayed with them. I soon grew weary of Grandma's "tongue lashings." Grandpa Booth, however, was a dear old man who was loved and respected by all. Grandpa worked for Uncle Elwood packaging embalmed cats to ship to medical schools. He did it mainly to escape from Grandma's tongue.

Lloyd and Sandy Cripe, a young couple who were friends of Mike and Bethel and were married about the same time, got it into their blood to go to Guatemala for a time and help with mission work.

Bethel and Mike planned to go after saving up some money, but Lloyd persuaded them to go sooner than had been previously planned.

Sherry and Lou, two girls of eighteen years, were anxious for some adventure and wanted to know if they could accompany the traveling caravan in a little old pickup that Sherry had. They were enthusiastically welcomed, and as preparations were being made for the journey, I saw my opportunity to escape Grandma's verbal assaults, so I asked my mother for permission to go along.

In my mind I contrasted the pleasant, smiling faces of the adventuresome young people to Grandma's scowling one. I told Mamma that I wanted to go along because I liked "the looks of their faces."

It must have been hard for Mamma to part with her small five-year-old girl. I know she would have loved to accompany us, but as mothers so often do, she was willing to stay behind and do what needed to be done while the young people went in search of adventure.

Grandma perceptively discerned my motive for going and had her say about it. She had a kind heart underneath her scowling exterior, and she would do no one wrong, but it was hard for a little girl to understand that. So bidding Mamma and the Booths farewell, off I went to Guatemala.

There were three pickups in the caravan: one belonging to Mike and Bethel, one to Lloyd and Sandy, and one to Sherry and Lou. Those old pickups could go as fast as forty miles an hour, and that was pretty fast for the kind of roads that Mexico had then.

We crossed the border into Mexico at Tijuana and began the long journey south. Each day was packed with excitement and adventure for the young people, with plenty of new sights to see. And never did a little girl have a big sister who took better care of her.

After a few days, I became deathly ill with dysentery. I couldn't hold anything in my stomach, not even water. In the years since then,

Some Adventure and Some Folly

I have seen children become dehydrated and die in a few hours time with the vomiting and violent diarrhea. My sister understood the gravity of the situation, and she constantly prayed for me. The little caravan parked in the desert, and I lay listlessly on a blanket in the shade made by the truck.

I believe it was the morning of the fifth day when Lloyd came to me with a small glass of water. Calling me by my nickname, he said, "Pumpy, here is a glass of water. Your body needs it badly. We are going to pray that you will be able to keep it down; then I want you to drink it."

Setting me on his lap, we bowed our heads while Lloyd prayed. Then I drank the glass of water, and from that moment on, I made a speedy recovery.

A few days later, Lloyd came down with dysentery, and the little caravan stopped again somewhere near the city of Tuxtla Gutierrez in Chiapas. Lloyd parked his pickup under a scrubby desert tree, and taking a blanket, he crawled up on top of his camper and laid down.

The *zopilotes* (vultures) flocked to the little tree and filled the branches only three feet above his head. They spread their wings as if ready to pounce on his flesh the very moment he died, and indeed, he felt like he was dying. The natives believe that *zopilotes* can smell death before it arrives. I don't know how true that is, but it sure looks as if that is the case sometimes. The others must not have been feeling so well themselves, because we saw very little of them. However, Bethel took her post beside the tree, keeping the vultures shooed away. But they were like flies, circling around for a few seconds, then coming right back and landing in the tree just above Lloyd's head again. She had to chase them away constantly.

After a time the rest of the group decided to go on to Guatemala and leave Lloyd to recuperate and finish the last part of the journey on his own. The border was approximately 300 kilometers away. A few days later Lloyd and Sandy came straggling in, somewhat the worse for wear. At least the vultures had not gotten to make a meal of Lloyd. He and Sandy were both just eighteen years old.

During the next three months, Mike and Bethel built a little two-room adobe house on the lower end of the Graves' property, within a few feet of the river, under the shade of the big sabino and pomarrosa trees. Lloyd built a small two-story adobe house next door with two rooms downstairs and two upstairs, with a ladder to go up and down on. Next door to them the doctor also built a little two-room house of adobes to be used as a guest house or hotel.

Mike and Lloyd had fun trying to help the hired native Guatemalans mix the mud with their feet down in the big mud pits they dug. They then mixed in the dry pine needles and set the mixture into the adobe molds to dry.

One day I was playing outside under a big tree that shaded the Graves' house when to my surprise I found a medium-size nest that had fallen out of the tree with a featherless baby bird in it. I gently scooped up the bird and, placing it back in its nest, ran with it to Bethel. She immediately took in under her "wing." She loved all of God's little creatures, and for several days she did a fine job of feeding it with an eye dropper. We kept it in its nest, and it seemed to be content there.

In the daytime we placed the nest in a small tree in the flower garden area in the middle of the Graves' house. At night we took it to our room upstairs in the clinic and covered it so it would be warm. It sang a lovely song to us early every morning.

One evening Lloyd said the bird was not getting enough to eat. So, taking it from its nest in the little tree, he began poking big pieces of banana down the throat of the unwilling baby bird.

The next morning our little featherless friend didn't sing its usual

Some Adventure and Some Folly

song. Wondering why, Bethel stood over its nest, which was cozy under a little doll blanket, and softly whistled a little tune similar to the one the little bird sang every morning. But our little friend was dead and couldn't wake up. We took it outside and sadly buried it. I will be so happy when we all go to that land where no one ever dies.

When the houses were nearly completed, my mother arrived on the scene, and my happiness was complete. About this time Bethel and Mike moved out of the upstairs room in the clinic and into their new house. Mamma and I took over the upstairs room in the clinic.

Shortly after that, a delightful lady by the name of Mary Lou Jones came to Clínica Valparaíso with her four sweet children—Linda, twelve, Melody, eight, Lula Mae, six, and Willy, just three years old.

Mary Lou was a big health fan, and at her instigation, she and her children and Mamma and I would sit on a blanket under the orange and mango trees behind the Graves' house and eat produce from the garden for our meals. Mary Lou believed in eating raw fresh food, but one day she wanted to try some black beans. She greatly enjoyed culinary experiments and thought of a way to eat black beans without cooking them. She was so happy. Now she could have her raw food and eat black beans too!

Now, black beans are good for you when they are thoroughly cooked, but they are high in uric acid and are poisonous when they are raw. But Mary Lou didn't know that, and besides, she was an adventuresome person. Perhaps it did not occur to her that the unknown could be dangerous. In order to succeed, we sometimes fail, and this little experiment proved to be a small disaster.

She soaked the beans overnight, then heated them to the boiling point, added some salt, and presto, lunch was ready. Little Willie and I ate the most. Perhaps it was because we were the youngest and craved protein on our all-raw food diet. Unfortunately, soon after lunch, we began to vomit and were quite sick for several hours. Maybe the others were sick, too, because I don't remember seeing much of them during that time.

Mary Lou later wrote and published a fine cookbook. It is obvious that those who never try, never fail—and never succeed!

It wasn't long until Mary Lou needed to go to the States, and she asked Mamma to keep her children until she returned. My mother generously obliged, and Mary Lou left on the bus. They were nice children, and I had a lot of fun with them. Mamma wisely appointed Linda as the "little mother," and she enjoyed the responsibility. With arms outstretched she would say to Willie or Lula Mae, "Come to Mother," and they would come running. They loved their kind big sister.

One afternoon Sherry and Lou went swimming in the river. While they were there, a carload of border officials came by on the little road that ran parallel to the highway across from the river. Seeing the girls, they stopped and proceeded to dive into the water to swim with them. The girls quickly got out of the water to go home, but not before the men informed them that they were coming that very afternoon to ask the doctor for their hands in marriage.

There were two guys for each girl, and I personally think they were just teasing them, but Sherry and Lou were frightened. So they decided to leave for the States that same afternoon. Harold and Rosalee were concerned for their safety. They didn't want them to drive across Mexico alone. So it was decided that my mother and I and Mary Lou's children would accompany them. Daddy had gotten a logging job in Alaska, and we wanted to go be with him anyway.

Melba, a young Guatemalan girl, wanted to go to the States and asked to go along. She had been helping in the clinic, but now saw a chance for some adventure.

The girls agreed to take her along, but my mother told them they

Some Adventure and Some Folly

needed to take her to the U.S. Embassy in Guatemala City 300 kilometers away and apply for a tourist visa for her. But the girls were too anxious to leave and thought they could take her to the U.S. Embassy in Mexico City on the way to the States.

Then Mamma told Melba that in all likelihood she would not be able to get into the United States. But Melba wanted to try anyway, so we all loaded up the truck and started on our way.

Yerba Buena Mission is about 240 kilometers from the Mexican-Guatemalan border, and Sherry's pickup was on the verge of breaking down, so we went there first and stayed for three days while kind friends repaired her truck.

From there we headed toward Pachuca where we would stay while Sherry and Lou tried to get a visa in Mexico City for Melba. A little ways into Oaxaca it began to rain. It was night, and the rain was so bad that Sherry and Lou, hoping to drive out of the storm, drove all night.

Mamma, the Jones kids, and I slept in the little makeshift camper that consisted of boards on the sides and a canvas over the top. We didn't sleep much that night because the rain pored in so bad it created a mini flood in the back of the pickup.

Everyone and everything was thoroughly soaked, so we stopped the next day at a river where we could bathe and dry our bedding. We hung the mattress, blankets, and sheets on the railing of the bridge to dry. It was Sabbath morning, so we stayed until evening. By Saturday night everything had dried and we continued on our way.

At Pachuca we visited Aunt Eva, and she helped us find a garage where we could get some more repair work done on the old pickup. After finding the garage, Mamma gave Eva some money to return home in a taxi, but she walked and saved the money. My mother and us children stayed with the truck to protect it while Sherry and Lou took Melba to Mexico City via bus to try and get her a visa at the U.S. Embassy.

That evening the night watchman at the garage talked to Mamma for quite a while about Christianity. He said that he too was a Christian. Later that night, however, he came to the truck and woke my mother and began to harass her. She reminded him of their previous conversation about Christianity, but it did no good. Then she said to him, "You are the night watchman here, and it is your responsibility to protect us. That is why we came to THIS garage, confident that we would be safe."

Upon hearing that, he went away and left her alone. He knew that if a bad report about him reached his employer, he would very likely lose his job. And he couldn't afford that.

The next day a forlorn threesome returned from Mexico City without the visa. They were told that Mexicans apply for tourist visas at the U.S. Embassy in Mexico City, and Guatemalans at the one in Guatemala City. But Sherry and Lou were determined to try to get her across the U.S. border.

Farther on the trip, a tire blew out one night. There was not much room to get off the road, and there were a lot of trucks going by. Sherry asked Mamma to pray that a truck wouldn't hit us while she changed the tire. Night vision was poor, and we were in a rather vulnerable position.

The door on the right-hand side of the pickup had been left open, and soon a car came whizzing right around us on that side away from the highway, ripping the door off as it passed. We were all very frightened, thinking that the police had come after us for some unfathomable reason. But it turned out to be a kind man who had stopped to help the girls change the tire. He didn't have any brakes, so he had to coast to a stop. The door, however, helped him to stop a little sooner than he had anticipated.

In Mexico accidents can result in jail time whether you are at fault

Some Adventure and Some Folly

or not. So neither the man nor we were anxious to have the accident reported. He worked for about three hours in the dark trying to repair the door. He finally got it so it would stay on if we were careful.

The next day the spare tire blew out, so Sherry bought a second-hand tire, but that soon blew out as well. Finally, she bought a new one, and that one stayed in-tact.

When we got to Mazatlán, Sherry stopped, and everyone had fun at the beach for a while. We all got a little sunburned, but poor little red-headed Lula Mae was blistered. After that we had to be careful how we moved about in the crowded little camper, so we wouldn't hurt her sore back and shoulders. She was a brave little girl who never cried once.

The problems with the pickup continued to increase. The radiator kept overheating, and the repair work done at the garages along the way would only last for a little while each time. Finally, we reached Tijuana and stopped to get the load "ready" for inspection. The girls cut up the sugar cane they had bought along the way and hid it in the bedding.

When we got to the U.S. border crossing, the officials said Melba could not enter the United States. They also found the sugar cane pieces and told us we could suck the juice out of them there but that we couldn't cross with it.

We went back into Tijuana to find a place for Melba to stay over the weekend until she could get on the bus and go back to Guatemala. But instead the girls decided to try to smuggle her across, so they hid her under the bedding with the luggage and boxes. But when we got back to the border, the customs officials, while pleasant, were not to be fooled. The man doing the inspecting began to take everything out.

"What do we have here? A dog?" he joked as he uncovered Melba's hair. Finally, he uncovered her completely and said, "OK, you can come out now."

Hope That Springs Eternal

Then they took Sherry and my mother into an office, and F.B.I. agents questioned them together and separately. Finally, they decided to overlook it since Sherry was a minor and my mother only a passenger riding with her. But they warned her that she could get into serious trouble should she ever try such a thing again.

Thus we went back to Tijuana to find a place for Melba to stay. We found one in the slums. The poverty was incredible. The family that Melba stayed with kept their baby in a dresser drawer instead of a bed.

While we were there, a little ragged boy came in with a note from his mother asking for contributions so she could buy some medicine. They dropped a coin into his cup, and he went on to the next house. The lady of the house where we were visiting told my mother that they all do that when they need something extra like medicine. Otherwise no one would ever have enough money to buy any.

So ended a memorable trip through Mexico, and Mamma and I went on to Alaska to be with Daddy. Later we all went back to Guatemala together.

Chapter Eight

Why Not Stay at a Hotel?

*W*e traveled many times through Mexico by bus. I was seven years old on one of these trips when my parents and I stopped at Tuxtla in Chiapas and stayed overnight in a hotel. A young Mexican girl by the name of Josefina was accompanying us. We were on our way to Yerba Buena Mission, and Josefina, needing to have her appendix removed, was traveling with us because it was neither safe nor considered proper for young ladies to travel alone in Mexico. Her mother was glad for the opportunity to send her to the mission for treatment. By this time the little hospital had grown quite efficient.

Needing to get something to eat for supper and some food to have with us on the bus the next day, we decided to go to the nearest market. The approximately 160-kilometer trip from Tuxtla to Yerba Buena over the rough roads would take all day.

We were just getting ready to step out of our upstairs room in the hotel when we heard two gunshots downstairs in the lobby. Rushing down to see what the commotion was all about, we saw a lady lying on the floor, apparently unconscious, and her husband kneeling over her. Her abdomen appeared to be rapidly filling with blood, and her breathing was labored and uneven.

There was a theater joining the hotel, and the entrance to the theater was only accessible through the lobby of the hotel. The lady and her husband had been in the midst of the crowd of people when she was shot.

A large crowd gathered, and a pickup soon came by and stopped to take her to the hospital. Two men picked her up and threw her into the back of the pickup as if she were a gunnysack full of corn. One of her shoes fell off, and one of the men picked it up and tossed it into the truck. Then her husband climbed in, and off they went.

The grapevine is quite efficient in those parts, and we soon heard that the lady was a schoolteacher and that she had sat in her classroom crying the day before because she heard that her husband had an enemy. Some of the people in the crowd, however, whispered that her husband had made up the whole thing and hired a man to get rid of his wife, pretending that he was the real target.

We shuddered as we hurried toward the market, and Josefina said, "It is not good to go to the theater. It is better to go to church."

We finished our journey to Yerba Buena Mission where we rested overnight before continuing our trip. Our next stop was Pichucalco, so we boarded a bus for the trip. We were traveling with Eva and Lucas. After quitting his job at the mine, Lucas heard of a "farm" for sale near a little town called Los Choapas in Veracruz, near the state of Chiapas in the lowlands. Lucas was considering the possibility of starting some mission work somewhere, and he wanted to go see it. So he, Eva, Mamma, and I were making a bus trip to that part of the country.

It couldn't have been more than a hundred kilometers, but the trip took most of the day. The bus was crowded with people and animals, and as we slowly descended from the mountains into the lowlands, the heat became intense. My neck broke out with heat rash, and the sweat trickling down made it burn.

It was a relief to arrive in Pichucalco and get off the bus. It was late afternoon, so we went to find a hotel. After renting a small room for the night, we went to the market to get something to eat. The cool, fresh tomatoes that we bought tasted good, and after eating, we retired for the night.

The room consisted of two narrow beds about three feet apart. Since sunset had brought no relief from the heat, we left the door open in the hopes of getting a bit of fresh air. My mother and I lay on one bed, and Eva and Lucas on the other.

For a while it was so hot that none of us could sleep. Not a breeze was stirring, and we lay uncovered. Being a child and tired from the long bus ride, I managed to drift off to sleep before any of the others.

It was about midnight, and Mamma was still awake, fanning herself with a newspaper. Suddenly she saw a dark silhouette of a hand reach up in the darkness over the foot of the bed and start to feel around her feet, as if searching for something.

Sitting up, she saw the shape of a man in the dark, crouched by her bed. Hitting him on the back with the newspaper, she yelled, "Lucas!" At that, the man jumped up and ran out the door. He was wearing nothing but a pair of undershorts. Lucas jumped up and sprinted out the door right behind him, but he could see no sign of anyone when he got out into the open enclosure of the hotel. Evidently the man was occupying a room near us and got inside before Lucas had a chance to see where he went.

In our room were a couple of old chairs and some glass pop bottles. Hoping to discourage any more would-be burglars, Lucas, Eva, and Mamma piled these in the doorway. When the burglar trap was finished to perfection, they went back to bed, but they slept very little for the rest of the night.

The next day we took an old, rickety train out to Los Choapas. It was a three-hour ride through the jungle, at about thirty miles an hour.

Hope That Springs Eternal

We rode in an open boxcar, crowded in with many smelly bodies, pigs, dogs, and chickens.

At length we arrived at the "farm" that was for sale. We found a tract of land cleared out of the jungle with a few banana, orange, and lemon trees growing on it. On a hill at the center of the property was a thatched roof hut. Lucas approached the hut and spoke with the man who wanted to sell the property.

We soon left because Lucas said the man was asking way too much for it. Before long, we discovered that the "farm" was government land and the man could not sell it legally. He was merely trying to cheat someone out of some money. We were all glad to start the return trip to Pachuca.

Chapter Nine

Hot Rice Beverage and Sweet Bread

By the time I was ten years old, my father was planting trees for the U.S. Forest Service in the northwest during the spring months of each year. Although he was earning a lot of money, we continued to maintain our simple lifestyle, and most of the money Daddy made was used for missions in Guatemala, Honduras, and Mexico.

He hired Navajo Indians to help him plant the trees. The Lord blessed his work. Many times God provided miraculous blessings through the weather, saving him from financial disaster.

At this time my parents decided to move to Guatemala on a permanent basis. Bethel and Mike were back in the States by this time, and they had a little blond, curly-headed girl. Evangeline Hope was one and a half years old at the time. They decided to make the move with us. It was decided that Mike would teach the little missionary school at the Graves' mission.

So we loaded up the truck and moved to Guatemala. Mike and Bethel traveled with us in their pickup. It was a long trip from Hamilton, Montana, where we had spent the summer of 1967, to Guatemala!

Arriving at the Graves' home, arrangements were made for us to occupy the three adobe houses by the river on the lower end of the Graves' property. Lloyd and Sandy were long since gone, and the little two-room adobe "hotel" had not brought any business, so the three houses stood empty. During some of our previous visits to Guatemala, Bethel and I had nicknamed that end of the property the "Tick Pasture," because Dr. Graves or "Doc" as we called him had pastured some horses there for a while, and the tall grass was full of ticks and chiggers, so that whenever we walked down there our bodies were covered with the little creatures within minutes. Fortunately, by this time the horses and the ticks and chiggers were gone.

Daddy had an adobe wall built around the three houses, encompassing about half an acre of land. It was plastered white with clay tiles along the top for protection from the rain, but Daddy didn't bother with the broken glass like Doc's wall. Instead, Bethel kept watchdogs inside to discourage anyone from climbing over our wall.

Daddy also built a little chicken house, and he planted papaya and banana trees inside of the protecting walls. The little houses had cement floors, but during the years that they had been unoccupied, the horses had gone inside and kicked up most of the thin layer of cement. For a long time, we had patches of cement and patches of hard packed dirt for floors. But eventually we had new cement floors laid, and downstairs in the "middle" house, as we called Lloyd and Sandy's old house, we had a mosaic tile floor. Besides all that, Daddy made an upstairs verandah of rustic lumber that overlooked the river.

Dr. Graves had built a church that also served as schoolhouse. It was located a few feet outside of his wall. The wall of this adobe building was only four feet high, with narrow sections built up to serve as pillars for the roof.

In Guatemala the school year begins in January, so in February of 1968 Mike started teaching school there. He taught grades one through six, which are all of the grades of elementary school there, and I attended classes along with the other children.

Hot Rice Beverage and Sweet Bread

My big treat of the week was Sunday morning market in La Democracia. Helping my mother carry her baskets and bags, my two best friends, Modesta and Elsa, and I would go out to the highway no later than dawn on Sunday morning and hale down the first little taxi that came by. (These taxis were all privately owned vehicles.) The adult fare was ten cents, but children could ride to La Democracia for five cents. Stopping all along the way to pick up more passengers, we would be crowded in like sardines by the time we got to La Democracia.

While my mother made the necessary purchases, my two little friends and I would hurry over to a stand where an old lady sold *arroz en leche*, a hot, sweet rice beverage made with milk. She kept it in a large clay pot wrapped in rags and sitting inside of a larger basket. Beside it she had a small basin of water and a dozen glasses. She also sold sweet bread to go with it. That was kept wrapped in a large cloth inside of another basket.

A glass of hot rice beverage cost two cents, and one piece of sweet bread cost three cents. We would each drink a glass of the beverage and eat one piece of the sweet bread. After each person emptied his or her glass, the woman would slosh it around in the basin of water, which became dirtier and dirtier as the morning wore on, wipe it on her dingy apron, and set it out for the next person in line.

We continued our tradition of purchasing our usual Sunday morning breakfast treat until I was about thirteen. At that time I was becoming more aware of contagious diseases such as tuberculosis (which was common at that time) and the need for sanitation and hygiene. On one particular Sunday morning, I was slowly imbibing my glass of sweet, sticky hot drink when I happened to glance around me. There I saw a topless Indian woman with a baby tied to her back in a very ragged *reboso*. She had pulled the baby around to the front and was chewing up the rice kernels in her drink and spitting them into the baby's mouth. At the same time I observed a man who I was quite certain was suffering from tuberculosis drinking a glass of rice beverage. That was the last time I had *arroz en leche* at the market.

After giving up our morning treat, we switched to ice cream. We would rush outside of the big market building to one of the ice cream venders and have a large five-cent cone of homemade ice cream. They peddled it in carts that they pushed around, ringing a little bell. I have never lost my taste for the exquisite flavor of that simple skim milk ice cream.

Across the little cobblestone street from the market was a meat house. The venders always wore dirty white aprons stained with blood, and swarms of flies crawled freely over the raw meat. A row of vultures always perched on the roof of the building, some of them with their wings outspread.

During the week after school, Modesta, Elsa, and I spent many hours of fun together playing and swimming in the river. Elsa lived with her parents, Tomás and Marcelina, in an adobe house near us on Dr. Graves' land. Tomás was a faithful, trustworthy lay evangelist who was much loved and respected by all.

Modesta was an Indian girl who lived in a hut on a neighboring coffee plantation. She was a constant visitor at the Graves' home from the time she could toddle over to the clinic. Modesta had learned to speak English quite well, besides Spanish and Mam, the local Indian dialect. She was younger than I by only a few months. Elsa was about two years younger than I.

In addition to playing with my friends, I had a few childish adventures with "critters." A pila is a set of cement tubs used for bathing and washing clothes and dishes. Water is stored in the deep tubs, and washing is done in a shallow sink-like one by dipping water from the deep ones and pouring it over whatever is being washed in the shallow

Hot Rice Beverage and Sweet Bread

one. Some have one deep tub, and some have two.

Occasionally I would find pink crabs in our pila about the size of a man's hand. I was told that they could pinch hard enough to sever the little toe from one's foot, so I always handled them carefully with sticks. I used to catch these crabs and put them in a kettle. Then I would carry them over to the neighboring coffee plantation where a community of Indian peons lived. They liked to eat crabs and always bought mine for one penny each.

Once when I went to sell crabs, a woman bought one and threw it, alive, into the hot coals of her fire. I watched it wave its pinchers up and down until it died. That was the last time I sold crabs.

Big black spiders the size of an adult's hand were also common. These spiders were not tarantulas. I was told that they secreted a fluid that if it got on you would make your flesh rot in that place. They said that the only cure was to put human excrement on the rotten sore. Otherwise it would continue to fester for years. Whether or not that was all true, I didn't know. But, needless to say, I always avoided the mammoth spiders.

One day Bethel was combing her hair when a big spider came down out of the rafters and landed on her head. She shook it off gingerly and continued combing her hair. I believe I would have panicked!

Another time Bethel woke up in the night and happened to flash her light on the ceiling. There she saw a cockroach six inches long. Not wanting to tackle killing it by herself, she called Mamma over from the other house. Between the two of them they got up the courage to squash the ugly giant.

I had gotten used to sleeping on the floor during our many travels, but now that I actually had a nice bed with a mattress, I just couldn't get used to sleeping on it. So I slept on the floor beside my bed in a sleeping bag. One night I felt something cold and smooth against my leg. It was about two o'clock in the morning. I jumped up, turned my flashlight on, and opened my sleeping bag. After inspecting it thoroughly and finding nothing, I got back in, ready to go back to sleep. But then I felt the cold, smooth thing against my leg again. Jumping back up to repeat the inspection of my sleeping bag, I again found nothing. After getting back in, I still felt it. This time when I got up, I saw a huge green worm hanging on the hem of the moo-moo that I wore for a nightgown. It was three inches long and was as big around as an adult's thumb. Maybe that wasn't huge, but it was just big, and I wasn't thrilled to share my bed with it. So I shook it off into the wastebasket, killed it—it was JUICY—and went back to bed.

We were also overrun with rats and big roaches. We did all we could to get rid of them, but we only managed to thin the population occasionally. One time we returned home from visiting a family to find an enormous black-and-yellow snake wound around the rafters above the door going into our compound from the end where Bethel and Mike's house was. It slithered on into the rafters of their house. Mike banged on the tin roof with a pole until it crawled out the back down to the river and slowly swam away. It was about nine feet long, but to me at ten years old, it looked enormous. I loved the water too much though to let the snake discourage me from swimming in the river, and I never encountered one in the water from that day to this. There were plenty of biting, stinging creatures around, but none of us were ever bitten by anything seriously poisonous.

Chapter Ten

Ahma Blommer

In the little township of Camojá lived a little girl of five years named "Tea," which was a nickname for Timotea. She was named after her mother, and indeed she looked much like her. She had big friendly brown eyes that looked right through you and a gentleness that could capture anyone's heart.

One day Mamma said to me, "There is something that little Tea wants more than anything else in the world, and I think you could make her wish come true."

Little Tea had deformed, crippled legs that bowed around in front of her, and she could neither stand nor walk. She had some trinkets and two or three little ragged dresses that she kept in a cardboard box. These were all her worldly possessions. Her mother would set her in the corridor of their hut inside the little box, and she would amuse herself playing with her things.

"What does she want, Mamma?" I asked.

"She would like to have a doll. Would you give her one of yours?"

I was happy to have the opportunity to do something special for sweet little Tea, so we looked at my dolls to decide which one would be most appropriate for her. We decided together that Ahma Blommer would be the most suitable for a small girl.

Hope That Springs Eternal

I had received Ahma Blommer as a gift when I was four years old. We were living in Pendleton, Oregon, at the time and Percy and Anita Wentlend surprised us by stopping by for a visit. They were aunt and uncle to some of my cousins, but I have always claimed them as my aunt and uncle, too.

It was nearing Christmas, and as they came in, Aunt Nita presented me with a beautiful package. My little girl heart was thrilled through and through, and I opened it, being careful not to tear the wrapping paper. (We always saved it to use again later.)

Inside was a new baby doll, and I hugged it to my heart.

"What are you going to name it?" asked Aunt Nita.

"Ahma Blommer," I quickly answered, saying the first syllables that came to my mind. I didn't know of many names, so I just made one up. Since Aunt Nita graciously approved of my choice of a name for the doll, Ahma Blommer it was from then on.

I took good care of the doll, and when we moved to Guatemala when I was ten, I took it with me along with several other dolls I had acquired over the years, although I no longer played with them.

So it was that I had a gift to give to little Tea. The next time we saw her, I placed the doll in her arms. Taking it, she held it to her heart, much the same way I had done several years before, and a new light of happiness dawned in her eyes. After that she would sit in her little box in the corridor of the hut each day rocking little Ahma Blommer in her arms, singing softly. I never found out what name she gave the dolly, but I do know that there was never a doll that was more loved.

A few weeks later, little Tea became sick and had to stay in bed. "Mamma," she whispered, "I can hardly wait for Jesus to come and take us all to heaven. There I will be able to run and play with the other children."

She had listened intently as the faithful lay evangelist, Tomás, had read to her parents from the Bible: "The Lord himself shall descend from heaven with a shout, with the voice of the archangel, and with the trump of God: and the dead in Christ shall rise first: Then we which are alive and remain shall be caught up together with them in the clouds, to meet the Lord in the air: and so shall we ever be with the Lord" (1 Thess. 4:16, 17).

With the faith of a little child, she believed. And how she loved to hear about that beautiful land where no one will ever die as written about in Isaiah: "Behold, I create new heavens and a new earth: and the former shall not be remembered, nor come into mind. . . . And they shall build houses, and inhabit them; and they shall plant vineyards and eat the fruit of them" (65:17, 21). Also, "the wolf also shall dwell with the lamb, and the leopard shall lie down with the kid; and the calf and the young lion and the fatling together; and a little child shall lead them" (11:6).

"If Jesus sees fit to let us die before He comes, we do not need to be afraid," Tomás explained patiently. "Death is like a peaceful sleep. And when Jesus comes in the clouds of heaven, He will resurrect and take all those to heaven with him who died trusting in Jesus."

He read from Ecclesiastes 9:5, 6, and 10: "For the living know that they shall die: but the dead know not anything, neither have they any more a reward; for the memory of them is forgotten. Also their love, and their hatred, and their envy, is now perished; neither have they any more a portion for ever in any thing that is done under the sun. . . . Whatsoever thy hand findeth to do, do it with thy might; for there is no work, nor device, nor knowledge, nor wisdom, in the grave, whither thou goest."

He also taught them John 14:1-3: "Let not your heart be troubled; ye believe in God, believe also in me. In my Father's house are many mansions: if it were not so, I would have told you. I go to prepare a place for you. And if I go and prepare a place for you, I will come again, and receive you unto myself; that where I am, there ye may be also."

"Mama," whispered Tea from her little bed, "I want to go to sleep so it will only seem like a short moment until I hear Jesus calling me to life to take me to heaven." A few days later little Tea fell asleep in Jesus, with the bright hope of the resurrection shining in her heart. Her parents purchased a small coffin fashioned of crude lumber. They gently laid her in it with her little trinkets beside her and the treasured doll in her arms. She was buried and sleeps peacefully, awaiting the voice of the Great Life-Giver.

> There is a land where all is peace,
> where stormy conflicts never come;
> Ten thousand times ten thousand
> praise the Holy Lamb.
>
> Their voices rise in perfect harmony,
> they never do each other wrong.
> The least is greatest in his gratitude,
> the greatest least in his own eyes.
>
> Oh princes of that mighty realm,
> they're rivals only in what's good;
> They ever seek each other's happiness,
> and live in perfect harmony.
>
> They know no sorrow, doubt, nor grief,
> for all is sunshine there.
> Love is alive in every heart,
> expressed in every look.

Ahma Blommer

Oh righteous kingdom, pure and blest,
my soul reaches out.
I praise the Lamb who died for me,
so I could enter there!

(Adapted from *Last Day Events* by Ellen G. White, p. 296)

Chapter Eleven

A Set of Dentures

*E*arly one Sunday morning, Mike took Elsa, Modesta, and me with him in his pickup and we went to the market in La Democracia. My mother usually went to buy the things that we would need for the week, but this particular Sunday Mike wanted to try his hand at buying the fruit and vegetables.

The Guatemalan currency was stable at that time, and the exchange rate was one *quetzal* to one dollar. Oranges, bananas, and avocados were all one cent each, and some smaller varieties of bananas were five for a penny. The merchants always asked for more, however, and you had to "jew" them down to the right price.

While living at the Yerba Buena Mission as a toddler, I had learned to speak Spanish right along with English. Children usually pick up another language quickly, but adults who go to another country for the first time struggle with it. Mike, however, earned our respect by becoming fluent in the Spanish language when he first went down to Guatemala with Bethel shortly after they were married.

This particular Sunday, besides the regular purchases of the week, he bought a fairly large amount of some greens he found for one penny a bunch. *Chipilín* is the name of that particular kind of greens, and they are delicious with black beans. They grow on large bushes and are usually grown near someone's hut.

A Set of Dentures

When we got home, Mamma steamed them, and she, Modesta, and I each had some for lunch that day. I ate by far the most, because my mother always gave me very generous portions of healthful things.

After lunch I went with Mike and Bethel in their pickup to Camojallito, a township about one kilometer past La Democracia. They had ordered some bricks from a brickmaker who lived there, and they were going to pick them up.

While we were there, I began to feel terribly faint, and I vomited. On the way home, Mike had to stop the truck for me to get out and vomit again. By the time we got home, I was vomiting green bile about every two minutes—I felt like I would die.

I lay on my bed with a basin beside me, vomiting all afternoon. For a while I felt like I was dying, then I began to wish I would die. The sick ache in the pit of my stomach was indescribable.

At that time we had the luxury of a flush toilet. (That was before it was ruined by visitors who threw everything imaginable into it.) When Mamma got sick that afternoon, she vomited in the toilet. After flushing it, she noticed that her mouth felt empty and realized that her dentures had fallen into the toilet, and she had flushed them away.

Modesta was also sick after she went home to her hut that afternoon, and her mother took her to the clinic. Emma Joe, the nurse, gave her lots of water to drink, and after vomiting twice, she recovered. I was miserable as I lay there on my bed. I was very thirsty, but I thought that drinking water would make my vomiting worse, so I didn't drink any. Perhaps I would have recuperated sooner if I had. After about three hours, my vomiting stopped, and I got up for a while that evening.

The next day we went to Comitán, a town about eighty kilometers into Mexico. It was time to renew our Guatemalan visas, and we had to leave the country for a few hours in order to get new ones at the border crossing on the way back in.

Unfortunately, Mamma had to go without her dentures. I still remember her explaining, with quite a lisp, to the border officials why she didn't have her teeth. Their eyes twinkled dangerously as she told them, but they were polite and didn't laugh.

For a long time we puzzled as to what could have made us so sick that day, but we finally came up with a likely explanation. In Guatemala the government required that every house and hut be sprayed with DDT every six months. It was believed that the spray would kill the anopheles mosquitoes that transmitted malaria.

Any cats that got the DDT on their paws would contract a shaking disease and die after about six weeks. Occasionally we heard of people who died from the "shakes," too. We figured that they must have accidentally ingested some of the DDT that was sprayed in their houses.

Anytime I went into a building that had recently been sprayed, I would immediately come down with a severe sinus attack. So Dr. Graves signed a statement saying that I was allergic to the spray. We would always show it to the uniformed men sent out to do the spraying.

Thinking back to the *chipilín* greens that made us so sick, we came to the conclusion that they had been grown near someone's hut and had gotten DDT on them when the hut was sprayed. My mother had washed them thoroughly, but chemicals may not always wash off. Perhaps we were lucky to vomit like we did, instead of getting the "shakes" and slowly dying.

Chapter Twelve

Eye Infection

When I was eleven years old, my mother and Dr. Graves arranged for me to work in the clinic as an interpreter. Bethel had made me a nurse's uniform and cap to play nurse with, and I was urged to wear it to the clinic that first morning. So off I went, a little girl in a uniform, trying to act grown up.

Emma Joe, the nurse, took care of most of the patients, but when one came in with an unusual ailment, I would run to find the doctor and call him to the clinic. I soon began learning how to treat common diseases such as malaria, dysentery, worms, impetigo, and scabies.

One day Doc called me into the medicine room where he had prepared a penicillin shot for a patient, and he said, "Take this and give it to that man in there sitting on the bench."

I began to object that I had not yet practiced injecting oranges and lemons, but Doc said, "You can practice on the patient then."

Nervously I went into the treatment room with the syringe in my hand. Since the man didn't seem perturbed in the least that a little girl was going to give him a shot, I began to feel more confident. I had seen both Doc and Emma Joe give many shots, so theoretically I knew how it was done. I proceeded to inject the penicillin into the man's arm, and he didn't even wince. To my relief, he actually looked rather pleased. I soon learned that to Guatemalan peasants an "injection" was the magic cure for anything!

After a few weeks, Doc began to occasionally leave me in charge of the clinic whenever Emma Joe wanted to go somewhere or do something else for the day. Morning was the busiest time, so I worked from 7:30 to 12:30, then spent the afternoons helping at home and swimming in the river with my two good friends, Elsa and Modesta.

One day a little man named Pastor Gil came to the Graves' place. He had been sent by the Guatemala Mission of Seventh-day Adventists to hold a series of evangelistic meetings in La Democracia.

Permission was granted to use a hall big enough to seat 500 people, and the meetings began. John Graves helped out by driving up and down the highway for several kilometers in each direction gathering up people to take to the meetings each evening. At the specified time, I would go out and wait at the highway for Dr. Graves' son John to come by and pick me up. Then I would climb into the board contraption that we called a camper and find a place among the many people that were already crowded in.

One night it was extremely dark when John stopped at our driveway to drop me off after the meeting. It had been raining, and as the pickup drove away, I was left in pitch darkness. I couldn't even see my hand when I held it up in front of my face. The driveway was about 500-feet long, and it curved around to the right. I crept along for a while, trying to feel my way home, and upon rounding the bend I saw the light from a little candle that Mamma and Bethel had thoughtfully left burning in the window of the *sala*, a little room that had been built to receive visitors at the entrance to our compound. It was still dark, but I walked toward the little light and was able to find the door.

The next morning my right eye was red and inflamed, so I didn't go to the clinic that day. I stayed home and rested, but the inflammation in my eye grew worse by the hour.

Eye Infection

Finally my eye was swollen nearly shut, and the burning pain was intense. A kind of acid pus oozed from my eye that burned more and more. I tried to keep it blotted up with a cloth, but it wasn't much use.

Bethel and little Evangeline stayed away from me, and it was a good thing because we didn't know it, but I had a dangerous, contagious disease.

After several days the pain had grown so intense it was almost unbearable, and I cried and moaned in agony that night. At about eleven o'clock, my mother decided to take me up to the clinic. We walked along the river trail, which took about five minutes. To go around by the highway would take ten minutes.

When we arrived at the Graves' home, Doc and Rosalee both got up and checked my eyes. By this time my left eye was infected also, but I didn't even feel it because the pain in my right eye was so intense. By this time, a substance that looked like raw meat had covered the white part and the iris of my right eye.

Rosalee fixed a charcoal poultice for me to put over my eyes through the night, and she gave me some anesthetic drops to put in my eyes to numb the pain. The Graves knew what was wrong with me, but they didn't want to scare us. It wasn't until years later that I found out that I had a disease that usually leaves its victims permanently blind.

I firmly believe that the charcoal poultice drew out enough of the inflammation to prevent the raw meat-like stuff from covering my pupil, which would have left me blind. Perhaps the inflammation in my left eye would have gotten bad enough to leave me blind in that eye, too. I believe the Lord saved my eyesight, because without a divine miracle, I would have been permanently blind.

I was very sick for three weeks. By the time my eye inflammation was completely gone, the evangelistic meetings in La Democracia were nearly over. At the end a number of people were baptized—I think it was about twenty.

This same eye disease plagued others in Guatemala. Over in the department of Petén there was an epidemic one year. More than one hundred people were left permanently blind before the doctors could get the epidemic stopped. Our SDA boarding academy is in Petén, and one of the students told me that they kept antibiotic shots on hand to treat the students. As soon as anyone's eyes would look red or a little inflamed, one of the other students would immediately give that person one of the shots. If one could get an appropriate antibiotic in time, the disease would not progress.

The Graves had also seen the disease before. In the clinic's early inception when they were serving people under a parachute, Dr. Graves had treated an old woman with the same eye disease in its advanced stages. Rosalee gave her anesthetic drops and put a cool charcoal poultice over her eyes. The old lady and a younger woman that accompanied her were given a place to stay for the night. By morning her eyes were completely free from the disease without a trace of inflammation! I believe in miracles, do you?

Chapter Thirteen

Clinic Days

*B*y the time I was twelve, I had been working in the clinic for some time and had grown quite confident. I cleaned out many ears full of wax and cleaned up many cases of nasty impetigo sores. Children would often be brought to the clinic who were filthy and covered with sores from head to toe. It was my job to shave their heads, heat water on the Graves' kitchen stove and carry it down to the clinic to bathe the sores and scrape off the scabs. I would then apply gentian violet and mercury ointment and bandage them up. Swarms of flies and gnats were attracted to the smelly sore-covered bodies, and I was always glad when the job was finished.

Most people suffered from malaria, and it was my job to take the temperature of every patient, inquire as to their symptoms, check them with a stethoscope for lung congestion, and if the symptoms were those of malaria, give them a shot and some pills to take home. The people proclaimed the wonders of the *gringo's* medicine. If you could rid their bodies of the hated malaria, Mother Nature would usually rally and their other ailments would begin to disappear as well.

I quickly learned that when I took the temperature rectally of babies with dysentery I had to look out or I might get sprayed in the face. Also, the little tots were frightened to death of the Americans, and they fought tooth and nail to avoid me. One child fought me so hard that the thermometer broke inside of him. Fortunately I was able to retrieve it without any injury to the child.

In an effort to protect myself, I studied an old nursing book that Doc had and learned how to hold down all of the flailing appendages quite efficiently. After that, things went much better, although the parents sometimes thought that I was going to kill their children. I was always gentle, but no child ever escaped having his temperature taken or swallowing his medicine, no matter how hard he struggled.

Tuberculosis was common, and Doc taught me to recognize it by listening to the patient's lungs through a stethoscope. During the rainy season pneumonia was quite common, also.

One day I gave some worm pills to an Indian woman to take home. I explained to her how to give them to her two tiny boys. The little tots abdomens were badly distended. She came back a few days later to report to me that one boy passed seventeen huge roundworms, and the other forty.

I also helped lance incredibly huge boils, and I learned to do sutures. One day a little four-year-old Indian girl was brought to the clinic. She had a big boil behind her ear. Doc lanced it, but he left me to squeeze out the dead blood and pus, which filled an emesis basin halfway to the top. I asked the parents if she had any more boils, but it didn't occur to me to check her myself. The parents said "no" and took her home.

The next day she suddenly grabbed her tummy and fell over dead. She had another huge boil on her abdomen, and it had drained into her abdominal cavity, killing her. The parents had wanted to see if our treatment would cure the one behind her ear before having the one on her abdomen treated. Those were the sad cases we dealt with and the skepticism of our treatments.

The next day I saw the little funeral procession going toward the cemetery at Camojá. The dead child was in a small coffin carried by two men, and the mother, weeping inconsolably, followed along behind with the rest of the people. I walked with her as far as the Valparaíso bridge, my heart wrung with sympathy.

Later that afternoon I took Modesta with me, and we went to visit the family in their hut. I spoke in Spanish, and Modesta translated everything I said into the Mam dialect. I told them of the second coming of Jesus and the blessed hope of the resurrection. They jabbered among themselves excitedly about everything I told them, and I would have to stop every little bit and wait for them to quiet down before I continued.

The father of that family was the son of a witch doctor, and I was overjoyed a few years later to hear that the whole family had been baptized and was attending church regularly. I always found it so delightfully amazing when someone accepted Jesus, how that dull look would give place to alertness and a clean, shining face. I give the faithful lay evangelists the credit for the conversion of that precious family and of many, many others.

One time an old Indian woman brought her daughter and tiny grandson to the clinic. The baby was about three months old, but he only weighed about seven and a half pounds. He was covered with huge black burns, and the grandmother of the baby said despairingly that her daughter would not tell her how the baby got burned.

The baby's mother had a faraway look in her eyes, and she would not look directly at me. I tried to question her, but she would only shrug her shoulders and say, "Saber," the Spanish infinitive of the verb "to know," which the Indians use to mean, "who knows."

Emma Joe and I dressed the baby's burns, but I really doubt that he lived. I personally believe the baby was burned in a witch doctor rite of some kind.

One really outstanding case was that of a lady who was brought from the border town of La Mesilla in a private taxi by her husband. She was nine months pregnant when a portion of the umbilical cord came out. She waited at home for a whole week in that condition, but the baby did not come. So they decided to come to the clinic. I called Dr. Graves, and he induced labor. In a few minutes a decomposed, dead baby was born.

To avoid the grim details, I will simply say that I will never forget the overpowering stench. How that poor woman lived through having a dead baby inside of her for a whole week, I will never know!

Dr. Graves placed the dead child and the placenta inside a paper bag, which was placed into a Mexican shopping bag with handles. The young couple wavered back and forth between taking it home and holding an all-night "wake," burning candles to it, or leaving it for the clinic personnel to bury. By this time yours truly was the main "clinic personnel," except for when Doc would come down to tend to an unusual case. The couple decided to let us bury their baby, but unfortunately, that job was left to me. At this time I was still just twelve years old, and the thought of burying that decomposed baby was a little too much for me.

Rosa, an orphan girl my age whom the Graves were keeping, took pity on me, her friend, and suggested a little scheme. Together we went outside and looked around until we found a pole about eight feet long lying on the ground under one of the orange trees. (It was used to knock oranges and lemons out of the treetops.) Hooking it through the handles of the shopping bag, we each carried one end, walking to the shop where Dick, Dr. Graves' good-natured younger son, was fixing someone's car. We dropped off the bag and said, "Here is something for you to bury!"

With that we both ran back to the clinic. I half expected to be

Clinic Days

dragged back by the ear to do my job, but Dick sweetly performed the unpleasant task himself.

Cleaning up the mess in the clinic still remained to be done, and although I had an iron stomach and was unmoved by most things of a medical nature, this was too much for me. I was wondering what to do when Inez, the kind old widow lady who served as the Graves' maid, offered to clean it up for me. I don't know how she did it, but she did. I have no doubt to this day that when she was converted to the Advent faith, she was really converted, heart and soul.

One time when I was fourteen, the Graves all decided to make a quick two-week trip to the States, and I was left in charge of the clinic during that time. I prayed that no emergency or obstetrics cases would come in.

One evening after dark a young Indian man knocked on our door and excitedly asked for the "nurse." I had packed a doctor's bag, which consisted of a paper sack containing a little bit of everything, and taken it home with me from the clinic just in case such a thing should happen. I was just getting ready for bed, but I quickly dressed, grabbed my "doctor's bag," asked Bethel to go with me, and headed out the door. The Indian man led us to Camojá, then off on a trail. We probably walked for about two kilometers.

Coming to a hut, he led us inside, and there was his sick wife lying on a little rickety wooden bed with no mattress and his mother tending to the fire. A small candle burned near the bed on a crude little stand.

Upon examining the patient, I soon concluded that she was only mildly sick but was having a good time scaring her husband and mother-in-law. Perhaps it was the only way she could ever get any attention or notice out of them. When I would ask her if she had a certain symptom, she would only groan in a fashion that could be either negative or affirmative. She bit the thermometer in two, and I had to take her temperature rectally, which was normal.

She would not hold her head up, and I finally guessed from the intonations of all the hollering and groans that she might have an acid stomach. I tried to give her some antacid tablets, but she clenched her teeth and rolled her head from side to side and would not take them. So I gave her some in liquid form, clamping her mouth shut and holding her nose until she swallowed it. She did not dare fight me too hard, or it would spoil her "sick" act.

Next I gave her an aralen shot for malaria and counted out some pills and gave them to her husband with instructions to give them to her morning and night.

"I will let him worry about how to get them through her clenched teeth," I remarked to Bethel in English. Turning back to the worried young man I said gravely, "Your wife is very ill. You must not beat her nor starve her. You must help her carry the wood, or she will die."

Blushing, the young man replied, "I do not beat my wife."

"Good," I said. "I commend you for that."

On the way home Bethel and I laughed so hard about the "sick" woman that we almost staggered off the trail. We made it home in record time though, in spite of our gales of laughter.

A few days after the Graves returned, the same young man came and asked the doctor to go get his wife in his car and bring her to the clinic for further examination and treatment. Daddy happened to be there and said he would go in Doc's VW and get her. I tried to tell them not to do it because she was not really that sick. But the "enfermerita" (or little nurse as Doc called me in Spanish) was not listened to that day.

Daddy tried to drive as far as possible up the trail off the highway so the patient would not have to be carried any more than necessary, and in the process he caught a part of the old VW on the rocks and tore it off. I am not mechanically inclined, so I cannot tell you just ex-

Clinic Days

actly what happened, but I do know that Daddy felt awfully chagrined. Doc, however, laughed it off good-naturedly and told him not to worry about it.

When the patient was helped out of the car and brought into the clinic, I noticed that her legs were strong although she leaned way over on her husband as if she were very faint. When he accidentally let go of her, she was able to catch herself very well, and she didn't fall over on the floor at all. Just as soon as she caught herself though, she quickly resumed her leaning position. Her husband did not seem to see through her act at all, and I decided that it was probably just as well that he didn't.

In the end, Doc didn't find anything wrong with her either, and he treated her for malaria. As I gave the husband a new packet of pills to take home, I lectured the patient severely. "If you do not open your mouth and take your medicine, you will die! When your husband or your mother-in-law bring you your pills twice a day, you must swallow them obediently!"

Near the clinic was a tree that once a year was covered with huge, green worms. They were about six inches long and as big around as a man's thumb. After a few days of hanging on the tree, they would all start dropping off, and scores of them would come crawling into the clinic through the doors. Inez and I would sweep them back out with brooms, and they would turn right around and start back. She killed a lot of them, but I was squeamish at the idea. Finally, one day I got up my courage.

A big worm was crawling in through the back door, so I grabbed a nearby brick and dropped it right on top of the enormous creature. Immediately I wished I hadn't. Its "juice" squirted out and hit me on the forehead. I had acquired some of the Guatemalan abhorrence of worms, and I nearly fell over backwards like Goliath when he was hit in the forehead by David's little pebble. When I picked up the brick, the worm looked like a tangled mass of white thread. I quickly swept the remains away, then hurried to wash my face.

For about three hours, no matter how much I washed, whenever I would run my hand over my forehead, it would leave a repulsive smell on my fingers. I washed and scrubbed with soap repeatedly, but the bad smell just had to wear away by itself.

One day I was out in the corridor of the clinic when I saw a little man riding down the highway on a horse. At the driveway to the Graves' home he turned in without hesitation and headed toward the big tree just across from the clinic that shaded their house. Stopping, he began to dismount in the same place where I had found the little featherless bird on the ground when I was five years old. I quickly turned around and went inside the clinic. A moment later the little man darkened the doorway.

"Come in and sit down!" I said to him as he hesitated for a few moments.

It wasn't until he bumped into one of the chairs uncertainly that I realized he was blind. "What brings you to the clinic my friend?" I asked in the most cheerful voice I could muster.

"Oh," he said stoically, "I was working clearing out weeds and brush with a machete when I made a wrong move and cut the fingers of my left hand."

I asked him to show me the hand. He had it wrapped in a dirty old cloth. I gasped as he unwrapped it. The "wrong move" he had made with his machete was one that people who have their eyesight make occasionally too when they are doing machete work. He had chopped the ends of his four fingers nearly off and they were just barely connected by a small thread of skin.

"Please wait here for a few moments while I go call the doctor to dress your hand," I said, trying to sound reassuring. "He will take good care of it, and you will be all right. You are a very hardworking man."

"Yes," he replied. "I know that if the doctor fixes my hand, I will still be able to work and support myself."

This poor man had ridden his horse clear from Peña Roja, a township far up in the mountains. It had already been about three hours since he had chopped his fingers. Fortunately, Doc said he would not lose them. They could still be sewed back in place. After the doctor was finished, the poor blind man mounted his horse and started the long ride home. Early the next morning, however, I heard a horse coming down the driveway. Going out to look, I saw the same man dismounting from his horse. This time I hurried across the driveway to meet him, and it was a good thing. He could just barely hobble on one foot.

"What happened to you?" I asked as I helped him across the driveway toward the clinic.

"Oh," he said, "I stopped yesterday at a little creek to let my horse drink water. But since I cannot see sometimes I step wrong, and the horse stepped wrong at the same time I did, and it stepped on my right foot. So now I cannot walk on it."

"Where did you spend the night?" I asked as I helped him to a chair inside the clinic.

"There by the creek with my horse. I could not go home with my injured foot, and it was too late to come back to the clinic. I had gone too far up in the mountains. So I stayed there until I felt the night air begin to change to the early morning air. Then I mounted my horse and came back to the clinic. The doctor here is very good. It is because he is a gringo. *Gringos* are very good."

"How could you mount your horse with the injured foot?" I asked him.

"I was very fortunate to have injured the right foot. If the horse had stepped on my left foot, it would be much harder for me to mount my horse."

"You are a very brave and remarkable man," I said as I went out to call the doctor.

This time the man stayed at the clinic until his foot was well enough so he could put his weight on it again. He slept in a room that had beds in it for patients.

He was given three good meals a day, and when he left, Rosalee gave him several *quetzals* to buy food with for a few days until he could work again.

The blind man was profuse in his thanks as he left. "That is why I came to the clinic," he said in parting. "I knew you would help me. May God bless you all and richly repay you for your kindness to me."

Chapter Fourteen

A Hole in the Wall

On the left-hand side of the property lived the Hidalgo clan. There were many aunties, uncles, and cousins. They owned a few *cuerdas* of land divided up among them all, so each had a small piece with a hut or small adobe house. At that time they all had mostly sugarcane growing around their houses, but later they pulled it up and planted coffee.

In the house nearest to the clinic just outside of the wall around the Graves' place lived Vitalino Hidalgo and his wife, Ventura. They had five children, ranging from ages eight to sixteen. The girl, Rosa, was my age.

Ventura was due to have another baby. One night the contractions started while the family was sleeping. Pretty soon she began to hemorrhage. She lay there in the dark beside her husband on the little wooden bed until she had lost about one liter of blood. Then she woke her husband and asked him to call Rosalee, who was an RN specializing in midwifery. She had safely delivered many babies at the clinic.

Rosalee hurried over to Vitalino and Ventura's house, but it was too late. Ventura had lost too much blood and was dying. "Please take care of my children," she whispered to Rosalee as she breathed her last.

The Graves took all the children to live with them. After a few months, Alfredo and Rigoberto, the two older boys, left to work on their own. Rosa, age eleven at the time, and her two younger brothers, Rocael and Leonel, ages eight and nine, stayed on at the Graves' home and attended the little school, which by this time was taught by Olive Mason, an American.

Vitalino, the father, was heartbroken after his wife's death, and he tried to drown his grief in *cusha*, the illegal native jungle brew. He soon became completely addicted and stopped working. After that he spent his days and nights drinking; he was never sober.

Needing money to support his habit, he made a career of petty thievery. He would steal a machete from the house of one of his relatives, take it to the house of another relative, and offer it for sale at a cheap price. The relatives, always greedy for a bargain, bought his stolen merchandise although each knew exactly who he had stolen each item from. Thus they made it possible for him to continue his thieving and his drinking.

One year Doc grew a lovely patch of big, beautiful tomatoes that were superior to any that anyone in that area had ever seen. As they began to ripen, Doc sold them for twenty-five cents a pound, the standard price for tomatoes in the market at the time. It became apparent though that tomatoes were disappearing from the garden, and they soon discovered that a hole had been dug through the adobe wall near the ground in a secluded place by the garden. The hole was big enough for a man to crawl through, and it made a dandy opening from Vitalino's land.

The identity of the thief was not known, however, and Rosalee decided that she was going to stand guard over that hole all night if necessary to catch the thief when he crawled through to steal tomatoes.

So, taking up her secluded post beside the hole, she waited patiently. About one o'clock in the morning she heard a rustling sound in the bushes on the other side of the wall. Soon the dark form of a man

A Hole in the Wall

crawled through. Rosalee quickly sat down on top of him, using her ample weight to pin him to the ground, and then she began to shout. Soon everyone inside of the house woke up and came running. Shining a light in the thief's face, they found him to be none other than Vitalino.

"How much have you been selling our tomatoes for?" they asked him.

"For ten cents a pound," he replied.

"Who have you been selling them to?"

"To my shameless relatives."

Perhaps Vitalino's relatives thought it wasn't so bad to buy goods that they knew to be stolen, so long as they didn't do the actual stealing themselves.

The Graves decided to keep Vitalino at the clinic for a few weeks and try to dry him out. His children helped to watch him, trying to keep him from sneaking out to get more drink. But after a few days he managed to make his getaway.

For years this poor man continued his drinking and thieving. His oldest son, Alfredo, married and lived in the house where the family had lived when Ventura died. Unfortunately, he set up a saloon and provided his father with free liquor. On the flip side, during those years the neighborhood had a respite from Vitalino's thievery.

The saloon prospered, and Alfredo tore the old house down and built a new one. He and his wife, Cory, had several children. Then he bought a used van and drove it up and down the highway, carrying passengers to and from the market in La Democracia like the other privately owned taxis. As the community thrived and prospered, the taxis ran every day, not just on Sunday.

Many of the smaller coffee farmers bought pickups as their possessions increased, but they could not drive them. Generally the younger men were adventurous enough to learn to drive and obtain a driver's license, but the older ones were afraid to drive, so they would hire one of these licensed "chauffeurs" to do their driving for them.

By the time the following story took place, I was married. One of my older brothers-in-law hired people to do his driving for him. He wanted to go to Huehuetenango one day, so he hired Alfredo to drive his pickup, and off they went. As was customary, they took quite a few passengers with them in the back of the pickup. No one knows what happened for sure, but after they had started back home in the afternoon, the pickup turned over, and Alfredo was killed instantly. Besides owning a saloon, he had done various things to earn himself a reputation as a confirmed atheist. I can remember him laughing at me when I was baptized in the river at age thirteen.

After his death, his body was brought home, and a *velorio*, a customary all-night wake, was held. They set the open coffin on a table in his house. The table was decorated abundantly with flowers and greenery. A thick layer of pine needles was spread over the floor. (This is customary for funerals, weddings, birthdays, housewarmings, and all special occasions.)

I attended the *velorio* for a few hours, and Rosa and I sang "Never Part Again." I had translated the song into Spanish, and the people loved it. Poor old Vitalino was there, weeping inconsolably.

He called me outside for a few moments and asked me, "Where is my son?"

"He is sleeping," I thoughtfully replied, "just like Jesus said Lazarus was when he was in the grave, just before Jesus called him back to life."

"What is it like to be dead?" he asked anxiously.

I quoted Psalm 115:17 to him. "The dead praise not the LORD,

A Hole in the Wall

neither any that go down into silence," I said. "It is silent in the grave. In Psalm 146:4 it says referring to man, 'His breath goeth forth, he returneth to his earth; in that very day his thoughts perish.'"

I continued, "Ecclesiastes 9:5 tells us this: 'For the living know that they shall die: but the dead know not any thing.' They are sleeping peacefully until the end of the world when Jesus comes. John 5:28 and 29 tells us, 'Marvel not at this: for the hour is coming, in the which all that are in the graves shall hear his voice, And shall come forth; they that have done good, unto the resurrection of life; and they that have done evil, unto the resurrection of damnation.'"

"About an hour ago I was walking out there among the coffee bushes in the dark," Vitalino said agitatedly, motioning with his hand. "There was a rustling behind me, and then I heard my son Alfredo's voice speaking. It said, 'Papá, I have died now and discovered that there is no God, no heaven, and no hell. Live it up! Drink! Do anything you want to. The message of the "Adventistas" and their Bible is a bunch of lies!'"

"I covered my ears and hurried inside as fast as I could," Vitalino continued. "But tell me, whose voice was that talking to me? It sounded exactly like Alfredo."

"It was the voice of that same deceiver called 'the Devil and Satan,' whose first lie was, 'Ye shall not surely die.' That is what he told Eve in the Garden of Eden, and that is what he tried to tell you tonight. But God has told us in the fourth chapter of Ezequiel that 'the soul that sinneth, it shall die.' The devil is a great mimic and deceiver. When it suits his purpose to do so, he and his demons can impersonate our dead friends and relatives very accurately. He can also 'appear as an angel of light' with 'the intent to deceive us to our destruction.' Second Corinthians 11:13 through 15 tells us that. And in the book of Revelation, God tells us that the 'spirits of devils' can work miracles to deceive. Satan convinced a third of the angels in heaven to become demons with his deceptive lies, and now he is trying to deceive and destroy each one of us in every way he can."

"Please pray for me," Vitalino said tearfully. "I want to be a Christian. I want to stop drinking and go to church faithfully. Will God forgive and accept me?"

"'If we confess our sins, he is faithful and just to forgive us our sins, and to cleanse us from all unrighteousness.' That is what 1 John 1:9 says. And Jesus said, 'Come unto me all ye that labor and are heavy laden, and I will give you rest.'"

Vitalino asked me to kneel and pray for him right then. We both knelt, and I prayed. Then he prayed a heartbroken, stammering prayer. "God help me," he cried.

Soon after Alfredo's death, the terrible craving for liquor returned, and Vitalino resumed his thieving and drinking. Around that time my father-in-law bought a couple of *cuerdas* of land in Valparaíso a few hundred meters up the highway from the clinic, and he built a large block house on it. There he and my mother-in-law lived for several years. During that time, whenever my mother-in-law saw Vitalino outside somewhere near her house, she would call him in and serve him a good, hot, nourishing meal. Once he bragged to bystanders on the road, "I don't steal from Doña Tona (referring to my mother-in-law) because she is good and kind. She gives me food when I am hungry."

My sister-in-law once told me that one weekend when she stayed in Valparaíso with "Mamma Tona" as we all call my mother-in-law, one of the Hidalgos celebrated a special occasion by making tamales. At that time a tamale sold for twenty-five cents.

Before long Vitalino managed to steal one of the tamales and took it to the house of a neighbor-relative and offered it for sale at the standard price. The auntie, knowing full well where it came from and who had made it, bought it and put it up on a board shelf in the kitchen. In a little while Vitalino spied his chance and stole it back again.

Taking it to the house of another auntie, Vitalino again offered it for sale. That auntie also bought it and put it up on a shelf. Vitalino soon stole it back from her, too. He re-stole and resold that tamale about five times. Finally, he stole it one last time, took it out into the coffee bushes, and ate it himself!

At one time he was sentenced to three years in the penitentiary at Quetzaltenango, a little over 200 kilometers from our area of the country. During those three years, he had no access to liquor, and his health improved tremendously. He gained some weight, and everyone hoped that he was cured of his drinking problem. He even dared to hope himself. He made hand-crafted curios along with the other prisoners and sold them. This way he was able to save up some money for when he got out of prison. But so-called "friends" could not bare to see him sober and prosperous, and soon after he was released from prison, they succeeded in luring him back to the old life.

Ever since praying for him at Alfredo's funeral, his face would light up with a smile whenever he saw me, and he would ask, "Are you still praying for me? I still want to change."

He would cling to my hand and say, "God knows. I was baptized again and went to church for a whole month without touching a drop of alcohol. Then I fell, and just look at me now!"

One time Bethel was walking to prayer meeting, which was held at the church, when a drunk Vitalino emerged from the coffee bushes by the road and announced that he was going to marry her. He even tried to hug and kiss her. (Several years before, her husband, Mike, had dropped out of the picture.) She hurried along ahead of him, keeping out of the staggering man's reach. Upon reaching the church she went inside and with a sideways grin crowded herself quickly in-between

Hope That Springs Eternal

Marcelina, the lay evangelist's wife, and Inez, the sweet little widow lady who helped the Graves' keep house.

A moment later, in staggered Vitalino, still saying thickly that he was going to marry my beautiful red-headed sister. Drunk beyond reason, he started to sit down on top of one of the ladies that she had taken refuge between. Seeing that, one of the deacons took him gently but firmly by the arm and sat him down on a different bench, then he sat beside him. Pretty soon the drunk Vitalino got up and left.

Vitalino often disrupted the church services, but the members were always patient with him and very compassionate toward him, although at times he had to be escorted outside.

He would quit drinking, take the baptismal studies, and repeatedly get baptized into the church, only to return to the old liquor habit again in a few weeks.

I was much saddened to hear that Vitalino had been hit and killed by a car in the border town of La Mesilla while we were in the States in 1991. Perhaps Vitalino was ready to go at the moment of his tragic death, and I hope with all my heart to see him in heaven.

Chapter Fifteen

Little Starving Girls

Shortly before my fourteenth birthday, a shy little Indian woman appeared in the door of the clinic one morning with a very small girl tied on her back in a *reboso*.

"Good-morning," I greeted her. "Please come in and sit down." I motioned her to one of the chairs for patients to sit in.

"What can I do for you?" I asked.

"My little girl is sick. I think she is dying. She won't eat."

"Why won't she eat?" I queried.

"Oh," said the little lady, "she only nursed, but when she had the measles, she couldn't nurse for two weeks, and my milk supply dried up. When she was over the measles, I tried to feed her other food, but she refused it. She wanted to continue nursing."

"How long ago was that?" I asked her.

"It has been six weeks now. During these past six weeks she has had nothing, not even one morsel of anything to eat! She refuses everything."

"How old is she?"

"Three years old," came the reply.

The little girl's name was Consuelo, which means comfort. The mother's name was María, the most commonly used girl's name among the Guatemalan Indians.

I directed María to unwrap the little girl so I could have a look at her. What I saw was shocking. She was as skinny and emaciated as any picture I had ever seen of starving children in Africa.

When I weighed her, the scales registered a mere ten pounds. The flesh hung loosely from her little skeletal body. Her mouth and throat were full of sores caused by scurvy, vitamin C deficiency, and she reeked with filth and stench.

After examining her, I tried giving her a small amount of milk. She fought it tooth and nail, but by this time I was well practiced in the art of giving little tots their medicine, and she soon swallowed it in spite of herself.

Her stomach, however, rejected it. She had been so long without food that by this time she couldn't keep down even one teaspoon of milk. I decided to try something else. I gave her one drop of milk with an eye-dropper; then five minutes later, I gave her one drop of orange juice. After another five minutes, I gave her another drop of milk; then in five more minutes, I again gave her a drop of orange juice. I kept this up the rest of the morning, giving her milk and orange juice alternately every five minutes. Apparently her stomach was able to handle that, because she didn't vomit again.

At 12:30 I went home for lunch, leaving María with instructions to keep feeding Consuelo in the same way as I had been doing. I led them to a bed in one of the back rooms where they could be as comfortable as possible.

In a little while I went back to the clinic, and Mamma came with me to see the little starving girl. What we found was very encouraging. Little Consuelo was holding a piece of orange in her hand and eating it herself! She did not vomit it up, either.

"It is going to take some time to bring this little girl back to life,"

Little Starving Girls

Mamma said. "We can keep her and take care of her until she regains her health."

I talked to María about it, and she was overjoyed to leave that little mite of a starving girl with us. Little Consuelo turned out to be quite a handful. That one little mite of humanity kept several of us busy almost night and day for several weeks. There was an American family staying at the Graves' mission for a few weeks at the time, and among us all, we took turns caring for her.

Feeding little Consuelo was an ordeal that sometimes took four of us to accomplish. Her throat would bleed when she swallowed, and she would fight taking any food for all her worth. We were gentle, but we had to get the food down her.

I slept in one of the rooms in the clinic with her for a number of nights. She slept in a crib, and I on one of the two beds in the room. She had a habit of getting up to play from one to two o'clock in the morning. She would holler for me to get up and play with her. When I didn't respond, she figured out how to reach the light string from her crib. When the light came on, that got me up in a hurry!

No matter where I moved her crib to, she always managed to reach that light string. When I tied it to my bedstead, she still reached out and found it in the dark. After two or three nights of this, I finally got the light string tied to something high enough to keep it clear out of her reach.

After a few weeks we took her home with us, and Bethel cared for her. Little by little she gained weight and filled out. She was the most stubborn little child that any of us had ever seen. Bethel gave her a little doll to play with once, and she threw it down. Bethel tried again and again to interest her with the doll, but she always refused to acknowledge it. It was only after my sister left the room and Consuelo couldn't see her that the little girl played with the doll. But anytime she heard the slightest sound of anyone coming, she would quickly drop it and resume her pout. She never would play with toys when any of us were around; she would only play with them when she thought no one could see her.

When she had gained enough weight and had gotten strong enough to walk, we gave her back to her mother. For two years Mamma kept her supplied with adequate food and clothes. But María wouldn't keep her properly covered during the damp, chilly weather. Every time María came to pick up the week's supply of food for the child, my mother would tell her to put shoes and socks on Consuelo and not let her out in the rain. But María didn't listen, and Consuelo developed an ear infection. By this time she was five years old.

For several weeks María didn't tell us about the ear infection. Perhaps she thought we would tell her that it was because she didn't follow our instructions for Consuelo's care. One day she finally brought her to us because Consuelo was having convulsions. Mamma and Bethel took care of her night and day for three days. We had her in the clinic in one of the in-patient rooms. Her parents and older sisters were all there.

Consuelo received the best treatment that Dr. Graves could give her, and Mamma and Bethel cared for her around the clock. In the afternoon of the third day, they both stepped out of her room for about five minutes. When they returned, little Consuelo was dead!

"What happened?" Mamma asked María.

"A bunch of blood and pus came running down out of her head into her mouth, so we sat her up, and she died," replied María tearfully.

The doctor was called, and after looking over the situation a bit, he concluded that the abscess in her ear had ruptured on the inside and drained down into her throat. Since she was unconscious, she choked

Little Starving Girls

on all the blood and pus when they sat her up. That was a sad day for us all. I saw my mother cry for the first time at the burial the next day in Camojá.

Not long after that, María had another baby girl who was born with Down syndrome. She named her Esther after me, but everyone called her Esthercita, meaning "little Esther." When she was three years old, she was in even worse condition than Consuelo had been at that age when María first brought her to us. She weighed nine and one half pounds.

Olive Mason, the schoolteacher, took her and kept her for two weeks. But teaching school and caring for a starved child twenty-four hours a day was too much for one person, so Bethel took the little mite of a girl and cared for her for about one year.

María didn't want to take her back for fear she might die like Consuelo had, and an American couple asked if they could adopt her. The Purdies worked with Lon Cummings (the man whose story is told in the book, *Ten Million Dollar Hostage* by Renee Noorbergen). They also started some mission work over near Lake Izabal, also in Guatemala.

Bethel and María both gave their consent, so "little Esther" was adopted by the Purdies and eventually taken to the States.

Chapter Sixteen

Man on a White Horse

*I*n September of 1907 a small, brown baby boy was born in a little hut in the mountains of Guatemala. His proud parents were an Indian couple who had abandoned the customs, costume, and dialect peculiar to the Indians in an effort to provide a better life for their children. The "Latinos," or what we might call "Hispanics," were and still are the privileged class of society, while the aborigine Indians adhere to the old ways.

Birth registration could be postponed for several months, and for many it was a long journey on horseback to the municipality, or county seat. Therefore, choosing a name for the new baby was not an urgent matter. If someone had asked them why they had not thought of a name before the baby's birth, no doubt the young parents would have explained patiently that in such a case, two names would have to be chosen: one for a boy, and one for a girl. Then when the baby was born, the appropriate name would be given to it, and the other discarded. Which would mean that they would have wasted their time selecting two names, when only one was needed. Besides, a baby doesn't really "need" a name until it is old enough to learn to respond to that name. Or so goes the reasoning of the peasants.

To us impatient Americans, it might seem that the baby would never be given a name. But let me assure you, I have never yet met a

Man on a White Horse

Papá Eustaquio (lived to be 99) and Mamá Tona (Petrona). She passed away in her 80s

nameless individual past six months of age!

In due time, Eustaquio (Yoo-stáh-kee-oh) was chosen as a distinguished sounding name for a promising baby boy whom his parents fondly hoped would grow up to be a coffee-plantation owner.

"Little Taco," as they called him affectionately, grew quickly. Soon after he was old enough to toddle around, it was decided that his little back was strong enough to carry small loads of wood in from the field. His parents were good to him. They carried big loads; he only had to carry small ones.

Brothers and sisters were soon added to the family, and it was urgently necessary for Taco to learn to work with a hoe and machete in order to help grow the corn and beans for the family to eat. Wiping the sweat from his forehead, little Taco would stand for a brief moment and watch with longing eyes as the children of wealthier parents would walk by on the path to or from school.

"I want to learn to read and write," he would say to himself as he returned to his work, a look of determination in his eyes. "If I could read and write and do mathematical figures, perhaps someday I could own a coffee farm."

As Taco grew to adolescence, he began to go out in the late afternoons after work and socialize with other young people. He still carried inside of him the longing to read and write.

"If only I had five cents, I could buy a notebook and pencil. But we must eat. My brothers and sisters must eat," he would say to himself, rubbing the hollow place in his middle. "So many children, and so little food."

Then there were the holes in their clothes. "Mother needs cloth to mend our clothes with," he would say to himself, fingering the most recent hole in his pants.

One day he said to another boy, "Show me how to write the alphabet." Taco handed him a stick. "Write in the dirt for me." The other boy obligingly showed him, and Taco struggled to make his marks on the ground look like those of the other boy. Each afternoon his friend showed him how to write and pronounce the letters. Taco learned quickly. When his friend was away, he asked other people to show him; even grown men.

Within a few weeks he could read, write, and do figures as well as anyone he knew. "Now I will work hard until I become a plantation owner," he solemnly vowed.

One day after Taco was eighteen, he was caught by the army recruiters and dragged away to serve his country. In the army he was found to be a young man of promise, and he was repeatedly promoted. At the end of three years he was offered an army career if he chose to stay.

Man on a White Horse

"I have had the honor of serving my country for these past three years," he said to his superiors, "but with all due respect, I don't want to make a career of taking human life."

With that he went back to work on the plantations. He soon married Petrona Morales, a young girl who had grown up as an orphan and had to forage for food. She was a resourceful young lady who knew how to make do with little. With much hard work and determination, they eventually acquired a few *cuerdas* of land in the township of Oja Blanca, which means "White Leaf." Their land was within one kilometer of the Mexican border, way back in the mountains thirty kilometers from where the highway was eventually built. (One cuerda is twenty-five square meters.)

Eustaquio and Petrona had thirteen children. Two of those children died while they were small, but Eustaquio and Petrona considered themselves fortunate because many other people lost more than half of their children to the grim reaper.

Eustaquio had an uncle who lived near Huehuetenango, about 110 kilometers from the township of Oja Blanca. Patrocinio, or Uncle Shino (Shee-no) as his nephews and nieces affectionately called him, occasionally made the four-day trip on horseback out to see Eustaquio.

In those days one had to be on the alert for the *choleros*, Indian witch-doctor headhunters. They would lurk along the trails at night, watching for lone travelers to kill with their big machetes to sacrifice to the devil.

Uncle Shino, however, believed in God with what limited knowledge he had, and he was not afraid. One day he said to his wife, Luisa, "I have some important business to discuss with Eustaquio. I must leave early tomorrow morning to go see him, and I will be back in a few days. I will need some *pishques* (peesh-kays) to eat on the way."

Pishques are made of corn tortilla dough shaped into loaves like bread, wrapped in corn husks or banana leaves kind of like tamales, and cooked. When traveling one simply stops and makes a little fire of sticks and twigs, unwraps one end of a *pishque*, cuts off some slices, and warms them over the coals. A *pishque* can keep for days, not getting old and stale like tortillas will.

Luisa made the *pishques*, then wrapped some refried beans in one corn husk, and some course, grainy salt and a few chili peppers in another. She packed them carefully in Shino's *moral*, a shoulder bag carried by the peasant men, and hung it beside his hat from a peg on the wall of their hut.

"Your food for the trip is ready," she told him that night. "Tona (short for Petrona) will surely prepare you something for the return journey."

Rising at three o'clock in the morning, Luisa got a blazing fire going and brewed some corn coffee for Shino to drink before leaving. "I hope you will be careful," she said as she poked a stick of wood farther into the fire. "I heard that the *choleros* have been out lately. They paid an old woman to lure a man who was traveling alone to sleep in the kitchen side of her hut by the fire."

She continued her story. "The man was a plain-clothes army commissioner. He carried a pistol with him, and he could understand some of the Indian dialect, but the old woman and her *cholero* companions did not know that. A little while after he had laid down to sleep, he heard the old woman whispering with some men outside that they were going to chop his head off at midnight.

"He lay there quietly until midnight. He knew that the men were outside in the bushes guarding the hut. He got his gun ready, and at midnight they suddenly burst into the hut, brandishing their machetes. The witch doctor was carrying a burning torch of pitchy pine wood, and before the men could come down on him with their machetes, he shot the witch doctor dead!

"The men quickly scattered, and he gathered up his things and left. The old woman also ran and hid when she heard the gunshot."

"I won't stop to sleep tonight," Shino said, looking into the fire as he sipped his corn coffee. "I am anxious to talk to Eustaquio anyway, so I will travel all night."

Bidding Luisa farewell, he mounted his horse and rode away. He stopped a few times that day to let his horse rest and to eat some slices from one of his *pishques* with the beans and hot peppers. But when night came, he traveled steadily without stopping.

At two o'clock in the morning he was passing through a narrow canyon called "El Boquerón." His horse was clopping along at a good pace when suddenly several men with sharp machetes stepped out in front of him and ordered him to stop.

"You must get off of your horse and come with us," the spokesman for the group said in Spanish that was heavily accented with the Indian dialect. Shino didn't know very much about God, but at that moment his heart reached out. A vision of Luisa poking wood into the fire flashed across his mind.

Suddenly his eyes were drawn to a man riding on a large white horse about fifty meters ahead of him on the trail. At the same time, the men who were blocking his way turned to look. In the brilliant moonlight, they could see the man motioning for him to come.

"Excuse me for a moment," Shino said. "I must go and see what my traveling companion wants."

The men stood speechless as Shino rode away. When he got to the place where the man on the white horse had been, there was no one to be seen anywhere. He turned and looked back. The *choleros* had disappeared into the bushes.

With a grateful heart Shino reigned his faithful horse to a gallop in order to search for the man who had saved his life, but he was nowhere to be found on the trail.

"God must have messengers that he sends to protect our lives," he mused to himself. "Just wait until Luisa hears this! And Eustaquio and Tona and the children!"

Uncle Shino heard the sweet old gospel story a few years later from some American missionaries who lived and worked in Huehuetenango for a time. When I met him, he was a loving, vibrant Christian. He lived to be approximately ninety-five years old.

Chapter Seventeen

A New Township

One day Eustaquio heard about a rich man who was offering large tracts of uncultivated land for sale at a cheap price. The land was in an area that had not yet been settled, and it was covered with virgin jungle. Not willing to let a good opportunity pass, Eustaquio rode his horse the twenty kilometers to the home of the landowner.

"Yes," replied *Don* Gilberto to Eustaquio's inquiry. "The land is up there in those mountains." He motioned with his hand. "Why don't you go see it?"

Eustaquio rode the ten kilometers into the mountains to inspect the land. He found rich soil and many monkeys and wild pigs. "This is my God-given opportunity to make plantation owners of my children," Eustaquio said to himself. "I will go back to see *Don* Gilberto at once and work out a deal with him."

"It is settled," *Don* Gilberto said after they had haggled over the price of the land for a while. "You shall have two *caballerías* for two thousand five hundred *quetzales*." That was approximately two hundred acres of land at twenty-five dollars an acre. A working man's wages were twenty cents a day at that time.

The *cuerdas* of land at Oja Blanca were sold and the money was used for the down payment on the new land, and the Matías family moved to the jungle to start a new plantation and a new township. A hut was immediately constructed to live in temporarily, and the family went to work clearing the land.

A man couldn't step outside of the hut alone, or he would be attacked and eaten by the wild pigs. So Eustaquio and all the boys would go out together to work. Clearing away the jungle with hoe and machete was not easy, but they were strong people who were accustomed to hard work.

More people bought land in the area and cleared it to plant corn, black beans, bananas, coffee, and tobacco. Many of the people killed the wild pigs to eat, and it wasn't long before only a few remained. After several years the wild pigs and monkeys were all gone.

One time Julio, one of the older Matías boys, shot one of the monkeys in the upper leg with Papá Eustaquio's pistol. The monkey quickly picked some leaves and, rolling them up, stuffed them into the wound. Then it pulled them back out and held them out so Julio and the other boys could see the blood on them. Then the monkey made another plug of leaves, again stuffing them into the wound.

Many other monkeys gathered around and, chattering loudly, broke off sticks and branches from the trees and threw them at the boys. After that incident, the Matías boys didn't want to harm any of the wild animals again.

After several years an American Catholic priest came to inaugurate the new township. He named it "El Chalum," after the chalún trees that were planted to shade the coffee bushes. Not knowing good Spanish, he made a mistake and put an "m" on the end of the word instead of an "n," so officially, the name of the township is El Chalum, when it really should be called El Chalún.

The Matías family planted tobacco to raise money quickly in order to make the payments on the land. During those first years food was

A New Township

scarce and they worked hard. Little Ismael, one of the younger sons, was six years old when they settled in Chalum. He was anxious to do his share of work and insisted on working hard all day, every day.

Sometimes Mamá Tona (as the children called her) would call him in and say, "You must not work so hard, my son. You should rest or play sometimes." But little Ismael would cry big tears until he was allowed to go back out into the field and work along with the older ones.

Ismael was nine years old when the highway was put through down in the valley, and the next year Dr. Graves set up his clinic. After some conversations with the American doctor, Papá Eustaquio requested Bible studies and baptism. Several years before, the family had joined the Central American Evangelical church, and Mamá Tona and some of the sons resisted the new religion for a while. But one by one, each followed the convictions of the Holy Spirit and asked to be baptized into the Bible believing Seventh-day Adventist Church.

"We will stop raising tobacco," Eustaquio told his sons. "It is better for Christians to raise coffee. And if we do not plant our own coffee, we will have to work on other people's coffee plantations in order to make a meager living. The way it is, God has given us the opportunity to have our own plantations. This way we will have more money to use to help spread the gospel in our own country."

Herculano, one of the Matías boys, worked as a lay evangelist for several years. The souls he led to Christ are numbered in the thousands. He is now a dentist. The rest of the family have done their share in the Lord's vineyard right at home. Many people have come to know the Lord through the dedicated efforts of the Matías family.

I remember visiting El Chalum when it was newly settled. What a contrast from the valley where it was hot and the people suffered from malaria and many other tropical illnesses. The mountain was similar in shape to Mt. Sinai in the Holy Land. At the top it looked like the Alps but with tropical vegetation. At those heights, there were no malaria mosquitoes, and the people were healthy. Chalum was nestled among the mountains along one side of that cliff.

The little rocky road leading up the mountain was more of a mule trail than a road. There were a few landowners who drove the road with four-wheel drive vehicles, but most traffic consisted of pedestrians carrying loads on their backs, occasionally someone on a horse, or someone leading a couple of mules loaded with beans, corn, or coffee.

The little road wound along the banks of the same river that ran along the edge of the Graves' property in the valley. In order to get to the township, you had to climb higher and higher until you reached a canyon with big cliffs towering above you. The cliffs lean over as if they are about to fall. In the rainy season sometimes big boulders came crashing down, rolling clear to the river. When that happened, it sounded like thunder echoing all through the canyon. No one had ever been hurt yet, but some people had some close calls.

On the way up the mountain was the township of El Sarral, where a few plantation owners lived along the river below the road and a few peons had their huts. This road went clear on beyond the township of Oja Blanca. Of course, it took the plantation owners three hours to drive the thirty kilometers from the highway to there. From the valley to this point was four kilometers. It was a bit cooler at this height.

At El Sarral you had to turn off of the little road onto a trail that went up the mountainside. The river was to the left. As the trail turned, you had to climb right up toward the cliff, which was very steep. To get to El Chalum you had to climb switch back after switch back. Young coffee bushes grew all over the mountainside.

On the trail was a place called "Mal Paso," or "Bad Pass." It got that name because one day a horse was carrying a load of coffee when

A New Township

it brushed too close to the mountainside and was thrown off balance, slipping off the trail and falling straight down for about 200 hundred feet into the rocky crevice below.

After the pass, the trail turned and suddenly went straight up the mountain. Climbing above the cliffs, the air was deliciously cooler, and the trail was not quite as steep as it was at Mal Paso. At the top you could see the township of Chalum. From here you had to walk down into the swale about one fourth of a kilometer. Although it was rocky, there were series of craters with little ridges in between them that were semi-flat on top. Here is where the adobe houses of the plantation owners were built, and coffee was planted along the steep sides of the craters. Eventually the mountainsides were cleared and planted too, but that happened later.

In the bottom of each crater was an opening down to an underground passage where the water drained into from the mountainsides when it rained, emptying out into the river below the cliff in the canyon. Of course, this caused the river to flash flood at times.

After all that walking, you would finally reach the Matías' home. Mamá Tona always served a fine meal from the *plancha*, an adobe fireplace with a wood stove top. Her black beans, rice, scrambled eggs, hot sauce, fresh tortillas, and hot corn coffee or lemonade were the best in the country.

The Matías children were a fun bunch. Francisco, the oldest, was quiet, shy, hard working, and kind-hearted. Next was Felipe who always had a mischievous twinkle in his eyes, then came Julio who sometimes talked before he thought, but he would give you the shirt off his back if you needed it.

Next came Benedicto. He was short, curly-headed, and quiet with bright, friendly eyes. After Benedicto or "Beno," as he is called for short, was Herculano who made you laugh all the time with his delightful wit and humor.

Then came Irene, a boy who was born spastic. You couldn't understand his speech until you'd known him for a while, and his movements were uncoordinated, but he would welcome you with a crushing embrace and inform you that if you wanted to live in Chalum, he would build you a house on his land.

Next came Reina, a quiet girl with long black braids. After Reina came Ismael, a strong boy who, in wisdom and maturity, was many years ahead of his age. Both Reina and Ismael have a tremendous sense of humor.

Next in order of birth was Efigenio who was a bit more feisty and aggressive than the rest. And last but not least, was Melca, who was somewhat feisty like Efigenio. Ranging in age from teens to early thirties, the family lived in two adobe rooms with many beds close together. Of course, as each young man got married, he would leave the house to build his own home.

Chapter Eighteen

Money to Throw Away

I have not always done things the traditional way, or at least not the American traditional way. God leads every individual over the path that is best suited to his or her needs, and where one can be of the most service to humanity.

One thing that I suppose was not traditional was when I married Ismael Matías two and a half months before my seventeenth birthday—he was twenty-five at the time of our wedding. We were married in Southern California. It was his second trip to the States, and by this time he could speak English quite well. We chose to have our wedding in Spanish, however, and were married by Iván Ruiz, a dear pastor from Costa Rica who had pastored Hispanic churches in the United States for many years.

When Ismael (or Ishmael as I call him in English) was born, a messenger was sent on horseback over the mountains to the municipality to register the new baby's birth. Forgetting the family name Matías, the man gave him his grandmother's last name, Recinos. At the time of our marriage, Ishmael asked me if I wanted his last name changed to Matías, but I liked the name Recinos just as well, so we left it that way.

After the wedding, my father offered Ismael a job if he wanted to stay in the States for a while before going back to Guatemala, but I

Ismael Recinos shortly after we were married.

was anxious for the adventure of beginning life on the coffee farm, so off we went to our home in Chalum.

Ishmael had started a house of adobes, then added a wooden upstairs made from lumber from the big trees on the mountainsides of Chalum. The adobes were made a few feet from the building site. The tin for the roof and tiles for the floor were hauled up the mountain on horseback.

When we first arrived in Chalum after our wedding, none of the rooms of our house were finished enough for us to move into, so my generous brother-in-law Julio offered us the use of his house until we could get a room in our own house ready to move into. Julio was living in the village of El Tablón that year and working as a lay evangelist. His wife, Catalina, and their three children were with him too.

Benedicto and his wife Petronila lived in a house between Julio's

Money to Throw Away

and our house. Julio's house at that time consisted of two adobe rooms with mosaic tile floor. Outside to one side of it was a little thatched-roof hut that was used as a kitchen and eating place. We had purchased a propane gas stove though, so we left the kitchen hut closed and used only the two adobe rooms.

Just outside and down over the bank was a water faucet and a table. Here I did all of our washing. Down the side of the crater a little farther was a prolific chayote vine that made a dandy outhouse. Ishmael hired several men to help him finish building our house, and I served them three meals a day. We all had a good time in those days. My family's old friend, Anastacio, was one of the hired men.

One thing I refused to do was learn how to cook the corn and prepare the masa to make tortillas. (I had learned to pat them out and bake them over the comal as a child over at Elsa's house, but I carefully kept that a secret.) The women there got up at three o'clock in the morning to start the tortillas for the day. We had company every night until midnight, and I decided to be a "rich" plantation owner's wife and buy our tortillas. That way I could be a popular hostess in the evenings and get my sleep as well. It has always worked out well for us that way, and my dear husband is very understanding. I often baked bread the American way to give to my neighbors.

One day I was washing at the little table when I heard a step behind me and felt hot air blowing down the back of my neck. I whirled around, and there stood a neighbor's curious run-away mule. It seemed like everyone always wanted to know how the American girl did things, and this mule was no exception! When I turned around, the mule whirled around and ran at the same time. I don't know which one of us was more startled.

At the same moment three pigs ran squealing out of the kitchen hut. Somehow they had pushed the door open and gotten in. They be-

People who cannot afford a pila often wash their clothes like this. When the stray mule breathed down the author's neck, this is how I was washing clothes.

longed to a neighbor who lived up the hillside and kept many animals. His grey water drain ran right across the main trail, and the pigs wallowed in it constantly. When crossing that mud hole, one would sink into the sour mud above the ankles, and there was no way around it. I once lost a shoe that the mud suctioned right off my foot—I was never able to locate it in all the muck.

Ishmael was the last of the Matías children to get married. However, his spastic brother, Irene, never married. At the time of our marriage, Papá Eustaquio and Mamá Tona had built a house down beneath the cliff near the river in Sarral. They now lived there, and Irene lived with them. He was an excellent errand boy and a help to them in many ways. He had a strange gait because of his spastic condition, but he could hike up and down those trails faster than anyone!

Eventually my parents-in-law had to abandon their house in Sar-

Money to Throw Away

ral because of land erosion. After that they built a nice modern block house in Valparaíso right beside the highway a few hundred feet from the clinic. But that was years later.

After two months we were able to move into the downstairs of our new house. We had a bed, a stove, and a pile of luggage in the corner. At that time a church was being built about 500 feet from our house. I had a little cedar chest of keepsakes from my childhood, and we put 300 quetzals in it that we had dedicated to the church building fund. Our windows had plastic glass in them and could be slid open. The bathroom windows were open, having no glass in them yet.

Sometimes when we made a trip to Huehuetenango (or Huehue as we called it for short), we would hike down the mountain to my folks' place in the valley, stay overnight, and then catch the early morning bus to Huehue out on the highway when it went by. Sometimes we got up at three o'clock and hiked down from Chalum, getting to the highway in time to catch the bus.

It was the day before Christmas in 1974. We had been married four months. We were in Huehue choosing paint for the house, when Benedicto snuck up behind me and pulled on my purse. I turned around and said, "Hey, what are you doing here?"

He grew serious as he told us, "Someone broke into your house. You must come home immediately so we can report it to the auxiliares (four men who are appointed each year as the local sheriff in the township). We've got to try to catch the thief. Maybe we can get some of your money back."

In my cedar chest I also had an old coin collection that had been given to Bethel at one time by one of our uncles, and she eventually gave it to me. He had collected coins from several countries when he was in the army many years before. I also had a collection of Guatemalan fifty cent coins that were made of silver. When they had been in circulation years before, Dr. Graves told me to collect all I could because someday they would be quite valuable.

"Do you know what the thief took?" I asked Beno.

"He took your cedar chest as far as we can tell," he answered.

"Oh no! The church money and the coin collection!" I exclaimed.

We all got on the next bus to Valparaíso. Benedicto had brought his three horses for us to ride up the mountain that night. The moon was full, it was Christmas Eve, and the air had that delicious December chill to it.

Telling Mamma and Bethel good-bye, we mounted the horses and headed for Chalum. We rode out to the highway and on past the clinic toward the gas station.

When we got to a place called El Jobal, we saw a crowd of people on the highway. They were celebrating Christmas Eve by drinking, dancing to marimba music, and burning firecrackers. As we approached on our horses, the crowd grew quiet. I began to feel apprehensive. It was around midnight.

When we were even with the fiesta crowd, some young fellows suddenly lit a bunch of firecrackers. The horses spooked at the pop-pop-popping sound, and they began to dance a jig of their own among the crowd. My horse kept trying to jump over the little bank at the edge of the road, and I held the reigns as firmly as I could. Four young men were underneath my horse, scrambling around and hanging onto their hats for all they were worth. I had to smile to myself. Pretty soon we got the horses calmed down and went on our way.

In a couple of hours we were home. "You mustn't sleep in your bed," Beno told us. "You can't touch anything until the auxiliares get here in the morning to inspect the evidence. I will get you a blanket to sleep on the floor with."

The thief had pried the window over the bed open and jumped in,

Money to Throw Away

**This may be why some people thought I
"shouldn't marry outside my race and culture."**

leaving muddy footprints and a smashed hat. If he had been a little more clever, he would have climbed in the bathroom window where there was no glass, and avoided leaving any noticeable evidence.

Benedicto ran over to his house next door, fetched a blanket, and brought it to us. Bidding us good night, he went home. Ishmael and I huddled together for the rest of the night on the cold tile floor with the blanket pulled around us as far as it would reach. Finally, daylight began to dawn, and a few minutes later the auxiliares arrived.

Ishmael's brothers and their wives came from their houses and gathered around, discussing the matter of the robbery. Each had a piece of evidence to contribute, and it was not hard to conclude that the burglar was Israel, (called Yeyo for short). He was a cousin to the Matías family.

Yeyo had left with his father the day before to go to Ixcán (Eeshcahn), a jungle area in the lowlands where land was being offered for sale at a cheap price. It was an all-day bus ride to the end of the road, then one could hike for days in the Ixcán jungle.

Two of the auxiliares went in pursuit of the young thief and his unsuspecting father. They overtook him a ways into Ixcán, and taking his father, Uncle Luís, aside, they explained the whole matter to him. In silent shock and anger, he immediately turned around and, taking his wayward boy, started back to Chalum with the auxiliares.

Yeyo was sixteen years old. "Your mother is very sick and needs you to return home at once," the auxiliares told him. They wanted to make sure he accompanied them willingly and did not try to run away.

The return trip took them a couple of days. Upon reaching Mal Paso during the hike up the mountain, the auxiliares pulled out a rope and proceeded to tie up the by-now-very-surprised boy. He was brought to our house, and someone was appointed to stand guard over him while the two auxiliares went home to eat and freshen up.

That year the road from Sarral to Chalum had been built. My father-in-law had a four-wheel drive Toyota station wagon, and Ishmael's younger brother, Efigenio, was his chauffeur. As the patriarch of the family clan, it was his duty to be present at the "trial" that was to be held that night. So Efigenio drove him up the mountain and brought him to our house.

When the two auxiliares returned, a crowd had gathered and Yeyo was brought inside. "Sit down!" ordered his father sternly, as someone pulled up a chair for him. Dangling a horsewhip in the boy's face, Uncle Luís asked, "Where is the cedar chest that you stole from your cousin, Ismael?"

"I did not steal the cedar chest," replied Yeyo with a wooden face.

"You shameless, ungrateful boy!" roared Uncle Luís. "Tell the truth at once!" With that he cracked the whip down on Yeyo's shoulder.

Witnesses then came forward and told of Yeyo tossing strange coins into the air and saying, "I have lots of money. I have money to throw away, and money from the United States. I am rich." They reported that he had thrown many coins out into the coffee plantation.

Others said that he had loaned them money. "I have plenty," he had said. But he had spent most of the money. His father searched his pockets, and finding one hundred quetzals, gave it to Ishmael. "Where did you get all that money?" Uncle Luís asked him.

"I sold three *quintales* of corn," the boy said. Three *quintales* or 300 pounds of corn was only worth twenty-four quetzals.

"Tell the truth! Tell the truth!" roared Uncle Luís, whipping him vigorously without regards as to where the whip should land. Yeyo put his arm up to protect his face.

"I took the cedar chest," he admitted, wincing with pain.

"And where is the cedar chest now?" interrogated Uncle Luís.

"I burned it."

"Tell the truth, you ungrateful, worthless boy! Where is it?" he bellowed, whipping him constantly.

"Down over the hill under a banana tree."

At that, the auxiliares tied Yeyo more securely with the rope, and taking him outside, ordered him to show them the exact whereabouts of the cedar chest. They returned with it in about three minutes. It was broken and the lock was gone, but some of my old pictures and letters were still in it. These were immediately given to me.

Over a period of three hours, Uncle Luís questioned and whipped the boy until he had extracted all the information we needed as to what he had done with the money and the coins.

Suddenly the door opened, and Concepsión, Yeyo's older married brother, stepped into the room. He was the only one of the family who

Hortencia at age 10 (my brother-in law Julio's daughter), and me a few months after Ismael and I were married.

had joined the church as yet. It was his duty as eldest son to help maintain order and discipline in the family, and he also believed it to be his Christian duty to demonstrate for all to see his disapproval of his younger brother's shameful conduct. He had a look of stern solemnity on his face, and everyone knew that behind it was deep sorrow and regret for Yeyo's misdemeanor.

With his jaw firmly set and without saying a word, he stepped over to his father. The room had become deathly silent. Taking the whip from Uncle Luís' hand, he gave his wayward brother a sound thrashing on his legs, but not all over his body and head indiscriminately like Uncle Luís had. After about twenty lashes, he handed the whip back to his father, and without saying a word, turned and left.

Then Uncle Luís fell on Yeyo, whipping him mercilessly in a rage of fury and shame. "I'm sorry your face ever appeared in this world!"

he shouted over and over again. "You are not worthy to be a member of this family! You are worthless dung!"

At last Papá Eustaquio decided that it was time to intervene. "That is enough, Luís," he said to his brother-in-law. "You have carried out your parental duty well, but you must not kill the boy. And do not worry about the money you could not recover from Yeyo. If Ismael becomes needy, I will help him. He is my son."

With that the trial ended, and everyone returned home. Over the next few days many people came, bringing coins or money that Yeyo had given or loaned them. Some of the children went out and searched the coffee plantation in the places where they had seen him throwing the coins from my collection into the air. I thought it was like searching for needles in a haystack, but to my surprise, they found a lot of my coins. Over a period of several months, children would come bringing more of the coins to me that they found when playing among the coffee bushes or running errands. In this way I recovered about half of my coin collection.

These children were mostly Ishmael's nieces and nephews, but there were other children in the neighborhood who brought the coins to me when they found them. I always gave them an orange or some other little treat as a token of my appreciation for their thoughtfulness. But they would have brought the coins to me anyway.

For years Yeyo drank heavily, but he would often have sudden seizures. He often bragged to his buddies that he was going to break into our house someday, steal a large amount of money, then leave the area for good.

When I heard of such things, I would smile and shake my head. Yeyo would never be able to figure out how to break into our house now that it was finished and had bars on the windows. And if he did get in, there would be very little money for him to steal anyway.

Catalina, Julio's wife, once planted an orange tree. When it was starting to bear for the first time, she proudly told her neighbors that she was going to sell the first ripe orange and give the money as a first-fruits offering. Hearing of that, one Sabbath morning while Catalina was in church Yeyo picked the biggest orange and slowly peeled it and ate it, throwing the skins high into the air. "So much for your first-fruits offering," he jeered.

Fortunately, Yeyo finally changed his ways and requested to be baptized. Ishmael was appointed to give him his baptismal studies. By this time he was married, and he and his wife were both baptized. At the present, their daughters attend our church school in Chalum and Yeyo no longer has seizures.

Uncle Luís was baptized before he died, and Aunt Beta, Yeyo's mother, was also baptized and attends church faithfully. Isn't God good?

Chapter Nineteen

We Want Blood

*B*y the month of February, 1975, we were moved into the upstairs of our house as well as the downstairs. The house still wasn't quite finished, but at last the end was in sight.

At this time the government of Guatemala was on the verge of declaring war with England. England claimed Belice as a colony, and Guatemala claimed it as a territory, and Belice had requested their independence from England.

Every day we anxiously listened to the news, hoping and praying that there would not be war. In such a case single and married men would be drafted alike, including Ishmael, and I was nervous about it.

By the evening of February 3, the tension had mounted in the country to a high intensity. Many people wanted war, and some, like us, did not. That evening a large number of prostitutes marched in the streets of Guatemala City, crying vehemently, "We want blood, we want blood!" The prayers of those street women were answered that night in a much different way than they had anticipated. Many of them lost their own lives!

I woke up at three o'clock on the morning of February 4, but I could not go back to sleep. I felt a strange, unexplainable restlessness. Suddenly at about three-thirty the house began to lurch and shake violently. There was a deafening underground roar at the same time. Ishmael woke up, and we clung to each other in silent terror. I expected the adobe downstairs to collapse beneath us, but it didn't.

The initial shock lasted for an eternity of thirty-nine seconds. After that, the upstairs windows continued to rattle and shake for another forty-five minutes. Occasionally there would be a lurch and the shaking would increase, then begin to die away again.

"There must be a lot of dead people somewhere," Ishmael whispered to me. "Let's pray." At daylight we got up and turned on the radio. All the stations thundered with news of the earthquake. "God, have mercy on us!" one reporter cried. Other stations played "Las Golondrinas," a good-bye or funeral song. Going to war with England was never mentioned again.

During the days that followed many people used the radio stations as a way to communicate with relatives in other parts of the country. "We are safe, but we do not have a house anymore," we heard over and over again.

A fault was discovered at Chimaltenango, a town about fifty kilometers from Guatemala City in the high country. The worst of the destruction was there. Nearly every family lost loved ones in the area surrounding that town. It was announced on the radio that the intensity of the quake was a 7.4 magnitude quake (if I recall correctly). At noon on the day after the earthquake there was an aftershock that brought down many buildings that had been shaken loose from their foundations by the initial quake.

Many people died from the clay tile roofs falling in on them. After the earthquake, no more tile roofs were made. Each day the number of dead bodies dug up from the ruins increased. The final figure that was announced was 22,000 dead, and 50,000 injured. I have always figured that the number of dead victims of the earthquake was greater. The authorities counted the number of bodies they dug up, but they

We Want Blood

probably did not know for sure how many actually were missing from among the Indian population in the rural towns and villages.

Other countries sent in food, clothes, and tents for the homeless. After several weeks the roads were repaired enough for travel to begin again. We ventured out to Guatemala City and saw many of the tent villages along the way. Some of the villages and towns that had been completely destroyed were rebuilt with money sent from other countries. As a result, many people had better housing after the earthquake than before.

The headquarters of the Central American Union were in Guatemala City at that time, and Robert Folkenberg was president. He organized the distribution of clothing, medicines, and other donated items. A village near Antigua that had been reduced to rubble was rebuilt by the Seventh-day Adventists.

Many buildings had fallen in Guatemala City, and many people had tragic stories to tell of digging out their loved ones. One story was told of a family living in one of the villages that was devastated by the earthquake. When the quake began, they all got up and ran outside, except for the old grandmother who announced that she wanted to die, so she remained inside, crouched in the corner. The house collapsed, and after the quake was over, they discovered that the beams had fallen in such a way as to form a teepee shaped shelter over her head, leaving her entirely unharmed.

In Chalum it shook hard, but no serious damage was done. Our house settled a bit on one side so that one of the plastic windows downstairs bowed out slightly and the doors were out of line, but otherwise there was no lasting damage. We were thankful for our blessings. Down in the valley, the shock was only a mild tremor.

During the following months, it was announced that another big quake was expected, and people were advised to sleep outside. We did that for many nights. I liked it better that way, because on the ground the tremors could not be felt as much.

At that time a comet could be seen in the eastern sky from our part of the world around three o'clock in the morning. The nights we slept outside we got to feast our eyes on it. It was the dry season, and the nights were clear. The comet looked to be the size of a basketball with a tail sticking straight up ten feet into the sky. It was bright and luminous, a sight more beautiful than I can describe. I will never forget it!

Chapter Twenty

Ixcán

"Your names are on the list," we were informed. "If you go back, they will kill you."

Around the time of the earthquake, my father-in-law became interested in some jungle land that was offered for sale at a very cheap price. It was in some lowlands called Ixcán, in a remote corner of the department of Huehuetenango. He had made a couple of trips out there, and now the fertile land was the talk of the entire Matías family. I reluctantly began to feel that it was my duty to go see the place.

Bethel was curious and enthusiastic to go on a jungle trek, so we got Ishmael to ask Papá Eustaquio if the three of us could go along on the next trip.

"Sure," he said. "The more people in our party, the safer we will be. I will send word for Luís and his son Yeyo to come and meet us where the road ends and the trail begins with mules for you to ride." (Luís had been so humiliated by Yeyo's burglary of our house that he had taken his family and moved to Ixcán where they remained in seclusion for several years until the communist guerrilla warfare forced them to return to Chalum.)

A date was set for a Sunday in April to start the trek. The rainy season would begin in May, and it was better to travel in the dry season. That Saturday night we took our backpacks and hiked down to

Sarral, where Ishmael and I, along with several of my brothers-in-law and some other men from the neighborhood of Chalum slept at Papá Eustaquio's house. Mamá Tona solicitously tended to our needs as best as she could. The men were told to sleep on the floor, but Ishmael and I were given a bed to sleep on.

At three o'clock in the morning we all got up, and after drinking some *mosh*, a sweet oatmeal and milk beverage that my mother-in-law prepared for us, we all climbed into Papá Eustaquio's newly acquired Ford pickup. It had a canopy on the back, and most of us rode back there.

It took us forty-five minutes of bouncing along over the rocky road to get to the highway, which was four kilometers away. We stopped briefly at my folks' place to pick Bethel up. She climbed into the back and sat down on the wooden bench beside me, and we were on our way.

We all dozed off and on as Efigenio drove the eighty kilometers to Huehuetenango. By this time it was starting to get daylight. From Huehue we turned onto a little dirt road that climbed quickly into the mountains.

"I wish the new land was up here," I said to Bethel. We strained to see through the cloud of dust.

"We haven't seen Ixcán yet," replied my sister. "It might be nice."

The road was rough, and progress was slow. We whiled away the hours chattering in English to each other about this and that. My in-laws and other friends didn't mind in the least. In fact, they were all a little carsick, including Ishmael. Some took Dramamine and dozed. (Motion sickness was something my family never suffered with, and it was a good thing with all the traveling we did!)

At length, Papá Eustaquio instructed Efigenio to stop. It was about ten o'clock, and we were still high up in the mountains. We had come

Ixcán

about fifty kilometers from Huehuetenango. Pine trees grew everywhere here, and I guessed that we were at about 10,000-feet elevation above sea level.

Ishmael felt better after walking around in the fresh air for a couple of minutes, and soon we began gathering sticks to light a small fire to warm our breakfast on. It is said in Guatemala that if women warm tortillas over a campfire, they always taste bitter. But if men warm them, they taste good. So the men warmed the tortillas and served them to us greenhorn American ladies.

"OK, folks," Papá Eustaquio announced after a few minutes, "let's get in and get on our way. We won't get there by staying here." Early that morning, he had offered Bethel and me a seat up front, but we had declined, saying that some of the ones who suffered from motion sickness should ride up there.

Now he asked us again, "Don't you want to ride in front?" Again we declined, and Ishmael rode in the back with us.

The road led down into a little valley where the little town of Soloma lies. Its inhabitants are mostly Indians, and it had cobblestone streets. From Soloma we climbed back into more high mountains. After a while the road took us down into another little valley where the town of San Mateo is. It looked much like Soloma. We slowly climbed from the little town back into the mountains. After what seemed like an eternity, the road began winding down, down, down toward the town of Barillas. There we stayed overnight with Atilano and Marta before starting the trek into Ixcán the next day.

Atilano is Ishmael's cousin, and he was working in the Barillas area as a lay evangelist at the time. His wife, Marta, is Catalina's sister. Atilano, Marta, and their little one-year-old daughter lived in a room they rented. Marta cooked on a kerosene stove they had in one corner. She made her tortillas every day at a neighbor's house over the fire.

We arrived in Barillas about three o'clock in the afternoon. The climate of Barillas, like Chalum, was pleasant—not too hot and not too cold.

We were all very dusty, and I was pretty tired, so we decided to walk down to the nearby river to bathe. It was not deep enough to swim in, but we could pour the water over ourselves and get clean. On the way to the river, two little girls about ten and eleven years old decided to follow us and find out who the new people were.

Assuming that Bethel and I could not speak Spanish, they walked beside Ishmael and asked him, "Are these white ladies your wives?"

"Only the younger one," replied Ishmael, smiling. "I have one wife." For a moment the girls looked at us wide eyed, digesting that bit of information as we walked along toward the river.

"Where do you live?" the older one asked Ishmael.

"We come from a township called El Chalum," he answered.

Putting her nose a bit higher in the air, the little girl said, "Oh. Is that jungle backwoods or a town?"

"It is jungle backwoods, just like Barillas, here," replied Ishmael with a twinkle.

"Oh," said the little girl, slightly nonplused. "Well, we will show you the nicest place to take a bath in the river."

After we had all bathed, the little girls returned home, and we went back to Atilano's room, and Marta served us a delicious dinner of spaghetti fried in mayonnaise. How different, and how tasty, I thought.

Soon the door and window were securely locked shut, and we all lay down to sleep on the cement floor. The air was stuffy, and I didn't sleep much. At four o'clock in the morning we got up and piled back into the pickup. It took us an hour to get to the end of the road. We were now in a lower elevation, and it was getting hotter.

Dawning our backpacks, we all started off down the trail. By this time it was starting to get light. The pickup was left in the care of some people living in a nearby hut whom Papá Eustaquio had become acquainted with during his previous trips to and from Ixcán.

The trail consisted of many boulders. Part of the time we climbed over them, but in other places we had to jump from rock to rock. The weight of my backpack threw me off balance a bit, and I was having a hard time keeping up with the men's fast pace. Bethel was doing fine though, and I was proud of her.

After about an hour we came to a hut on the trail where an old Indian woman lived. She sold food and lemonade, and everyone bought some from her. I wanted plain water, but she didn't want to let me have any. She spoke very little Spanish, but Ishmael succeeded in getting the message across to her that we would buy plain water at the same price that she sold her lemonade for. Beaming with pleasure, she quickly poured the water from her old clay pot. She had to walk two kilometers down the mountainside to a spring to get water, and carry it the two kilometers back up to her hut in a heavy clay pot on her head. I did not blame her in the least for not wanting to give her water away!

While we were at the hut Uncle Luís and his son Yeyo appeared on the scene leading two mules. I wondered to myself if this boy who had broken into our house and then been soundly whipped for it in our presence would be reluctant to see us again. However, he greeted us in the customary way for close friends and relatives by patting us each on the back. But I thought his attitude seemed shameless and defiant.

Uncle Luís walked slowly toward us. He looked older and more tired and careworn than I remembered him. Perhaps life in the lowlands was not so great after all. I patted him warmly on the back. My heart went out in sympathy to this poor old man who had been so desperately humiliated by his youngest son.

The mules had "arquillos" on their backs in place of saddles. An "arquillo" is a rough wooden frame similar in shape to a saddle. It is used to tie one hundred pound sacks of corn, beans, or coffee to the mules' back.

Bethel was offered one mule, and I the other. We settled ourselves as best we could on our wooden perches atop the mules and began the long ride down the steep mountainside into the lowlands. Bethel soon tired of riding on the crudely shaped arquillo and got off of her mule. I was determined to ride though, so I stayed on my mule. The trail was still strewn with big boulders, and in many places it branched out into several trails. One had to pick the right trail, because they all dead-ended a hundred or so feet farther on, and the space between the rocks was too narrow to turn the mule around in. At one place, my mule was determined to go down a dead-end trail, but after a battle of wills, I prevailed and got us back on the right path.

My mule seemed quite reluctant to have me for a passenger, and it would often crush my legs and feet against the boulders if I wasn't on the alert to pick them up out of the way.

The heat was intense, and I could see heat waves radiating from the jungle vegetation all around us. After six hours, we got down into a valley. About noon we came to a little river, and we all stopped for a swim.

Ishmael was looking flushed and overheated, so I insisted that he ride the mule. After another hour's steep climb up a hillside, we came to some huts where we were to spend the night. The girls that lived there were delighted to see Bethel and me. They fingered our braided hair and gently stroked our sticky, sweaty skin.

There were no lemon trees around there, so the girls made "vina-grada," or vinegarade, for us to drink. I about choked on it, so I asked for plain water.

"Oh, no!" The girls exclaimed almost in unison, one of them grinning toothlessly. "It would be an insult to our hospitality to serve you plain water. We want to give you vinegarade!"

I managed to sneak away to the spring a few times and drink my fill of water, but I got thirsty again in a few minutes and had to try to sneak back to the spring. The girls kept a sharp lookout, and usually caught me and dragged me back to the kitchen hut for a big glass of vinegarade. Eventually Ishmael, Bethel, and I managed to convince them that we really needed plain water, and that it would be very hospitable of them to let us have it. After that they served both water and vinegarade, so that everyone in the group could take their pick. They were sweet and well meaning. It just takes people time to digest a new concept or idea sometimes.

We slept that night in the large hut that had many wooden beds in it. The flees chewed on us all night, and I was glad to get up early and leave the next morning. I wore a pair of knee-length shorts.

Papá Eustaquio shook his head. "You need to wear your long pants," he told me. "The blades of grass will cut your legs."

"I cannot tolerate the heat," I replied. "I will be careful of the grass."

I had braided my hair the day before, and the sun had burned me where my hair usually covered my neck and shoulders. Now I found that I could not carry my backpack. The men in the group distributed my things into their packs, and we were on our way. After a while we came to a large pasture with cattle. Someone said that there was a bull at the other end of the pasture. I asked if it was mean. "If we walk along quickly and quietly, it will not chase us," Ishmael and Herculano said evasively.

Bethel was keeping up fine, backpack and all, but I kept tiring and lagging behind. But when I thought about the possibility of the bull chasing us, I forgot my weariness and hurried along for a few minutes.

Suddenly I looked up and saw Ishmael and Herculano exchange a knowing glance.

"You are taking advantage of my fear of bulls to make me walk faster!" I exclaimed crossly. Ishmael, as usual, was patient with me, and Herculano said gently, "We meant no harm." I quickly forgave them, and we continued on.

Before long we came to a mud hole on the trail, and I got some of the gritty, grainy mud in my shoes and in between my toes. After an hour the mud had rubbed some pretty good-sized blisters, and I had to remove my shoes. I found that barefooted I was able to keep up with the rest easily. Or maybe they just slowed down some for me, now that I had an apparent reason to go slow.

We hiked through flat, swampy lands and up and down hills until late afternoon. Finally, Papá Eustaquio announced, "This is the land that I am buying. We have reached our destination."

In the center of the property was a small hut with some Indians living in it. The Indian women in the Ixcán area generally went topless, and the little lady of this hut was no exception. We had a nice time visiting with these gentle-natured, friendly people, and we set up our little camp a few feet from their hut.

The men made a shelter of banana leaves supported by four poles for us to sleep under. Then we all gathered sticks for a campfire to keep the bugs away and to warm our pishques for supper.

When it grew dark, the dew fell heavily, and the damp clamminess chilled us to the bone. We laid down sheets of plastic, and each person took out the blanket or sleeping bag he had brought along, and we all retired for the night. I didn't mind the lumpy hard ground underneath me, but I detested the clouds of mosquitoes and gnats that severely attacked any exposed area. I had to sleep with my head under the sleeping bag, without leaving the slightest air hole where the bugs could get in. Once in a while I would stick my nose out for a breath of fresh air, and the gnats would instantly swoop down on me. The mosquitoes were right behind them, and I decided that I was going to have to choose between itching to death or suffocating. I ended up being tortured by both in equal amounts. For some strange reason the bugs picked me for their prime target and left the others alone.

Early the next morning, I went out to the trail to sit in the sun for a few minutes. A couple of men came along who were all bent over with big loads of corncobs on their backs. They stopped to talk with me for a few minutes. They looked and talked like Latinos, but they were dressed in Indian clothes.

"Good morning," they both said politely.

"Good morning. Good morning." I replied in the customary way of greeting each one individually.

"Do you like our lovely Ixcán?" they asked.

"It is very beautiful," I answered evasively. (South of the U.S. border, one must always be polite.)

"Are you going to live here?"

"Perhaps," I replied, thinking, More likely I will die here before we ever leave to go home!

"Who are the people with you?"

"My father-in-law and some of his family," I told them.

"Is he buying land here?"

"Yes."

"Is he going to move here?"

"I think he would like to."

"Welcome to Ixcán," they chorused. "Adios, adios."

"Adios, adios," I echoed back.

I whiled away the day soaking in the stream that ran across the property and sleeping in the cool, chigger-infested grass in the shade.

Hope That Springs Eternal

The others went off to inspect the land, and some of the men in the party who were no relation to the Matías family had brought rifles and were killing off the wild life ruthlessly and indiscriminately, feasting on everything from possums to deer. I was sickened when they brought a beautiful toucan bird to camp that they had killed and ate it.

Bethel and I went together to the stream for a while, and finding a deeper place, sat in water up to our necks and tried to imagine what a blizzard would be like. The very idea seemed extremely remote and far away, and we could not even muster a shiver.

"This is green hell," I said to my sister. "During the day the devil cooks you, then at night he turns off the fire and sends out the bugs to chew on you until you lose your mind!"

"I rather like it," replied Bethel. "For once the chronic ear infection has 'cooked' out of me, and I can hear decently. I don't have to try to guess what people are saying."

As we sat I began to hear the flies. There was a kind of fly in the jungle there that the people referred to as the *chiquirín* fly. These flies were about two and a half inches long and one inch wide. They looked like giant houseflies, and I abhorred them. They inhabited certain trees that were scattered through the jungle, and at certain times they would all start "singing" together in a constant, high-pitched screech that made ones ears ache. They would keep this up for an hour, then rest for an hour.

Thinking about the flies reminded me of Ishmael's nephews, Oziel and Amilcar, twelve and thirteen years old at the time, who had accompanied us on the excursion to Ixcán. They were sons of Gomercinda, Ishmael's older sister who had died in childbirth. These two boys and their siblings had been left motherless at a very young age.

Oziel caught a "chiquirín" fly and tied it to a string and carried it with him. It would fly in a circle as he held the end of the string. Once he put the fly on me, and I made the mistake of jumping. I have never been fond of insects, and I realized that now that he had discovered my aversion to them he would have ample opportunity to drive me berserk with bugs out here in the jungle where "critters" of every description thrived in abundance. I also knew from the mischievous look on his face that I would need to take some decisive action to banish all plans from his mind in order to preserve my own sanity.

Accordingly, I began to watch for an opportunity, and one soon presented itself. I discovered a couple of toads near the fire, and grabbing one of them, I took off after Oziel with it. Guatemalans detest toads, and I chased him round and round the fire. I stepped on a hot coal with my bare foot, but I didn't let that discourage me. I didn't catch him, but I chased him with the obnoxious toad until I was sure that all thoughts of scaring me with bugs had abandoned him.

We slept there one more night, then headed for home the next day. At one point we crossed the Rio Ixcán, a beautiful wide river that is lovely for swimming. We stopped for about an hour to enjoy it. I went upstream about one fourth of a kilometer and floated on my back toward the rapids, which were just below the river crossing. When I was still about thirty feet upstream from them, Ishmael and Herculano grabbed me and pulled me to my feet.

"Are you alive?" one of them asked me.

"Very much so!" I sputtered, upset at having been so rudely extracted from my blissful trip downstream.

"You were so still in the water, and you almost hit the rapids," Ishmael said.

"But I was still thirty feet above the rapids!" I protested.

None of the Matías family had been around water very much, and they were distrustful of it.

Bethel's hair was a dark, auburn red, and her skin very fair. Her legs burned to a deep brick red color in just a few minutes that day. I still don't know how she tolerated her jeans on the hike out of Ixcán.

We spent Sabbath at the huts. At sundown Saturday night, we all decided to hike on to the next village and sleep in the corridor of the little public schoolhouse. Someone led the way with a dim flashlight, and the rest of us followed along behind, feeling our way in the dark.

When we arrived at the little schoolhouse, one of the men went to find the schoolteachers and get permission to sleep there that night. The two schoolteachers came over to see the new people. They were both drunk, and in their delirium, they made quite a nuisance of themselves trying to be hospitable. They dragged out a blackboard and insisted that Bethel and I sleep on it. It had a crossways ridge in the middle and was not quite long enough.

We were all sitting on a couple of long, backless wooden benches in the corridor with a small candle burning for light. The intoxicated schoolteachers lingered, talking nonsensically and stepping on our feet in an effort to get closer to us. In order to get them to go, Bethel and I finally said that we would sleep on the blackboard. After what seemed like a long time they left for the night, and some of the men in our group carried the blackboard back inside for us. Then everyone lay down on the dirt floor of the corridor to sleep for a few hours.

At two o'clock we got up and started on our way. It was pitch black. Someone handed me a stick to pick my way with, and we went up the trail single file, each following in the steps of the person just in front of him. The lead man carried the dim flashlight. I was so sleepy I just plugged along with my eyes shut. It was too dark to see anything anyway even if I had tried to open them. I was thankful it was so dark. Otherwise I would have had a hard time keeping up with the men's fast pace on the steep climb out of Ixcán. With it so dark, they had to pick their way slowly.

We came to the end of the trail and the beginning of the road right at the crack of dawn. I was deeply grateful to climb into the pickup and ride. An hour later in Barillas, Marta served us a big breakfast before we started the long ride home.

Felipe came over to see us a few weeks later. "I was in Huehue," he told us, "and met an acquaintance from Ixcán. He told me that the communist guerrillas sent him a message to tell us that they have all of the names of those of us who made the last trip out, and if any of us goes back, they will kill us. They are trying to prevent the land owners from selling the land, and new people from moving in, because they want all of Ixcán for a guerrilla hideout. The man told me that he saw the leader of the guerrillas in Ixcán and his nostrils are as big as those of a horse."

I laughed loud and long. "If Mr. Horse-Nostrils only knew, he could not tempt me to go back to his old steamy jungle, even if he offered me all of Ixcán as a gift!"

Unfortunately, Papá Eustaquio was never able to get the money back that he had paid down on the land in Ixcán.

Chapter Twenty-One

Because of a Ride

*F*ive years after Ishmael and I were married, we bought a Toyota Land Cruiser pickup made especially for the rugged terrain of the mountain coffee farms. We chose a diesel rig, and years later during the guerrilla uprisings of the 1980s, we were glad we had. Gasoline was rationed until there was none left in the country, but we were always able to get enough fuel for our missionary trips.

The road to Chalum was the most frightening mountain road. Many of our friends only visited us once. My mother always said that the only other road she knew of that would compare to it was the road into Hunza Land. Uncle Ernest Booth, who was a world traveler, agreed with her. He and Aunt Dorothy, his wife, and my two cousins, Lowell and Laurie, and Lowell's wife, Marcia, came to visit us several times. Those were always exciting times. (Uncle Ernest and Aunt Dorothy have both fallen asleep in Jesus, and I can't wait to see them again.)

I had very little opportunity to drive. By this time I was twenty-one years of age, and I was anxious to have a driver's license of my own, like other American ladies. So with our new pickup, I learned to drive on our mountain road to Chalum. Ishmael patiently taught me exactly how to negotiate the narrow switchbacks. After practicing, I got a Guatemalan driver's license, that I drove with for several years

Because of a Ride

in the U.S., Mexico, and Guatemala. For a while I much preferred to drive on those mountain roads than to negotiate traffic. It all depends on what one gets used to. To me the mountain roads were not scary.

Other people who had pickups made their living by hauling loads of coffee, corn, young coffee plants, or supplies to stock the small country stores, and sometimes they were called upon to provide transportation to the hospital or doctor for the sick. We could have made money in the same way, but our conscience would not permit us to charge the poverty stricken peasants what to them were exorbitant prices.

For several years Ishmael gave many rides to people traveling up and down the Chalum road on foot, stopping to pick them up as we passed by in the pickup. I especially remember one family who had left their native village in the mountains another hour's hike past Chalum and moved to Ixcán in the hopes of obtaining some land and bettering their circumstances in life.

About seven months after they moved to the lowland jungle, they were obliged to return home. They were all sick with perhaps hepatitis and malaria. They were yellow, emaciated, and skinny, and they could not have lived much longer if they had stayed in Ixcán. So they packed their few belongings, hiked out of Ixcán, and rode the rickety buses as far as the gas station where our road turns off. From there the father, mother, and each of the children shouldered their loads and began the hike to their village that would take a healthy person about four hours.

We overtook them about one kilometer below Sarral. We were returning home in the pickup from some business errands, when we saw these poor people who were barely staggering under their loads. To look at them, one would have thought they would drop dead any minute.

It was a hot day, so I was riding in the back with some of our relatives who had accompanied us. Paco, a young man who had married one of Ishmael's nieces, stood up, leaned into the driver's window, and suggested to Ishmael that he stop and offer these poor people a ride.

They were soon helped aboard with all their packs and baskets, the rest of us moving over to make room for them. We invited them to sit clear down in the middle of the pickup bed, and we healthier ones sat along the sides, hanging on tightly to keep from bouncing off.

"How much do we owe you for the ride?" The gaunt-faced father asked Ishmael when we had arrived in Chalum.

"Nothing at all," he replied with a sunny smile. "May God bless you and restore your health soon." The family had been given some medicine to take at a free government clinic.

"The old yellow truck" taking a group of our church school kids for an excursion. Usually, we filled the truck like this, only with adults, children, babies, and animals such as chickens, turkeys, etc., that people took to market, or brought back from market.

Our church group in Chalum got together at the first opportunity and took up a collection for the family to buy food and medicine, and

Because of a Ride

one of the more swift-footed young fellows carried the money in an envelope to the family up in the village of Chicharro. I really didn't expect them to live, but a few weeks later I heard that they were regaining their health rapidly. About six months later I was introduced to a robust-looking peasant man whom I did not recognize and was told that he and his family had all made a complete recovery. I stared at him in amazement. Could this be the same man who had been so emaciated and hollow-cheeked months before? Indeed, it was!

As time went on, we continued to use the pickup for missionary purposes to help the needy. Ishmael often drove sick people long distances to the doctor. Dr. Graves was not always available these days, and the nearest hospital was in Huehuetenango.

Then the recession of the 1980s hit Guatemala, and we, along with everyone else, began to feel it. We had been charging a small fee to people who could afford it, and now Ishmael wondered if he should begin charging everyone the full customary rate for the privilege of being transported in our by-now-not-so-new pickup.

We prayed about it, and waited for a time. Then one day Ishmael said to me, "You know, Esther, I had a strange dream. I wonder if it might have been from God."

"What was it about? Tell me!" I exclaimed.

"Well, I dreamed that Jesus came in the clouds of heaven, the dead were raised, and we were all taken to the New Jerusalem. It was all lovely and beautiful. The streets were of gold, and there were flowers and fruit trees. And there were lots of people who had been saved from earth, walking and talking with the angels and with each other. We were all wearing shining white robes, and everyone was so very happy. Suddenly a man walked up to me and warmly shook my hand. He then said, 'You gave me a ride in your pickup, and that is why I am here.' Then more and more people came to shake my hand, profusely thanking me for introducing them to the gospel story by letting them ride in my pickup."

He continued, "One man said, 'The day was so hot, and the hike so long, and then you came along in your Toyota truck and offered me a ride. I hesitated because I couldn't afford to pay for a ride. But you said, "It won't cost anything. Just come and get in." So I got in, and when we came to where my trail turned off, as I got out, you smiled and wished me a good day. And that is why I am here. Thank you my brother.'"

Because of that dream, we decided to continue using the "old yellow truck" in the same way as we had until now, and the Lord has never let us down.

At the time of this writing the pickup is doing faithful service on the Chalum road. It has had to have much repair work done on it over the years, and it is badly worn from the rough road. But it still runs, and one of Ishmael's nephews drives it now.

I am so happy because the day is getting nearer when Ishmael's dream and those of many others will come true. I can hardly wait!

Chapter Twenty-Two

One Tiny Baby

*I*t was April 22, 1979. Mamma, Ishmael, and I were getting ready to make a trip in the yellow Toyota pickup to the States. We planned to be gone for two months. Bethel and Evangeline had already left on the bus to California, and Daddy and Jordan were in Montana getting ready for spring tree planting. We planned to go to California, then on to Montana to plant trees for a few weeks.

Grandpa and Grandma Booth had come down to Guatemala to live with my folks a few months after Ishmael and I were married. Grandpa Booth lived for two years in Guatemala before dying of cancer at the age of ninety. He died in my house, and we buried him in the Chalum cemetery up on the mountainside under some beautiful cypress trees.

Grandma Booth lived for several more years. At the time of our trip to the States in 1979, Mamma got Anastacio and Rosaura Martínez to come over from the village of Tablón where they lived to care for Grandma and watch the place in Valparaíso while we were all gone.

Anastacio and Rosaura had just gotten settled, and we were ready to tell Grandma good-bye and climb into the pickup and leave when I heard a knock at the outside door. I ran to open it, and there stood a young girl holding a small mite of a baby in her arms. She was also accompanied by a little boy who was about four years old.

She looked a little scared and confused, and I invited her in. She made the little boy stay outside to his extreme dislike. He cried and screamed, and I told her she could bring him in, but she refused. Perhaps she didn't want him to see what she was about to do.

"Could I have a drink of water?" she asked timidly after she had been seated. "Of course," I said, hurrying inside the middle house to the kitchen to fetch it for her.

I brought her the water, and she took a couple of sips before saying, "I need to give this baby away. Would your mother take it?"

"How are you related to the baby?" I asked.

"He is my little brother."

"Why do you want to give him away?"

"Because my mother died during childbirth, and I have to support the bigger children."

"How old is the baby?" I asked.

"One week old," she replied.

"Where is your father?"

"He died one month ago."

"And your mother died during the birth of this baby?" I asked again.

"Yes," she said. "She was weakened by the shock of my father's death."

I looked at the tiny baby. His little face looked yellow, but he was sleeping. I called Mamma. She hurried out to see the baby.

"I hate to turn this child away," my mother said. "Maybe we could find someone to take care of him until we get back from the States. Then we can find an Adventist family to adopt him."

Anastacio suggested that we take the baby to his sister, Amalia, who lived in La Democracia. So, after discussing the matter, we told the girl that we would take the baby. With a great air of relief, she

One Tiny Baby

handed him over and left. Then we all piled into the pickup, baby and all, and went to La Democracia to see Amalia.

"If Amalia cannot take care of the baby, then I will," Rosaura said. "But if she can do it, it would be better, because I am going to have my hands full enough with Grandma to care for."

Amalia agreed to keep the baby for us until we returned, and we left her enough money to buy milk for him until we came back. Then we left for the States. In California I told Bethel and Evangeline about the baby. "Why don't you adopt him?" Bethel asked me.

"I am not ready to commit myself to caring for a child," I told her. "Maybe someday I will be, but not now."

"I hope Amalia knows how to take care of a baby," Bethel said. "He could get sick or even die before we get back."

"Amalia has several teenage children of her own," I commented.

"Breast-feeding a baby is different from raising one on formula," Bethel informed me. "She nursed her own babies, but I'll bet she won't know to increase his formula. She will probably feed him like a newborn until we get there."

"I hope not," I said.

But Bethel turned out to be right. When we arrived back home, we discovered that the baby was sick and nearly starved. Bethel took the baby and began to care for him. She named him Louis Frederick, but called him Freddy. "If I give this baby to anyone else now, they won't know how to cope with the dysentery and malaria. He will die, so I must keep him until he can regain his health."

But little Freddy didn't get well right away, and after several months Bethel decided to keep him. "It is too late to give him away now," she said. "To him, I am his mother, and to me, he is my baby, so I will keep him."

After securing Guatemalan papers for him, she took him to California and stayed with my cousin, Flora Richards, until the U.S. adoption was finished. Freddy was sick during all of his childhood years, but eventually he outgrew it and became a sturdy, strong young man. At the time of this writing, he is almost fifteen years old, and we are all proud of him and happy to have him in the family.

Chapter Twenty-three

No Laughing Matter

*R*umors of the communist guerrilla warfare in Guatemala were multiplying rapidly. In our own part of the country, people began to disappear mysteriously, and at the same time, mutilated, unidentifiable bodies would be found in conspicuous places.

Life in Chalum continued about the same as usual, and we continued to help with evangelistic meetings in different places in the department of Huehuetenango, the same as we had done for several years. We had a music group that consisted of three singers—Paco, Julio Ramos (a relative of the Hidalgo clan), and me. There were other people in the group who played instruments. Paco played a big bass guitar, Julio played a melodica in between singing, Ishmael played a little concertina accordion, a couple of boys played harmonicas, I played my autoharp, and some others played guitars.

The district pastor asked us to be present at as many of the evangelistic meetings as possible. He held them constantly in different towns, and we always did our best to go to as many as we could with our music group.

We would all pile into the truck, filling both front and back with people and musical instruments. When it rained, we would put a canvas over the back to protect the instruments and people as much as possible. We would leave Chalum about four o'clock in the afternoon after the day's work in the coffee plantations was done, and we would usually arrive at whichever town the meetings were being held in around seven o'clock in the evening.

The meetings were usually over at ten o'clock. Then we would load back up and go home, arriving about one o'clock in the morning. It took about three hours from Chalum to get to most of the towns or villages where the meetings were held.

One time meetings were to be held in Malacatancito, a small town about eleven kilometers beyond Huehuetenango. It was the rainy season, and there was danger of landslides and rocks falling down the mountainsides onto the highway in the afternoons and evenings when it had rained. Also, we had to put chains on all four tires in order to negotiate our steep, muddy road from Chalum. But the pastor sent for us, and we decided to go, at least to one meeting.

After loading the truck with people and instruments, we left Chalum in the late afternoon of the day that the first meeting in Malacatancito was to be held. There was a small church in the town, but the meetings were to be held in the town meeting hall at the town square. Accordingly, we arrived there about seven o'clock. The meeting was to begin at about eight o'clock, so after helping the pastor set up the loudspeaker equipment and movie screen and projector, we got together to tune up our instruments and get in a little last-minute practice.

Every few minutes the pastor would announce the meetings over the loudspeaker, inviting people in the streets to come to the meeting and find a seat. People began coming in a few at a time, most of them anxious to get good seats in order to see the movie on the life of Christ that would be shown after the sermon.

We were standing at the back of the meeting hall tuning our instruments when a drunk man staggered over to where we were, and weep-

No Laughing Matter

ing aloud, he threw his arms around my neck. "Oh," he cried, "I had eight airplanes, and crashed them all! Now what can I do?"

It is not wise to anger a drunk person, so a couple of the boys began talking soothingly to him while they gently pulled him off of me. Then I quickly sat down on a nearby bench, and one of the fellows sat close to me on each side so that the drunk man would not be able to sit down beside me. But the poor man seemed to have an answer to every difficulty that presented itself in his way, and he tried very hard to sit on my lap. I had the autoharp strapped to me, and this particular situation was not working well for me or my instrument.

"We need a director for our group," Paco said brightly to the man. "Would you please stand up here and direct the music?" He took him firmly by the arm and stood him several feet away, showing him how to move his arms like a choir leader.

To our relief, the drunk man was delighted with this new turn of events, and he cooperated beautifully, going through every bodily contortion imaginable in an attempt to "direct" the music. This way we were able to practice for a few minutes before the meeting began.

Before we were through practicing, the man tired of "directing" the music, and he went to the door. There he began to bawl in a high-pitched voice, "Pasen adelante, pasen adelante." (Come in, come in.) Then he staggered about outside the door, grabbing people by the shoulders, steering them inside toward the benches, and almost forcibly sitting them down. The people that he brought in stayed, however, and I was surprised at how many this self-appointed "usher" brought to the meeting.

After a while we moved toward the platform, waiting to be called on to sing and play. The pastor started the meeting, and we all forgot about the drunk man. The hall was packed, with many people standing by this time, and none of us noticed that the drunk man had obtained a seat for himself near us.

After awhile the pastor called on us to sing, and we all stepped onto the platform. We were quite well into the first part of our song when the drunk man stood to his feet, and facing us, began to "direct" the music, going through even more ridiculous facial and bodily contortions than he had before.

In this particular song I did not sing, and it was surely a good thing because I would have gone into gales of laughter at the sight before me. The way it was, I turned my face away from Paco and Julio who were doing the singing, and prayed silently that they would be able to resist the urge to laugh. The audience was not aware of the drunk man who stood with his back to them, facing us. They were listening intently to the song. I don't know how Paco and Julio did it, but they made it through the song without bursting into laughter, and we sat down, immensely relieved.

We had another song coming up in a few minutes though, and we wondered what to do to distract the drunk man. We all groaned silently as the pastor announced our song. But then he said, "My friends, you are at a great vantage point in the audience, where you can see this wonderful music group perform. With your indulgence, I am going to step down where I can not only hear them, but watch them as well."

So saying, he stepped down, and as we all walked onto the platform, the pastor took the drunk man by the arm and engaged him in conversation while we sang. We were relieved, and the drunk man, obviously pleased by the pastor's kind attention, soon forgot all about us. After the song, he listened intently to the sermon, sitting quietly.

By the time the meeting was over, our inebriated friend had sobered up considerably, and approaching the pastor, he shook his hand warmly and expressed a desire to study the Bible and be baptized. He bid us all goodnight by patting us each on the back in the customary way of close friendship and begging us to return.

"Your music is wonderful, and I want to have the happiness of Christ that you have," he told us in parting.

It had rained hard that evening during the meeting, and the pavement was wet as we drove home. Much of the highway ran through a long, narrow canyon along the high, steep banks of the Selegua River. In several places rocks had fallen down from the mountainside onto the road during the heavy rain, and a couple of times we had to stop and the fellows had to move some of the big rocks out of the way so we could get through.

By one o'clock in the morning we were about two-thirds of the way home. About fifteen minutes before, we had met one car that was headed in the opposite direction from us. Usually I would take over the driving after Ishmael got sleepy during those late night drives home, but tonight, Ishmael was wide awake.

"Are you sure you don't want me to drive?" I asked him.

"I am sure," he replied.

The boys and musical instruments were covered with a heavy canvas in the back.

The rain had stopped, but occasionally it still sprinkled. Suddenly we rounded a bend in the road, and there were a bunch of more big rocks that had tumbled down from the mountainside. In between all of the rocks was a strange object wrapped in cardboard. It was about five and one half feet long, wider at one end, and very narrow at the other. Ishmael carefully steered the little pickup between the rocks around it, and we went on. Paco was riding with us in the front seat, and none of us said what we were thinking. It was too awful to talk about then.

We went on, keeping the conversation pleasant, and at last we were home in our safe little mountain village.

The next day we heard that two people had been murdered and

mutilated the night before. One was impaled on a fence post in a conspicuous place by the highway near La Democracia, and the other was wrapped in cardboard and placed among rocks that had fallen onto the highway from the mountainside. In all likelihood, the one lone car that we met on the road that night was driven by the murderers who had put the bodies in the particular places of their choice before driving out of that part of the country before morning.

In the following years, thousands of innocent people were mysteriously murdered, their mutilated bodies dumped into the Selegua River. The communist guerrillas were trying to overthrow the Guatemalan government, but the ones who suffered were the innocent citizens. They were abused, mistreated, and murdered by the guerrillas, and the Guatemalan army as well. It was the beginning of an era of terror when anyone could be shot dead on the slightest suspicion or tortured with the object of extracting information.

Approximately thirty kilometers from our home village were some villages that became the "hot spot" of guerrilla warfare in Central America for a while. But the object of the following stories is not to play up the violence and terror that reigned but to show God's overruling providence and loving watch care over his people.

Chapter Twenty-Four

Holdup

*T*hings were going from bad to worse. The communist guerrillas were becoming more numerous by the day, and the army more violent. Everyone was required to carry identification, and anyone caught without it could be shot on the spot as a guerrilla insurrectionist. Questions were not asked, and proof was not "needed." Many of the peasant women and children were not even registered, and therefore, they did not have so much as a birth certificate. But after a number of killings of innocent people, the population in general began to get wise to the ways of war and violence.

Many people whose relatives were shot by the army joined the guerrillas, and many whose loved ones were shot by the guerrillas joined the army. Many others were captured and forced to serve on one side or the other. All who were not guerrillas obtained and carried proper identification. For a man to fail to do so meant death at the hands of the army, and for a woman it could mean rape by a large number of soldiers, or death, or both.

The guerrillas hid out in the jungles and did not keep up their *cédulas*, or Guatemalan identification booklets. It was rumored that they assaulted foreigners and stole their passports for the terrorist leaders to carry as ID.

Around this time the Graves family decided to close the clinic and move back to the States. Someone planted a homemade bomb in their powerhouse that caused some damage, and that among other things led them to decide that it was time to leave. They sold a lot of their equipment and other things, and the rest they stored inside of their house. Before they left, a peasant man and his wife who were strangers in the area presented themselves to the Graves, and claiming to be Seventh-day Adventists, asked it they could live on their place as caretakers. Doc agreed, and after the Graves left, it became apparent that these people were guerrillas. They held midnight meetings in the Graves' house. Cars with their motors and lights off were seen by the local neighbors coasting silently down the driveway from the highway into the yard, and mysterious things began happening around the community that the people attributed to the strangers in the Graves' house.

These so-called caretakers stripped the place of everything valuable, even pulling out sinks and toilets. When Inez, the little lady who had served so long as the Graves' housekeeper remonstrated with them, they threatened her, and the man handled her roughly and told her to keep out of it. Eventually the army came along and took over the Graves' property and made an army base and barracks out of it. The soldiers lived in the clinic, and the officials set up their living quarters and offices in the house. The "caretakers" of the Graves' place had suddenly disappeared, and it was believed that the army had done away with them.

About this time my folks donated their place down by the river to the Guatemala SDA Mission, and they prepared to move out. Grandma was ninety-one years old and moving her was unthinkable because she was in a wheelchair.

Anastacio and Rosaura had come from Tablón several months before to help care for her, and it was just as well for them because their village was in the area that was fast becoming the "hot spot" of Central America.

Grandma had a kidney disease that caused terrible sores all over her body. They were gangrenous and deep, and one had to wear a mask in order to be in the same room with her, because the stench of the terrible sores was overpowering.

Daddy, Bethel, Evangeline, who was sixteen by this time, little Freddy, and Jordan had all left for the States, taking books and a few other valuable items with them.

By this time Felman was about sixteen years old. He was going to our SDA boarding academy in Petén and was on vacation visiting his folks, Anastacio and Rosaura, for a few weeks. It was November of 1981. In Guatemala school lets out in October and starts in January or sometimes February.

About this time the Guatemalan economy began to go down, and it was no longer possible to exchange Guatemalan currency for U.S. dollars at the banks. The black market exchange had not yet come into being, and Daddy had loaned us ten thousand dollars to invest in some land in Chalum some time before.

We now had the money to pay Daddy back, but he was in the States and our Guatemalan quetzals were useless to him. But we found a solution to our dilemma. Daddy needed a car, and he wanted a VW diesel rabbit, and we could buy one in Guatemala brand new for ten thousand quetzals. So that is what we did. And now we had the beautiful new little car. We just needed to get it to the States to Daddy.

We needed to go to Guatemala City in order to take care of some business after we had the car for a few weeks. We had heard of buses being stopped and held up, so we decided to take the car.

During our previous trip to Guatemala City, a couple of men staying at the same hotel where we stayed had questioned us, and I was certain that they were guerrillas who were up to no good. On this trip, however, everything went smoothly in Guatemala City, and on the morning of November 5, my twenty-fourth birthday, we were ready to start home.

It was a beautiful day, and we were in good spirits. I had a one hundred dollar bill in my purse that I had brought along for "emergency money," and suddenly I had a strong urge to take it out of my purse and tuck it in my Bible, which I kept in a special little basket with my hymnal and Sabbath School lesson. But I was busy, so I dismissed the urge as a silly thought and went on my way. That money is safer tucked away in my purse than it would be in my Bible, I reasoned.

The highway through the high mountains from Guatemala City to Huehuetenango is scenic and beautiful, and the day was lovely as only a day in November could be, with the sky a brilliant blue after the last of the rainy season was over and flowers blooming in abundance everywhere.

After a while we came to the Sololá junction in the mountains. The beautiful Lake Atitlán, nestled at the foot of some volcanoes, is in the department of Sololá. The Sololá road winds around through the mountains, down around part of the lake, then back up to the main highway. Ishmael pulled over and stopped.

"I can't give you a present for your birthday, but I could take you for a scenic drive today," he announced. "Mamma has never seen Lake Atitlán, so she would get to see it, which would be something special for her, too."

I turned to Mamma who was in the backseat. "What do you think?" I asked.

"It's fine with me," she answered with her usual adventurous enthusiasm.

Holdup

So we turned sown the Sololá road. I still don't know whether that was a good choice or not, at least it might have been the lesser of two evils.

I don't believe in hunches and impressions, but this particular day I kept having a feeling that we were going to encounter some kind of violent situation before the day was over. I suppose common sense and the amazing power of reason that God has given to human beings would have told most anyone the same thing.

On our way to Guatemala City a couple of days before, there had been logs of trees that had been cut down and fallen across the highway to block the road. It was the work of guerrillas to keep the army trucks from getting through so they could have full run of the mountain towns, entering them and taking over in the usual ways of war, terror, and bloodshed.

By the time we got there, the army men had sawed enough of the logs away so that the traffic could squeeze by. In the following months, the army cut away all of the vegetation from the highways for several hundred feet on each side in order to prevent such a thing from happening again. Due to the warfare of the 80s, Guatemala has lost much of its original, natural beauty. But I am getting ahead of my story.

The breathtaking beauty of the November day was so intense one could almost reach out and touch it. And also there was the uncertainty . . .

The drive through Sololá was every bit as beautiful as we had expected, perhaps more so. At length we came to a scenic overview of the lake and stopped for a few moments. There were some friendly Indian women there displaying beautiful Indian-made garments for sale. Pretty soon we got back into the car and continued on our way. I had been keeping my door locked, but this time I forgot to lock it.

The road wound down a mountainside toward a town on the shores of Lake Atitlán. It was paved, but very narrow, full of big holes and sharp curves. The vegetation closed in over our heads so that we could not see the sun.

We were nearing a bend in the road again. Cows were sitting here and there across the road in front of us, and there were some deep potholes just ahead of us. Suddenly a man dressed in a red shirt and blue pants jumped down from the bank above the road and landed right in front of us. He was carrying a small old-fashioned pistol of some kind, and he stood in front of us, arm outstretched, with the pistol.

This is it, I thought.

Another man emerged from the jungle growth below the road. He was dressed the same as the first man in a red shirt and blue pants. He held the same kind of pistol and blocked the other side of the road, standing opposite the first man with arm outstretched with the pistol in the same way.

Ishmael saw that he could not outrun them because of the cows and potholes, and what if there were more armed men around the bend? So he began to slow. Just then three more men jumped down from the bank and landed halfway on the hood of the car.

They were dressed the same as the other men and carried the same kind of pistols. The first man, who apparently was the leader of the gang, yanked my door open and held his pistol across my chest, pointed at Ishmael. The second man menacingly pounded on Ishmael's window for him to open it. Thinking that the man might break the window, Ishmael rolled it down, and the man jabbed his pistol at Ishmael's head.

From the very first second, Mamma had started saying, "We have the Lord. He will not let anything happen to us that is not His will. The angels are all around us. We are in God's hands."

Holdup

Hearing that coming from Mamma in the backseat was reassuring to me. She switched to Spanish and continued repeating the same things as Ishmael said to the men, "What do you want?"

"Get out of the car!" ordered the man on my side. He was somewhat drunk.

"No!" said Ishmael. "This is my car. I don't owe you anything."

"Get out or we will kill you!" several of them said at once. "Do you want to die?"

"OK, guys. What do you really want?" asked Ishmael, gripping the steering wheel firmly.

"Give us all your cash and valuables!" they demanded. Three of the men began clawing around, searching the bags in the backseat around my mother.

"God is with us, and you can't touch us!" Mamma was saying emphatically. "His angels are all around us, and you can't do anymore than they permit. You need God, too. Do you know God?"

The man who was holding the gun to Ishmael's head began to tremble. His hand shook so that it looked like he might drop his gun. Meanwhile, the man on my side picked up my purse, then set it down and picked up the little basket with my Bible, hymnal, and lesson quarterly. Then he set it back down and picked up my purse again.

I remembered my morning impression to put my money in the Bible. Fascinated, I watched as he vacillated back and forth between taking my Bible or my purse. Didn't it occur to him that he could take both? Finally, he decided to take my purse. The guy on the other side took Ishmael's wallet.

"Just let me keep enough money to buy diesel to get home on," Ishmael said in the tone of voice of a market vegetable vendor.

"None of that," roared the man. "I will kill you!" He had an Indian accent, and Ishmael was speaking to him in the Indian brogue, which he can mimic to a tea. At length they said, "Get out of here! And don't report us to the authorities in Panajachel."

They had taken Ishmael's wallet, my purse, another handbag of mine, which they thought might have money in it, and my melodica. Fortunately, they did not get my autoharp with my notebook of songs that I had written and could not replace. (I decided to make an extra copy of my songs after that.)

Mamma had thirty quetzals in her pocket, and they did not touch her, so we had a little money to buy diesel fuel to get home on.

As Ishmael shifted the car into gear with his right hand, he moved his left hand up higher on the steering wheel, and the man on my side, spying his watch, suddenly yelled to the other guy, "El reloj, el reloj." (The watch, the watch.)

The man on Ishmael's side grabbed at his arm. Ishmael let him take off the watch, but not without protesting reproachfully.

As we drove away, I turned to look at the men. One was holding my handbag, and on a sudden impulse, I smiled and waved in the Guatemalan custom of waving good-bye to friends. The man started to wave and smile back; then apparently remembering his wretched role as thief and bandit, quickly looked down. I will never forget the look of guilt and dejected misery on that poor man's face. The very last glimpse I got of them they were scrambling up the bank into the jungle growth about as fast as they had jumped down on us. And that by no means concluded the events of the day.

As we drove on down toward the little lakeside town of Panajachel, we stopped every vehicle that we could and warned them to go back, telling them what had happened to us. Several of them looked frightened and concerned, and thanking us, they turned back. Among them was a car full of American tourists. One young man on a motorcycle, however, jeered at us and went on, and we figured that he, too,

Holdup

was a member of the gang.

My papers were in the purse that the bandits had taken, so I now had no ID. Pretty soon we met a couple of policemen on a motorcycle, and we waved them down. We were in the outskirts of Panajachel by this time. Ishmael told them what had happened to us, and asked where we could find the police station.

The two policemen were very kind. With concern they told us, "We are just on our way up there again to try to catch those guys. They've been at it all morning. You are not the first people that were attacked, and you were very lucky. They have been taking people's cars."

Then they told us to be sure and report the incident, and they gave us directions to the police station.

"Be sure to ask them to write a special report for you to show to the military as ID," they told me.

When we parked the car and I got out, I noticed that my legs were shaking. Everything had happened so fast that I hadn't had time to panic or be afraid.

Inside the station, the police were angry and refused to write the report. They did have to radio it into Guatemala City to army headquarters, but they were happy to let me go on without any ID. We were quite certain that they were in cahoots with the bandits, and we could have reported them to the military, but for the sake of the two kind policemen on the motorcycle, we didn't. The innocent might suffer along with or instead of the guilty.

We went as far as the town of San Cristóbal, near Quetzaltenango, that afternoon. Dr. Albertson used to run a missionary clinic there, but by this time it had been shut down for several years. It was being used this particular weekend by the Mission for a mini camp meeting. We stopped there that evening, intending to stay until Sunday.

Julio Juarez, our district pastor, was there along with two or three other pastors that we knew, and some whom we were not acquainted with. One of them told us that he had driven out from Guatemala City that day also, and guerrillas armed with machine guns had tried to stop him. However, he had stepped on the gas and managed to outrun them.

"They would have killed me anyway, so they might as well kill me for trying to get away," he told us. "But our kind heavenly Father protected me, and helped me get away, so I am here to continue serving Him until my work is done. You were better off getting held up on the Sololá route with pistols than if you had been stopped on the main route and killed like they tried to do to me."

Another pastor who was supposed to be at the camp meeting had died in a bus wreck that morning on his way there. But the worst thing of all was the mysterious killing of a young pastor who was also on his way to the camp meeting that morning. He was dragged off of a bus that he was riding down from a village he had visited somewhere in the vicinity of the Tacaná volcano. He had visited the SDA church there the day before, held a meeting, collected the tithes and offerings to take back to the mission in Guatemala City, then left on the early morning bus the same day that we were held up in Sololá. Two of the church members were on the bus, and they reported that a group of people with masks and machine guns stopped the bus and climbed aboard. Looking around, they said, "We want to talk to the Seventh-day Adventist pastor."

The pastor quickly stood to his feet and said, "I am he. Please do not harm anyone else." The men dragged him off the bus and beat him to a kneeling position. The last thing people saw was the pastor praying.

For a long time no one knew whether he had been kidnapped and held somewhere or killed. Pastor Emilio De León was pastor of the

Holdup

San Marcos district at the time, which included the church that our pastor friend had visited the day before he was dragged off the bus. Pastor Emilio De León was supposed to come to the camp meeting too, but instead he was sent to investigate as to the whereabouts of the missing pastor. Now everyone prayed for the safety of Pastor Emilio, as he was affectionately called.

There were about 300 people present at the camp meeting. We all stood around outside for the evening meeting, and the events of the day were shared. We held a minute of silence in memory of the pastor who died in the bus wreck, then we prayed, and after that everyone began to sing, solemnly, reverently. One of the pastors had a guitar that he played to accompany the singing.

The whole congregation linked arms and sang "Side By Side." Then to my surprise, I was called to the front of the group, and everyone sang "Happy Birthday" to me. Then the pastor made a speech and wished me many years of life and happiness. I must say that it was a memorable twenty-fourth birthday.

Sometime later I heard that an unidentifiable body had been found in the woods near the place where the young pastor had been dragged off the bus with some torn pieces of tithe envelopes around it. It was concluded that the pastor had been murdered and the tithes and offerings that he carried were stolen. During the following years, there was quite a bit of speculation as to who was responsible for his murder, but that secret still remains with God and no doubt will until the judgment when all things will be revealed.

We had met that dear young man a couple of times, and I will always remember his kind sincerity and his earnest Christian manner. He was a humble young man who lived to serve others, and I expect to meet him in that wonderful land where no one will ever again follow Lucifer's example, become a guerrilla insurrectionist, and try to

Hope That Springs Eternal

overthrow God's government of liberty, justice, and love.

After our refreshing visit with the fellow believers at the camp meeting, we headed on our way. But before we did, the next day we heard that two American tourist women were held up at the same place we were; however, their car was taken, and they were left standing on the road with nothing but the clothes they had on. Several weeks later it was reported in the newspaper that ten dead bodies were found in that place, dressed in blue pants and red shirts like the guerrillas sometimes wore. Had the army killed the bandits? If they did, there were plenty more to take their places.

Chapter Twenty-Five

Angels

*G*od's mercy to us undeserving human beings and His protection and loving watch care are marvelous. As I look back over the past experiences of my life and those of my dear friends, I can see it so plainly. Surely in the future God will lead His people in ways even more special than in the past.

The people at the little San Cristóbal camp meeting stayed in tents. One row of tents was for the women, and the other for the men. These camp meetings were usually called youth camp meetings, but anyone who considered him or herself a "youth" was welcome to attend. There were many young people there, of all ages! My mother and I were given a place to sleep in a tent with some girls, and Ishmael slept over on the boys' side.

After the morning meeting the next day, everyone divided up into small groups, and the pastors and their wives taught classes on marriage and raising children. The material being covered that day was excellent, but my nerves were agitated from the experiences of the previous day, and I felt strongly that we needed to get right home to my dying grandmother and the Martínez family.

After talking it over, we bid our friends farewell and left for home. It was almost a three-hour drive, and I prayed that we would not find any military roadblocks along the way, because I had no ID. The bandits had not searched Mamma's pockets where she carried her ID and some money, and Ishmael's papers were not in the wallet that they stole, so I was the only unidentified person in the car. But God heard our prayers, and there were no military roadblocks set up anywhere along the highway that day.

Upon arriving home that evening, we gathered around Grandma's bed with the Martínez family for Friday night worship. We all thanked God for our blessings and for the new Sabbath that was beginning. Then we told them about the events of our trip. Felman was sixteen, and his little sister, Magda, was eleven at the time.

When we had finished our story, everyone was quiet and thoughtful for a few moments, and then Felman said, "You know, we can't see God's angels, but they are all around us like a protecting wall. Only those things that God in His wise providence permits can happen to us.

"One day a few months ago, two men from the town of Poptún, twelve kilometers from the academy, came out to the school on a business errand, and saw a girl they liked. They determined to kidnap her, and they somehow found out which room in the girls' dormitory she stayed in, and even which bed she slept in.

"They planned to crawl in her window at midnight on a certain night, roll her up in her blankets, and carry her away to the jungle. They met near the school as planned on the designated night and crept down the long driveway to the gate that is kept locked at night. They planned to go through the fence, then over to the girls' dormitory. But when they got to the gate, they found in place of each fence post clear around the school property a tall, shining angel—a whole wall of tall, shining angels—and they could not get through.

"In fear they went quietly away. Within a few months, one of the two men was killed by the military, and the other one requested Bible studies and was baptized into the Adventist church. He is the one who

Angels

told us this story as a testimony."

After worship we parted to get some sleep. Mamma and I slept at the far end of the place in the little house that had been Bethel's, and Anastacio and Rosaura slept closer to Grandma in a separate building. No one could tolerate the stench of the sores for more than a minute or two, so Grandma had to sleep alone. Grandma's sores were even worse now, if such a thing were possible. We knew she couldn't last much longer. At least she wasn't in any pain, and she slept most of the time.

One night Mamma got up and went to check on Grandma. To her horror, she found the army ants invading the little house that Grandma stayed in. When the army ants come through, everything alive has to get out quickly or be eaten alive. They were crawling up the bedposts, and Grandma was sound asleep. Mamma got a jug of kerosene and began pouring it on the floor around the bed and rubbing it on the bedposts with her hands. She stomped her feet constantly to keep the ants from crawling up her legs. Even at that, a number of them got on her and were biting her.

The ants seemed to be attracted to Grandma's sores like a magnet. Mamma battled them for hours in the dim light of a kerosene lamp. The rest of us slept peacefully, but she didn't dare to leave Grandma alone with the ants long enough to go and call us. And the roar of the river behind the compound was so loud that we could not have heard her even if she shouted. So she fought the ants bravely for several hours, picking the ones that got past the kerosene out of Grandma's sores.

Grandma slept peacefully on, and finally the ants went away. Then Mamma went back to bed to get in a few winks of sleep before daylight.

A few days later, early on a Sunday morning, Grandma peacefully breathed her last as some of my in-laws from Chalum watched beside her bed. Shortly before, she had rallied sufficiently to pray a

Spirit-inspired prayer of surrender to God's will. Grandma always had a buoyant spirit and a great desire to live. It was hard for her to relinquish life, even at ninety-one.

Now we had another problem. It is illegal in Guatemala to transport a dead body from one municipality to another. Valparaíso is in the municipality of La Democracia, and Chalum in the municipality of La Libertad. At the local cemetery in Camojá, in order to bury anyone, someone else had to be dug up, the newly dead person placed in the grave, then the bones of the one that was dug up were thrown in on top of the new coffin.

Grandpa had been buried in the little cemetery in Chalum on the mountainside under the beautiful cypress trees. Now we wanted to bury Grandma beside him. By Guatemalan law, the dead must be buried within twenty-four hours. The putrefying sores also made it necessary to bury her immediately. To try to get a permit to move her body to Chalum was virtually impossible, and with the guerrilla warfare going on, it was best to just do things quickly and quietly without attracting attention. On Sundays there were usually policemen at the gas station where the road to the mountains turned off the highway, and they would stop and check every car that went by. Today we hoped and prayed that there would be no policemen. Grandma was wrapped in a roll of blankets and placed in the back of Julio and Catalina's station wagon. Anastacio straddled the tailgate, and off to Chalum we went.

There were no policemen that day at the gas station, and our trip was uneventful. No one suspected that we had a dead body on board.

Pastor Julio Juarez came to be with us, and he conducted the funeral service at our house. We put the coffin in a room downstairs and all went to bed. We didn't observe the custom of holding an all-night wake. The next morning we all marched up to the cemetery on the mountainside, and after a graveside prayer, buried her. Grandma's cof-

Angels

fin was borne tenderly to the gravesite by Guatemalan hands, and her passing mourned by many Guatemalan heartfelt tears.

On Christmas Eve, a band of about forty guerrillas suddenly interrupted a Christmas program in an evangelical church in Camojá, and at gun point they made all of the members plus a couple of bystanders move a bunch of blocks that were stacked beside the road into the highway, making a sort of wall across it so no traffic could get through. Their purpose was to slow the progress of any army truck that might come after them, in case the army was alerted to their presence and activity in the area that night.

At exactly midnight, when all the people were eating tamales, burning firecrackers, and giving one another the traditional Merry Christmas hug, the forty guerrillas entered La Mesilla by surprise with a shout. In the general panic and confusion, no one could say for sure what kind of explosives they used, but they entered the customs building and killed all of the police-guards that were on duty that night. Not only had the poor men not gotten to go home for Christmas to see their families, but they were killed as well!

One of the guards was an old man. He and two or three others had not died from the explosion, so the guerrillas got ready to shoot the survivors. The old guard knelt and begged the terrorists for his life. "I am not into any kind of politics," he exclaimed in anguish. "I am just trying to make a living for my family."

Anyone employed by the government was considered by the guerrillas to be a traitor to their cause, but the leader of this particular bunch began to soften and had decided to spare the old man when another guerrilla fighter, a woman, came over to him and said sharply, "No! All of the guards must die! That is our mission, and the old man is a liar. Kill him!"

Upon hearing that, the leader raised his gun and shot the poor old man.

One old lady had taken some tamales to the guards for a Christmas Eve treat a couple of minutes before the guerrillas arrived. She was still there passing out the tamales when they attacked. She was beaten and both of her legs broken for committing the "crime" of extending a little Christmas cheer to the government employees.

With their mission in La Mesilla accomplished, the guerrillas left as quickly as they had come. Not long after that a seven o'clock curfew was imposed on all citizens. Anyone out after that hour of the night was considered a guerrilla by the army or was considered to be some kind of army personnel by the guerrillas and therefore was liable to be shot either way.

Between Christmas and New Year, we had a double wedding in our church in Chalum. In fact, we were in Chalum making wedding preparations the night of the attack on La Mesilla. One of Ishmael's nieces, Hortencia, married Paco, the young fellow who sang in our music group. And Ishmael's adopted nephew, Mario, married Marta, Ishmael's young cousin. Paco was Rosaura Martínez' nephew, and was from the village of Tablón. But he had worked and lived with the Matías family in Chalum for years, until he actually became one of us. It was right that he marry Hortencia, Julio's beautiful, quiet daughter.

Catalina sewed beautiful wedding dresses for the two young brides. The material for the dresses cost only a few quetzals, and with Catalina's artistic expertise rivaling the most elaborate, expensive wedding dresses to be found anywhere, the girls were beautiful. She could sew anything without a pattern.

A thick layer of fresh pine needles was spread on the church floor and platform, and the walls were decorated with so many palm branches that the place seemed like a fragrant garden. Many flowers were placed among the palm branches as well, and fourteen girls and fourteen boys were selected to be bridesmaids and groomsmen. They carried fragrant cypress branches decorated with flowers and marched down the aisle to the tune of "The Little Drummer Boy." The attendants then formed two lines down either side of the aisle, and holding the branches up so that they touched at the top, formed a long archway for the two couples to march under.

Pastor César Santos conducted the wedding ceremony, marrying both couples at the same time. Rubelín, Paco's brother, and Felman and I sang a couple of songs that I accompanied on my autoharp. Then we turned "The Little Drummer Boy" march back on, and reversing their formation, the two couples marched out under the archway made by the bridesmaids and groomsmen. The whole procession marched out behind them, followed by the congregation who also marched out in order. Outside everyone was served tamales, hot chocolate, and cake.

Anastacio, Rosaura, and I had made the cake—it was big enough to feed 600 people. One of the neighbor ladies had beaten all the egg whites for the frosting in a tin tub with her bare hands, whipping them in a circular motion. We baked many little cakes in Reina and Jorgelio's big clay oven and put them together in layers to make one giant cake. It was a major operation, but lots of fun. Those were days of much happiness and laughter. We all treasured every peaceful moment in one another's company.

The day after the wedding, Paco borrowed our old yellow Toyota pickup to take all of his relatives and friends who had attended the wedding back to Tablón. In Valparaíso they urged me to ride along with them, but fatigue from the fun but strenuous activities of the preceding days was setting in, and I decided to stay at the old place that by now was property of the Guatemala SDA Mission and rest. Mamma was there getting ready for us to leave the sweet old place for good.

After leaving his friends and relatives in Tablón, Paco and his precious little bride started the trip back. It was only about thirty kilometers, but because of the rough road, it took about three hours to drive from his village to Valparaíso. On the way, they passed an army jeep. There was prolific jungle growth on the mountainsides above them, and the road ran along the banks of a river.

Presently they overtook a big army truck that was carrying soldiers. The jeep was close behind them now. Knowing that it was not safe to be near an army vehicle on the road, especially sandwiched in between two of them, Paco pulled around the truck at the first wide place, waving to the soldier boys as he passed.

During the next couple of minutes he put as much distance as possible between himself and the army truck. Then it happened! They heard a deafening explosion from behind. A quick glance over their shoulders told the newlyweds that the army truck had been blown up by explosives thrown down from somewhere in the dense jungle growth on the mountainside by guerrillas hiding there. The young people were thankful to be alive!

The political unrest was getting more out of hand now, and in Valparaíso and the surrounding area people were being mysteriously murdered every day. Many mutilated bodies were seen floating down the Selegua River a few kilometers away, and it was suspected that many of these bodies were those of the people that were so mysteriously disappearing. We decided that it was time for us to join the rest of the family in the States for a few months, until the political winds in Guatemala should change. There were things that needed to be taken care of before we left though, so we stayed for a few more days.

Early in the morning on January 2, 1982, we loaded up the little car and headed for the States. Our destination was Alice, Texas. It

Angels

was with some trepidation that we undertook the trip through Mexico. The year before, we had been falsely accused of smuggling contraband into Mexico at the Brownsville-Matamoros border crossing on our way down, and Ishmael and Jordan spent nearly a week in the crowded Mexican jail.

I had barely escaped arrest myself, and it was only by the providence of God that we found an honest Mexican lawyer, and got them out. Daddy's Ford pickup that we were traveling in at the time was impounded, but after three weeks, we got that back, too. Our financial losses were heavy, but Ishmael and Jordan would have been in jail for years and our pickup never returned if it hadn't been for the Lord's merciful interposition on our behalf.

Now we prayed for a safe journey through Mexico with Daddy's new little car that we were taking to him. I don't remember which city it was in Mexico, but we were going through it at night. It was about one o'clock in the morning, and Ishmael was driving. Traffic was somewhat heavy, so I was very alert. I saw a fork in the road ahead of us. The fork to the right went up a hill, leaving a drop-off between it and the left fork. There was no sign to tell us which road to take, and I watched, wondering what Ishmael would do.

We came closer and closer. He was headed straight for the drop-off between the two roads. I looked to see if he was awake. His eyes were open wide. I waited another second then yelled, "Ishmael, what are you doing?"

He yanked the wheel to the right, barely missing the drop-off, and went on. So we had taken the road to the right. I wondered if it was the right one, and it turned out to be. "Why did you go straight toward the drop-off like that?" I asked Ishmael when we got out of town.

"What drop-off?" he asked.

"Didn't you hear me holler?"

Hope That Springs Eternal

"No, I heard you say, 'Ishmael, go to the right.'"
"Didn't you see the drop-off?"
"No."
"Did you see the other road?"
"What other road?"
"Why did you suddenly swerve to the right if you didn't see it?"
"Because you said to."
"Well," I said, "I really don't think you heard me, because I didn't say, 'go to the right.' I said, 'Ishmael, what are you doing?' I think you heard an angel say, 'go to the right.' And you obeyed, just in time to save us from having a wreck." An accident in Mexico could have meant a long prison sentence for Ishmael, maybe even twenty years if anyone was killed.

The rest of our trip was uneventful, and we arrived late one night in Alice, Texas. Bethel, Evangeline, and Freddy were staying in Humberto and Barbara Martínez' house. Humberto, if you remember, was Dr. Graves' first convert many years before. His brother, Anastacio Martínez, was the one who, with his family, helped us take care of Grandma. Humberto and Barbara were away planting trees for the winter with daddy in Louisiana, and because we did not have a vehicle of our own with us, I stayed with Bethel in the Martínez' house.

We had made it safely to the States. Now what did God have in store for us? And what about our dear ones back in Guatemala?

Chapter Twenty-Six

The Blood of Jesus

It was good to look down on the familiar terrain of Guatemala once again after being gone for a year and a half. Our flight had taken us to Belice, then San Salvador, and now at last we were landing in Guatemala City. My family now lived in Tennessee, but Mamma had decided to go to Guatemala with me for a few months. She couldn't bear to not be able to see what was happening to me with the guerrilla warfare going on.

During the time we were in the States, Ishmael had made a trip back to Guatemala, intending to stay for one month to record a tape of the marimba band. We had had a large marimba handmade for us by a man in the Indian town of Colotenango. It took seven people to play it, besides one on the big bass vile, and we wanted to make a professionally recorded tape of the band.

Pastor Alvarado, an accomplished musician, helped the boys with their arrangements and style for the hymns they played, and he played with them whenever he could. So while Ishmael was in Guatemala, they got together to make a tape of their marimba music. But they didn't get it done in one month. There were many delays, and it took six months to get the recording made. But they had finally achieved their goal. Then Ishmael telephoned and asked me to choose a name for our marimba band. We settled on "Jungle Inspiration," and everyone was happy with

Hope That Springs Eternal

Our marimba band. At the time this picture was taken, some of the players were children.

the name. As I had looked down on the jungles of Guatemala a few minutes earlier, I thought how appropriate the name was. Now we were landing, and I was excited at the prospect of seeing "our" relatives again.

Benedicto, Paco, and several others (who were really relatives of relatives, but very much loved by all of us) had come to meet us at the airport. I thought we would never get through customs, but at last we did, and I was being hugged and picked up off my feet by everyone at once.

That night at the hotel, conversation soon turned to tales of guerrilla warfare and terrorism. We talked in whispered tones. The new president, Ríos Montt, was trying to put a stop to the uprisings and killing. The army was not killing as ruthlessly anymore, but every man and teenage boy were required to do guard duty as a civilian patrolman.

Along the roads and highways, checkpoints were set up every few

The Blood of Jesus

kilometers, and all traffic had to stop and everyone was searched for weapons and required to show their *cédulas*. All passengers were required to get down off of the buses while they were searched.

Every village had to be guarded twenty-four hours a day, and every man and teenage boy had to serve one day or night a week. Every village was visited by the army, and the civilian patrolmen were all trained in warfare. And it was helping. Attacks on villages were not so common anymore. The army under Ríos Montt was working toward establishing a degree of rapport with the civilians, and that was also helping considerably.

All of the people of the Nentón area (about forty kilometers from Valparaíso) and Ixcán had fled to Mexico. Most of them were guerrillas, and the army under Lucas had threatened to come in and completely destroy them. The Adventists among them had to flee along with the rest of them and were not heard from again. If they had remained behind, they would've been killed by the army. Or their fleeing guerrilla neighbors might have killed them before they left. But by going with the refugees, they were automatically classed as guerrillas. None of them could return to Guatemala.

The refugees set up camps in the Mexican jungles along the border, and from time to time, they attacked the villages over on the Guatemalan side. The army would come out to route them, but they could not chase them any farther than the border. Therefore their casualties and losses were low, while the people they killed were many. The Mexicans didn't help matters any by granting these people asylum and by treating their wounded ones for free in their hospitals. In this way Mexico was an accomplice to the guerrilla warfare, while professing to greatly fear the guerrillas. (Or maybe that is why they granted them asylum and free medical care!) Finally, the Mexican government gave the Guatemalan army permission to fight the refugee guerrillas on Mexican territory. After that the raids along the border stopped.

A few weeks after returning to Guatemala, Lucinda, Rosaura's sister and Paco's mother, told my mother the following story: "One day some men dressed in ragged clothes came to Tablón and engaged a neighbor man in conversation. They looked like guerrillas, all filthy, dirty, and ragged from living in the jungles. But they were army spies.

"They said to my neighbor, 'Come and work with us, and we will pay you well.' He was afraid because he thought they were guerrillas, and if he out and out refused to join them, they would kill him. Or maybe they would kidnap him into their ranks. So he tried to put them off for the moment, stalling for time until he could figure out what to do. Maybe if he fled the area for a while, they would eventually forget about him.

"So he said to them, 'I don't know. I would have to think about it. Can I talk to you later?'

"He went home to his wife and children, trying to decide how to get the guerrillas off his back. That very night there was a loud knocking on his door. He and his family were quiet for a while, but the men outside said, 'If you do not come out to us, we will break the door down and go in and kill all of you. Come out like a man and face us!'

"So the man went around and kissed his wife and each of his children good-bye. Then he stepped out into the black night, and all was quiet. The family didn't dare go to the door to see what had happened, so they waited quietly in their beds until daylight. They were very frightened.

"Early in the morning they went outside, and found him lying on the doorstep. He had been bayoneted to death, and there was lots of blood everywhere. I went over that morning and helped his wife clean up the mess and bathe his body.

"They didn't dare have a burial for him or take him to the cemetery. Anyone seen caring for his body could be killed because he was considered a political offender by the army, since he had not said 'no' in no uncertain terms when asked by the army spies if he would join the guerrillas. So they simply had to dig a hole in a hidden place and bury him like they would have buried an animal."

"What did you and his wife think about while you cleaned up the blood?" my mother asked Lucinda.

"Oh, we just cried and cried," she said, "because we thought about how Jesus shed His blood for us. We felt like we were cleaning up the blood of Jesus after the crucifixion."

One day I went to Huehuetenango with Ishmael. Benedicto, Petronila, and some others also went along. On our way home, when we were driving by the steep banks of the Selegua River, we saw a police jeep and a couple of policemen. They stopped us and asked Ishmael to pull over. We expected the usual hassle over car papers, so Ishmael was prepared to give the usual tip. But they didn't ask for car papers. Instead they acted a little scared and hesitant.

"Would you please go down to the river and investigate a dead body that is caught in the bushes at the edge?" they asked. "We don't want to go."

The two cowardly policemen waited while Ishmael and Benedicto started off down the steep bank. I started to follow after them, but then retraced my steps. I had already seen enough dead people over the years without looking at a murdered mutilated one.

After a while they came back, reporting that they found a decapitated body that appeared to be that of a tall white man. The body was all bruised as if the man had been beaten. The policemen wrote down everything on their report that Ishmael and Benedicto told them as if they had done the investigating themselves, and then thanked them for their cooperation.

Ishmael's cousin, Rómulo, whom we call "Chomo," was made commander or leader of a civilian patrol group in Chalum for a while. At one time all of the bridges between Valparaíso and Huehuetenango had been blown up and completely destroyed by the guerrillas, making travel very difficult. Whatever buses or private vehicles happened to be in the areas between the bridges at the time they were destroyed served as public transportation for the people. At each place where a bridge had been destroyed, one had to wade the river, then ride in another vehicle to the place where the next bridge had been destroyed, get out and wade again, and then ride for another little ways to the next place, over and over, all the way to Huehuetenango. That made it especially hard for people who had to transport merchandise and supplies to their stores from Huehuetenango and for people hauling coffee or corn to Huehuetenango. I heard that an American tourist once broke his leg trying to wade one of the rivers that was high, swift, and muddy from a recent rain. But now temporary wooden bridges had been sent from the States and were erected where the old ones stood. They made a loud rattle when one drove over them, but it sounded like music to our ears, believe me!

Once a month, it was Chomo's job to take the civilian patrolmen from Chalum who were under his command and go guard the bridge at El Cable for twenty-four hours. It belonged to our municipality of La Libertad, although it was down on the highway about thirty kilometers away.

Superstition about the departed spirits of the dead is strong in Guatemala, and the devil certainly does all in his power to encourage it. Chomo told me that one night they were guarding the wooden bridge when they saw the headlights of an automobile coming down the highway. It didn't slow to a stop as all traffic is supposed to do at the checkpoints of the civilian patrolmen. They waved the Guatemalan flag as an authoritative signal for it to stop, but it just came faster and faster. When it got to the bridge it accelerated and started across at breakneck speed.

"I raised my rifle and shot at the tires," said Chomo, and the car vanished into thin air before my eyes. Then I knew it was the devil playing tricks on us. At the sound of the rifle shots, all the other patrolmen came hurrying down from their posts of duty on the mountainsides to help us fight off the guerrillas, but there weren't any.

"It happened not once, not twice, but four times. Finally, we were all so scared, we quit guarding the bridge. The other fellows said it was the spirits of all the dead people who had been murdered and thrown into the Selegua River that runs under the bridge there. So after that we would all hide under the bridge instead of guarding it, and the devil would come every little while and shake it and rattle it above our heads so much that we felt like we would die of fright. We would just cover our heads and wait for morning light."

When the guerrillas were spotted somewhere, or when there was a guerrilla invasion, all of the civilian patrolmen of the area would be sent out on what was called a "rastreo." They would walk through the jungles combing every inch thoroughly, looking for the guerrillas or their hideouts. They captured many of them this way.

They were also ordered to confiscate any native jungle brew that they found. Unfortunately, many of the civilian patrolmen greatly enjoyed this task because they got to drink it themselves. But not Chomo. He wouldn't touch the stuff.

Once he and the men under him were sent on a rastreo somewhere in the municipality of Cuilco. They searched the jungles and also investigated some out-of-the-way villages. In one village he found an Indian woman living in a small hut with her children. This woman's husband had been an active guerrilla and was killed by civilian patrolmen. Chomo searched her hut for weapons, ammunition, and explosives, and asked to see her *cédula*.

"I don't have one," she said, weeping. "It is true, my husband was a guerrilla, but that was my husband, not me! I want to live so I can take care of my children!"

"Kill her!" some of the boys under Chomo's command hissed. "She is just conning you. She is a guerrilla. Who knows how many heads she may have already severed and hid somewhere in a cave!"

But Chomo was moved to compassion by the woman's pleadings. "I will not kill you," he told her. "I have never killed and never plan to. I would turn you over to the army."

Before he could say more, the woman resumed her pleadings. "Please don't turn me over to the army! Please! My children, my poor, fatherless children need me! I am not a guerrilla! I only want to take care of my children!"

"I am not going to turn you over to the army," Chomo said when he could get a word in edgewise. "I am going to let you go free. But don't you ever, ever have anything to do with politics, and you must really dedicate your life to caring for your fatherless children, as you have said."

"Oh, I will, I will," said the woman, tears still running down her cheeks. Her half-naked children looked on, wide-eyed.

That same day Chomo and his men captured a guerrilla in the jungle. Chomo refused to kill him, ordering the men to securely tie him up and guard him with their lives until they could turn him over to the army. If the man escaped, they would have to pay with their lives because they had the opportunity to kill him, and did not. The army would think that they were undercover guerrillas masquerading as civilian patrolmen.

Needless to say, the man did not manage to escape, and when

Chomo turned him over to the army officials that evening, he was commended for his service to "La Patria" (the country).

"We prefer to capture them alive," they told Chomo. "That way we can extract information from them about the others. Just don't ever let one escape!"

Chomo was thankful when the time came for him to be released from his responsibilities as commander of a civilian patrol group. He still did guard duty one night every week, but he was thankful to be relieved of the headaches of making dangerous decisions and choices.

"I hated every minute of it," he told me. "But I never killed anyone. And I wasn't killed either, as you can see, or any of the men under me."

Chapter Twenty-seven

Santa Ana Invasion

*O*ne Sabbath early in the morning, a bunch of us from the Chalum church drove over to the village of Santa Ana, which is about four kilometers from El Tablón. It is located in a canyon with a river running along one side of the little town. There is a small adobe church there with a tin roof, tile floor, backless wooden benches, and big windows way up high covered with chicken wire. At the time this story took place, there were only two Adventist families living in the village who attended the little church.

Sister Hermila was the main pillar of the church, figuratively speaking. There had been guerrilla invasions the year before in the village of Santa Ana, and one day an army truck had come through. Every so often the truck would stop, and the soldiers would grab a man from the side of the road, throw him facedown in the bottom of the truck bed, and go on. Sister Hermila's husband and son were taken in this way. As the truck bumped along the road toward Tablón and San Antonio Huista (the municipality or county seat), the soldiers jumped and jumped on the backs of the men they had lying face down in the bottom of the truck. By the time they arrived in San Antonio Huista, the men they had picked up were all dead, including Sister Hermila's husband and son. After that the army sent her a message to go to San Antonio Huista to get the bodies of her loved ones to take home to bury.

Following the burial, she and her daughters fled the area in order to avoid further persecution of their family by the army. For several months, they lived with an Adventist family in Mexico. When enough time had passed for all the army personnel in the vicinity of their home and surrounding villages to be replaced, the widow and her daughters ventured to return home to Santa Ana.

News had reached us that they were back, and that was why we decided to go visit them this particular Sabbath, in order to offer our support and encouragement.

Ishmael and I took the old yellow truck, Benedicto drove his jeep, and Julio his station wagon, with as many people as could be crowded into the vehicles, plus quite a few more.

Anastacio and Rosaura hiked down from Tablón that morning with some of their friends and relatives from their little home church in order to meet with us. Felman and Rubelín were on vacation from the SDA boarding academy in Petén at the time, and they accompanied them as well. The sun shone brightly that day, and we all expected a wonderful season of fellowship together.

We parked our vehicles along the street by the church and walked to Sister Hermila's home. She welcomed us gravely, and then we all walked to the little church, which was just a few feet up the street from her house. It was almost time for Sabbath School to begin, so we all went in and sat down quietly. Rosaura sat beside me for a few moments, then, in typical Martha-style, remembered something that she had left undone at a house two blocks away where she was going to graciously provide a meal for everyone that afternoon.

She leaned over and whispered in my ear, "I have to go tend to something at the house of Araceli's mother-in-law. Would you please walk with me?"

I nodded my head and rose to follow her. In a few minutes we returned to the church and took our places on the bench where we had been sitting before. Suddenly Rosaura put her hand on her head. "Oh no! I forgot something else," she said in a low tone. "What an empty head! Will you go back with me?"

"Well," I answered, "Sabbath School has begun, and they may call on me for something. I had better stay here."

"OK, Felman and Rubelín can go with me."

The two boys obligingly accompanied Rosaura back to the house where she and I had gone just a few minutes before. About fifteen minutes later, Rosaura came in and sat down beside me, pale, shaking, and very much agitated.

"Give me some paper, quick! I must write a note," she said.

I looked at her blankly.

"The guerrillas have surrounded the church. They are carrying big guns and have masks over their faces!" she said. "I must write a note to pass to Julio on the platform so he won't say anything that might get himself or us killed." Julio was up front teaching the Sabbath School lesson.

Then Ishmael whispered, "No! We mustn't write a note. If one of them were to find it later, we would be killed for sure. Let's just be quiet and pray, and otherwise proceed as though everything were normal."

As we sat there, I looked up through the window above my head. Way up high on a hill overlooking the village, I could see a red flag blowing in the breeze. It had been put there by the guerrillas to show that they claimed Santa Ana and the surrounding area as their territory. Although I could not see them, I knew that the flag had E.G.P. written on it in big, black letters. These initials stood for "Ejercito Guerrillero de los Pobres," meaning "Guerrilla Army of the Poor."

At the end of the sermon, Rubelín and I got up to sing a song we had prepared. I played my autoharp, and Rubelín played a melodica in certain places through the song. From the platform one could see out the windows around the church, and I was relieved to not see anyone standing outside.

During the meal that afternoon, Rosaura and the two boys told us what had happened. First of all, Felman and Rubelín had left the house before Rosaura to return to the church. As they were walking, a man with a machine gun suddenly stepped from behind a building and blocked their way. He had a cloth tied over most of his face and was wearing a hat so that only his eyes showed.

"Go to the plaza at the center of the village!" he ordered the two boys as he prodded them along with his gun. At the same time other people were being herded in the same manner to the same place from all directions.

A crowd of people were assembled by about thirty guerrillas who consisted of men, women, and children. (The only requirement to be a guerrilla is to be strong enough to carry a machine gun or rifle.)

The head guerrilla made a speech. "We are the army of the poor! We are your friends! We are here to help you regain the property that is rightfully yours. The rich have no right to the land they hold. It belongs to the poor!

"We do not kill people! We do not torture people! We do not harm anyone. If you cooperate with us, your benefactors, you have nothing to fear from us.

"We give you permission to be non-political, or to choose a neutral political position. But if you do so, you must not report us, or anything you may know about us, our whereabouts or activities, to the army, or you will be killed!

"As has been stated, we are your friends. And now we must go before the murderous army discovers that we are here. Good day to you."

With that they disappeared from the village as quickly as they had come. Felman and Rubelín made their way back to the church. They were brave boys and took the whole experience in stride without becoming excited or overly alarmed, although they were fully aware of their danger.

During the speech by the guerrillas at the town plaza, Rosaura started back toward the church, unaware of what was happening. Suddenly a man, armed with a machine gun and with a bandanna tied over his face stepped out in front of her. Rosaura was terrified, but she kept her composure.

"Buenos días," he said gruffly.

"Buenos días," she replied.

"What is your name?" demanded the man.

"Rosaura," she said, trying to look and act as dull eyed and ignorant as possible.

"Where are you going?"

"That way," she said, motioning with her hand.

"Whose cars are those?" asked the man, pointing toward our vehicles that were parked down the dirt street by the church. Knowing that the guerrillas often burned or stole automobiles and sometimes killed the owners, Rosaura tried her best to act all the more dull-witted.

"They belong to some señores," she said, gaping at the man.

"Are you one of the long tongues?" he asked her now.

She continued to gape, slouching her shoulders.

"I have a list here," he continued. "I am going to read this list of names to you. Maybe yours is on it. The people on this list have used their long, gossiping tongues to give the army information about us. We are going to kill them. Perhaps your name or that of someone you

Santa Ana Invasion

know is on this list, and if so, you can give me information about these people so that we can find them and kill them."

With that the man pulled a folded sheet of paper from his pocket, unfolded it, and began to read. Rosaura trembled. The names he read were those of people she knew, both from El Tablón and Santa Ana.

Presently the man finished reading the list, folded it, and put it back in his pocket. "Do you know any of these people?" he asked.

Rosaura shook her head, praying silently that she would not be questioned any further. After scrutinizing her face for a moment, the man said, "You may now continue on your way." With that he walked on down the street.

As we discussed the events of the morning over lunch that afternoon, Julio told us that from the pulpit on the platform of the church where he was speaking, he had seen three of the armed guerrillas standing outside, listening. He had not shown even by the flicker of an eye that he was aware of their presence. I hope and pray that a ray of the good old Gospel Light shone into those poor men's hearts that day during the fifteen or so minutes that they stood around the little church.

That afternoon Ishmael took most of the folks from Tablón home in the pickup, and Anastacio saw to it that I stayed inside the house where we had lunch in Santa Ana. "You need to keep out of sight," he told me. "I would hate for you to get shot. El Tablón is not a safe place for foreigners these days. It is even more dangerous than Santa Ana. And it's a good thing you stayed inside the church this morning."

The drive home that late afternoon was uneventful. The scenery was beautiful, the atmosphere quiet and peaceful. Everyone was cheerful. Could it be possible that there was a war going on? No doubt those who have lost their loved ones are painfully aware of it, I thought.

Chapter Twenty-Eight

Some Battery Acid and a Prayer

It was October, and it was graduation time at the Instituto de Capacitación Adventista del Petén, the SDA boarding academy in the department of Petén. This graduation was special to the Martínez family and us. Felman and Rubelín were graduating as elementary school teachers, and we were all excited. The oldest of Ishmael's nephews and nieces were going to school there, too, so a number of us from the Matías family, besides Anastacio, Rosaura, and Magda, were anxious to go to the graduation ceremony. Among us all, we rented a van and hired a chauffeur to drive it. Herculano followed us in his little Chevy LUV pickup that we sold him one year after bringing it down from the States. It is a long, hot, tiresome journey from our part of Guatemala over to Petén, but we were all enthusiastic and excited, and we whiled away the hours by singing, telling stories, and finding things to laugh about.

    A couple of years before, we had made a trip to Petén, and had sunk clear up to the axle in the mud several times. But now the road had been greatly improved, and there were no mud holes. However, the van began overheating, and we had to stop several times. Paco was with our group on that trip, and during one of our stops, he took the battery out of Herculano's Chevy LUV and put it in the van. We were all walking around outside trying to cool off, and as I watched

Some Battery Acid and a Prayer

what Paco and the others were doing, I suddenly pointed at his shirt in alarm.

"Look at your shirt, Paco!" I exclaimed. It was all covered with battery acid, and so was the front of his pants.

A look of dismay crossed Paco's face. "Oh no, this is the shirt I wore to my civil wedding three years ago!" (In Guatemala Protestant ministers are not licensed to perform marriage ceremonies, so when a couple wants to have a church wedding, they go to the municipality and get a civil marriage first. Then the pastor performs a wedding ceremony for them in the church on their wedding day, and that is considered to be the "real" marriage by church members.)

"What will Hortencia say when I get home and she sees this shirt?" Paco continued. He looked so stricken that I began to feel really concerned.

"Oh, Lord, I prayed silently, "it would be such a simple thing for you to send an angel to remove all that battery acid from Paco's shirt. You provided wine by a miracle for a wedding feast once when you were on earth. I know you can do this just as well."

We arrived at the school that evening and all of us slept on the floor in a vacant house. The next morning Paco came over to me and said, "Look at this shirt. I don't understand why, but it is perfectly clean and looks brand new. There is no sign of the battery acid at all. Yet I had to throw my jeans away because the whole front of them was eaten away and completely dissolved."

I looked at the shirt. It looked brand new all right. It even looked like it had been washed and ironed! Then I told Paco about my prayer the day before. He shook his head. "Your prayer was certainly answered," he said. Years later he still had that same shirt.

The graduation program that weekend was beautiful, and we were so proud of "our" boys. That next year Felman and Rubelín taught our church school in Chalum. "Colegio Sinaí," as our school is called, was never blessed by better teachers. The next year after that they attended the University of San Carlos in Quetzaltenango. God was with them in their struggle to maintain their faith amid snares, trials, and political dangers as they struggled to gain a higher education. We would have sponsored them to go to the Adventist college in Costa Rica if we could have, but the declining economy made it impossible for us to do so.

Felman won first place in the field of mathematics in the entire university, and he was offered many tempting scholarships and a high position at San Carlos University. But he turned it all down to go into denominational work, which had been his lifelong desire. He receives a low salary, but he is doing what he loves best—using his teaching skills to help teenagers learn to know Jesus better and to become workers in God's vineyard. He is also earning his master's degree at our college in Costa Rica. And last but not least, he recently married a beautiful young Christian lady!

Chapter Twenty-Nine

Soloma

One Friday druing the late rainy season, 1983, Ishmael and I were eating lunch in our kitchen when we heard a gentle knock on the door. Then it opened and in walked Benedicto. Mamma must have been upstairs, because she was not eating with us in the kitchen.

"Buenas tardes, Ismael," Benedicto said in the customary way.

"Buenas tardes, Beno," replied Ishmael.

He turned to me. "Buenas tardes, Esther," he said politely.

"Buenas tardes," I smiled back. "Pull up a chair and sit down. Have you eaten lunch yet?"

"Yes, I have already eaten lunch," he said, sitting down. "But if you don't mind, I will have an orange."

"Sure," I said, starting to get up to get him a plate and a knife.

"Don't get up," he said pleasantly. "I will put my peelings on Ishmael's plate."

When I had finished eating, I excused myself from the table and started tidying up the kitchen while the two men talked. Presently Benedicto pulled out a telegram and showed it to Ishmael. It was from our new district pastor that we had not met yet.

"Please-come-help-evangelistic-meetings-soloma-this-weekend." It was signed by Pastor Rudy Garcia.

"Well, let's go," I said.

Ishmael and Benedicto both agreed, and in a little while we were all bumping down the road in Beno's little black jeep. I had my Yamaha keyboard, and several people accompanied us. Mamma was along, too. She stayed with us that summer, and she never liked to miss out on any adventure.

In Valparaíso, Julio Ramos joined us, and we continued on our way. It was slow going. Every few kilometers along the highway going toward Huehuetenango, we were stopped and inspected by civilian patrolmen who were on duty. It was a nuisance, but we were glad to see that they were doing their job, and we cooperated enthusiastically. The guerrilla warfare was still in full swing, and so was President Ríos Montt's "beans and bullets program." (The civilian patrolmen could not afford to spend time away from their work to do guard duty or it would mean that their families would suffer for lack of food, so the president gave them each a ration of black beans for their time spent serving the country and community in that way. The black beans were provided out of funds sent from the U.S. as foreign aid to Guatemala during the guerrilla warfare.)

From Hueuetenango we turned onto a dirt road leading up into the high mountains called "Los Cuchumatanes." It couldn't have been more than sixty kilometers through the mountains to Soloma, but due to road conditions, it took a couple of hours to get there from Huehuetenango. The narrow, bumpy dirt road wound along up near timberline in some places. The mountains were rugged and majestic. About the only livelihood for the Indians who live there is herding sheep. It gets cold up there, and sometimes there is a heavy frost. The Indians wear coats made from the wool from their sheep.

Every few kilometers we would show our ID to the civilian patrolmen at the checkpoints along the way. As we rode along, I remem-

Soloma

bered when we had driven this same road to go to Ixcán when I was seventeen, and a newlywed. There had been no civilian patrolmen then, nor guerrilla warfare to speak of.

About an hour before dark we started down the long hill into the town of Soloma. There were pine trees on the mountains surrounding the little town, and we could see the cobblestone streets and adobe houses as we got closer. There were apple trees everywhere, it seemed to me, with big clusters of apples starting to turn red.

"Why can we only get apples that are small, lumpy, green, and sour at the market when such lovely ones grow right here in Soloma?" I asked Ishmael.

"Because we Guatemalans export the best things to other places and keep the worst for ourselves," he said matter-of-factly. "Our people want things dirt cheap, but foreigners will pay more for them."

In a little while we found a hotel and rented a room with several beds in it for us all to sleep on. The adobe hotel was damp and chilly with a cement floor. The structure was built around an open place that was brightly adorned with flowering bushes.

We were used to the warm climate of the lower altitudes, and I shivered with cold. "I need something to warm me up," I said. "I feel sick from the cold, like I will have to go to bed." It was foggy and a slow drizzle had begun to fall, typical of the mountains. "If I could have some hot water to drink, I think I would be OK," I said.

Ishmael called the young man that had showed us to our room and asked if I could have some hot water to drink. The young man looked at me a little strangely, then said, "Sure. Follow me to the kitchen."

He led me up some steps around a big pila, by the bathrooms, and along some clammy corridors into another part of the building. There he took me into an old room with a dirt floor. There was an adobe plancha with a big fire blazing in it. Several women stood around it. They were friendly and talkative and began to ply me with questions about myself. It was not often that a "gringa" visited their little kitchen. I stood as close to the fire as I possibly could. How funny, I thought. When we camped in a tent in the snow in Montana, I never got this cold!

Pretty soon one of the women said, "You are cold. And you came to get something to warm you up, and we keep talking and talking. What would you like? Coffee, hot chocolate, atole, or milk?"

I smiled. "I want a cup of hot water to drink," I said.

"Hot water!" they chorused in surprise.

"Yes, hot water," I repeated.

They gave me the hot water, and we talked while I drank it. They wanted to know who I was, where I came from, how I had come to marry a Guatemalan, and how many children we had. In that country, people could never understand why I thought we were not ready for children yet, so I usually just said that we didn't have any yet, but maybe someday we would. If they questioned me further, I would just shrug my shoulders.

After I finished the water, they offered me more, but I needed to get going with the others to the meeting, so I told the ladies goodnight and hurried back to our room.

When Benedicto stopped the jeep outside of the old building where the meetings were being held, the first thing I saw was a little man not even five feet tall, wearing an old sweater with a necktie, a tuke on his head, and big thick glasses. I guessed him to be about forty years old, but I was wrong. He was twenty-six, just one year older than myself. I am usually a bit hesitant to approach strangers, but this one did not look in the least bit intimidating, so I climbed out of the jeep, went over to him, and held out my hand.

"Are you our new pastor?" I asked.

Soloma

"Rudy García, at your service," he said, shaking my hand politely. I told him my name, and Ishmael and the others all came over and introduced themselves, warmly welcoming the new pastor to our district, and he warmly welcomed all of us to Soloma. Pastor Rudy turned out to be one of the most dynamic, fascinating people I have ever met.

The room where the meetings were being held was about twenty feet long and fifteen feet wide. The cement floor was cracked, and so was the dingy plaster on the walls. There were rickety backless benches for people to sit on and an old wobbly table up front with a cloth over it to serve as a pulpit. There was a lovely bouquet of flowers in a Coca-Cola bottle in the middle of the table. When not being used for meetings, this room was actually the living room of the family who resided in the house. The front door opened right onto the dirt cobblestone street, and in the back there were rooms that served as a bedroom and kitchen. The bathroom was a separate small building. There was a pila outside, and the rooms were in an L-shape around it so that the extension of the roof covered it. A little ways behind the house were a couple of apple trees and some flowers and greenery.

The people didn't seem to notice the dingy appearance of the room, and it was soon packed until there wasn't even standing room. About fifty people stood outside, as well. The audience listened with eager attention, and no wonder! Pastor Rudy was a fantastic speaker. He easily carried his listeners with him back to Bible times, the dark ages, and on into the future.

Whenever he would ask a question referring to another sermon he had already preached, the people would answer enthusiastically. But the first to wave his hand in the air was always a twelve-year-old boy who sat as close to the front as he could. He seemed to have Pastor Rudy's sermons memorized from beginning to end. I later learned that this boy's name was Pedro.

The next morning the living-room-turned-temporary-meeting-hall was packed again for Sabbath School and church. After I had accompanied the singing on my keyboard and Julio Ramos and I sang a couple of special songs, Pastor Rudy asked me to take the children out back and have a Sabbath School class with them. Pedro helped me herd the fifty-some children along, insisting that they be quiet and orderly.

The children sat on the ground or stood, and I observed that my audience ranged from ages two to fifteen. The little ones were looked after by their older siblings, and they stared at me with as much wide-eyed interest as the older ones.

I had not had time to prepare anything, and I had not thought to bring along any pictures or children's Sabbath School materials. As I took my place in front of the children, not knowing what I would say, I prayed silently, "Lord, please give me some of the new pastor's ability."

I noticed that Pedro's face was radiant with eager anticipation. I was thankful there were no adults there. I could talk freely to children, but not if adults were present.

Actually, teaching children's Sabbath School was nothing new to me. I had been leader of the children's division in Valparaíso since I was thirteen, and in Chalum ever since Ishmael and I got married. But today, I had nothing prepared, and I had no pictures.

I flashed the children a smile, and they smiled back. Then we sang and prayed. Then it was time to start talking. I smiled and opened my mouth, still not knowing what I would say.

"How many of you have been coming to the meetings?" I heard myself ask.

Nearly all of them raised their hands.

"Who can tell me who Elijah was?"

Pedro was standing a little to one side of the rest. He immediately answered in a clear voice, "A prophet of God who carried an important message to his people to repent and return to the Lord!"

"You have listened well to Pastor Rudy," I said.

"And it was prophesied that Elijah would return," Pedro added.

I ventured to ask him, "Has that prophecy been fulfilled?"

"Yes. John the Baptist was the symbolic fulfillment of that prophecy. He also carried a message of repentance to God's people. He told them to repent and be baptized, because the kingdom of heaven was at hand, and God's people on earth today are supposed to carry an Elijah and John the Baptist message to the world to repent, believe the Gospel, and get ready for Jesus to come."

Pedro had listened well. The ice was broken, and I began to talk. I don't know what I said, but the children were quiet and attentive.

That morning we had left the jeep at the hotel and walked to the place of meeting. After church, as we walked back, Pastor Rudy and Pedro accompanied us. At the center of every Guatemalan town is a park with flowers and cement benches to sit on. We stopped at the park and sat down on the benches for a few minutes that day.

My mother pointed out some men and a boy about fourteen years old who had followed us at a distance. Now he was standing with a couple of men just far enough away so we couldn't hear what they were saying. They were looking at us. The boy would smirk and say something, then they would all laugh.

We turned to Pedro. "Who are those people over there that keep looking at us and laughing?" Mamma asked him.

"Well," he said, "you see, there is a division in this town. Some of the people love the meetings, but others hate the 'Elijah message' and do all they can to oppose it and keep the people from going to the meetings. Perhaps those men and that boy over there think that if they

Hope That Springs Eternal

laugh at you enough you will give up trying to preach in this town and leave."

When we were ready to go back home, Pastor Rudy asked if we could come back the next weekend, and Ishmael and Benedicto said yes.

And that is another story.

Chapter Thirty

Providences

The next Friday we did our best to get off to an early start for Soloma, and by late afternoon we were bumping along through the Cuchumatanes. Today only Benedicto, Ishmael, my mother, and I had come along. My keyboard and autoharp were in the back. The mountains were foggy this particular afternoon, and as we climbed higher, a slow drizzle began to fall.

I glanced at my watch. Five minutes after four. *We will have just enough time to get a room at the hotel and then eat something at one of the little restaurants before sundown,* I thought. We were about an hour from Soloma. We were at the highest point on the road. Pretty soon we would start the several kilometers descent toward Soloma.

I was wrapped in these thoughts when suddenly the motor quit and the jeep came to a stop. We were in a lonely area, and I had heard that these mountains were infested with bands of guerrillas. The fog was rolling in closer, the drizzle increased, and it seemed to be getting darker by the minute. I knew that we were in a potentially dangerous situation, although before I had a child, I never really took danger too seriously. However, this afternoon I had a feeling that some kind of danger was lurking nearby in some way.

Ishmael and Benedicto got out and raised the hood. They couldn't find anything wrong, and for twenty minutes they tried in vain to start the jeep.

"Lord," I prayed, "why has this happened? Don't You want us at the meeting? What could possibly be Your purpose in allowing the jeep to quit like this out in the middle of nowhere when You could so easily prevent it? Are we going to have to sit here all night?"

My mother was quiet and serene, no doubt praying silently. She always had such faith! We didn't say anything to each other. We just both sat there quietly while the men worked. They knew little about mechanics, and Mamma and I knew even less.

Suddenly the motor started again and off we went. Normally we would have overtaken the late afternoon bus and passed it, but because of the twenty minutes delay, we never caught up to it.

When we got to Soloma, it wasn't raining anymore, and the clouds were high. After leaving our things in the hotel room, we hurried toward the meeting place, carrying our Bibles and the keyboard.

At the town square we saw a car with a loudspeaker attached to the top of it. A man inside the car was announcing that every civilian patrolman in Soloma must present himself at the town square at six o'clock sharp the next morning. The car went down a side street with the man inside making his announcement over and over again. Before the evening was over, everyone in Soloma would have heard the announcement.

"The civilian patrolmen must be going on a *rastreo* tomorrow," Ishmael commented under his breath.

The meeting that night was good. Ishmael and Benedicto talked with a number of people who were interested in receiving Bible studies in their homes. This interest would be followed up by Tomás Martín, the local self-supporting lay preacher and evangelist.

The next day after church Pedro sidled up to us after most of the people had left. After the customary greetings had been exchanged,

Providences

he said, "Yesterday afternoon about four fifteen the guerrillas stopped the late afternoon bus that came just a little while before you got here. They made everybody get out, and then the guerrillas searched the bus. I guess they were looking for something or someone. After searching the bus, they ran back up the mountainside into the forest above the road. Today the civilian patrolmen all went on a *rastreo* looking for them."

"OK, Lord," I breathed silently. "I get the message now. You had a reason for letting the jeep quit and then start again so mysteriously twenty minutes later. We might have overtaken that bus at the wrong time otherwise."

Some things will remain a mystery until Jesus Himself explains them to us when we walk and talk with Him beside the River of Life. But sometimes He lets us see a little glimpse in this life of His providences, so that we can believe and trust Him all of those other times when we don't know the reason why.

Pedro was speaking again. "It's a lot better now than it was a year ago," he was saying. "We used to have to go inside of our houses here in Soloma at four o'clock in the afternoon, shut and bolt the doors, and not make a sound. We didn't even dare to light so much as a candle after dark.

"In the late afternoon the guerrillas would come down from the mountains and walk up and down the streets carrying their big guns. Their hair was long, filthy, and matted; they had dirt caked onto their necks from going for months at a time without bathing or changing clothes. They wore old, crude looking sandals, and their clothes were filthy and full of holes.

"If they found anyone out on the street, they took them to their mountain hideouts and made guerrillas out of them. They would even kidnap small children. That is why everyone had to hide in their houses in the late afternoons. But now the guerrillas are afraid to come down into the town because of the civilian patrolmen. Ríos Montt is saving our country by organizing all the civilians to do guard duty under the supervision of the army. In just a few more months, I will also become a civilian patrolman," Pedro said eagerly.

Meetings were not held on Saturday nights, so we drove home that afternoon. The civilian patrolmen at the checkpoint along the way seemed nervous. Who could blame them? The guerrillas had a reputation for being vicious fighters, and everyone feared them. Once in a while someone would laugh and say, "The guerrillas? Why they're nothing to be afraid of. They wouldn't hurt anybody!" After that, everyone would be quiet around that person and watch him suspiciously.

We were past Huehuetenango just a little ways on the highway going toward home when we saw the pickup of *Don* Javier from Chalum stopped beside the road facing us. Ishmael pulled over and asked, "Do you need help?"

"Need help!" exclaimed *Don* Javier. "You are lucky you were gone this weekend. The army called us all out to go to a place near Nentón to fight the guerrillas. It was some battle! The guerrillas were all up on a hilltop. They were some of the refugees who fled to Mexico.

"There were women and even children too, all with guns, yelling insults at us. The shooting back and forth was awful. Even the little children were shooting down at us. Some of the soldiers were killed. Then the army official radioed for a helicopter, and when it came, it almost got shot down. It had to go back, and then he radioed for a plane to fly out from Guatemala City. When the plane came, it began to bomb the hill where the guerrillas were. Then the same ones who had been yelling insults at us began to scream and cry, saying, 'We are just women and children, and you are murdering us!' When it got to be too much for them, they ran back over to the Mexican side, carrying their dead and wounded with them. Now the Mexicans will treat them in their hospitals," he said with distaste.

Then he said, "I've got to get going. I'm carrying a couple of wounded men to the hospital in Huehue. Adios."

During that particular encounter, a number of soldiers were killed, but none of the civilian patrolmen lost their lives.

Chapter Thirty-One

Pastor Rudy

The next Friday afternoon we arrived in Soloma about three o'clock in the afternoon, and Pastor Rudy invited us to go to the house of Tomás Martín, the local lay evangelist, for a late afternoon meal and sundown worship.

Tomás had a sweet wife named Marta and three children. I had known her several years before when we were both teenagers. Her family lived in La Democracia. She had three sisters all nearly the same age, and occasionally they would come out from La Democracia to visit the Valparaíso church. Then the handsome young man from Soloma came along and swept her off her feet. She married him with her parents' blessing, and eventually they moved to Soloma to live and raise up a new church in the town.

Their house consisted of non-plastered adobe walls, a dirt floor, and a tin roof. Out back was—you've already guessed it—an apple tree with lots and lots of rosy apples on it. The house was made up of two small rooms—the kitchen and the bedroom.

Tomás told us all to sit down at the table in the kitchen, then he and Marta began to serve us the meal of hot black beans, rice, scrambled eggs, hot sauce, and tortillas. They had a fire going, and the atmosphere was pleasant. Our host and hostess stood by while we ate, watching to make sure we had everything we needed.

Pastor Rudy

"You know," commented Pastor Rudy, "we are living in an important era of this world's history. Life is not like it used to be, but God will watch over and protect us as long as we endeavor to carry out the great Gospel Commission. As yet there are so many people in the world who do not know that Jesus is coming soon."

"Pastor Rudy," my mother said enthusiastically, "tell us about yourself."

The talkative Pastor Rudy rose to the occasion. "I am an Indian from the mountain department capital town of Totonicapán. I come from a poor family. My mother wears the Indian costume, and I learned to speak the Indian dialect." (Later I discovered that he could speak several dialects and quite a bit of English as well.)

"My father died when I was small, and my brother, my sisters, and I suffered much from poverty. Once my mother was falsely accused of committing a crime, and she was put in prison for several months. During that time we suffered from hunger and loneliness. Another time I was accused falsely of a crime that I did not commit and was put in an underground prison for six months. It was dark down there, and I never saw the light of day until it was 'discovered' that I was innocent, and I was brought out. The sudden change from being in the dimly lit prison for months and then stepping out suddenly into the brilliant sunlight caused permanent damage to my eyes, which is why I have to wear these thick glasses.

"When I was thirteen years old, I was studying to be a Catholic priest. We were given a twelve-weeks course called 'Heresies.' We were taught the doctrines of every major Protestant denomination, including those of the Seventh-day Adventists. By the time the course was finished, I had decided that my favorite 'heresy' was the Seventh-day Adventist 'heresy.' So I went home and told my mother that I could not be a Catholic priest.

"'Then you will leave my house immediately,' she said stoically.

"I knew she would not change her mind, so I left that same night. I went to the mountains and roamed around for three days without anything to eat. 'God', I prayed, 'I am suffering because I want to be a Seventh-day Adventist, but I don't even know who the Seventh-day Adventists are or how to find them. Please lead me to your people.

"The morning of the third day, I heard someone chopping wood in the forest with a machete. I followed the sounds until I found the man that was cutting up firewood. When he saw me he laid down his machete.

"'*Buenos días*,' he said.

"'*Buenos días*,' I replied.

"He pulled out an old worn Bible. 'Do you know how to read?' he asked me eagerly.

"I said yes, and he handed me the Bible. He motioned for me to sit down on a rock and told me to read to him. He sat down near me, and I read to him for about forty minutes. Then he invited me home for breakfast. That man was a Seventh-day Adventist.

"Eventually a way was found for me to attend the Seventh-day Adventist boarding academy in Petén, and later I went to our college in Costa Rica and took theology. So, instead of becoming a Catholic priest, I am a Seventh-day Adventist pastor.

"God has been with me in my work as a pastor," Rudy continued. "Just a few weeks ago a church member from Huehuetenango accompanied me on a visit to El Rosario."

"Do you know where El Rosario is?" asked Pastor Rudy, looking at me.

"Yes," I answered. "We have been there before. It is a town up here in these same mountains. We went there to help with a meeting once. There is a small group of believers now, isn't there?"

Pastor Rudy

"Yes," said Pastor Rudy. "You are right. As I was saying, a friend from the church in Huehuetenango accompanied me recently on a visit to El Rosario. When we got off the bus with the rest of the passengers at the checkpoint of the civilian patrolmen just before entering the little town, the commander ordered me to open my bag, which I did. I was carrying some *El Centinela* magazines (similar to *Signs of the Times*), and the commander grabbed them angrily. Waving them around, he demanded that I tell him who I was and why I had come to his town.

"However, we already knew each other. He was the Pentecostal preacher of El Rosario. I answered that I was a Seventh-day Adventist pastor and had come to visit my members and give them some *El Centinela* magazines.

"'Ah yes,' he said. 'Adventism! Communism! They both end with "ism," so you must be a communist guerrilla!'

"'Men,' he shouted, 'tie these two strangers up to be shot!'

"The men brought some ropes to tie us up with. I said to my friend, 'You are a married man with children. I am single. I will try to distract them, and you run for your life!'

"Just then an army truck came along raising clouds of dust, and it suddenly came to a halt right there in front of us. To my amazement, an old friend, Ricardo, from my army days jumped down from the driver's seat. I had served my obligatory three years, but Ricardo stayed on and worked his way up to a higher rank.

"'Rudy!' he exclaimed. 'What are you doing here all tied up?'

"'These men have accused my friend and me of being communist guerrillas', I told him.

"His lip curled in anger. He turned to the civilian patrolmen.

"'Why do you have these two men tied up like this?' he demanded.

"'Official,' said the commander, 'they are guerrillas. We were just going to turn them over to the army.'

"Ricardo flew into a rage. 'Turn them over to the army indeed!' he shouted. 'You were going to shoot them! And Rudy here is a military man. He was my best friend in the army! You are the communist guerrillas going around trying to shoot good men who have served their country faithfully in the army! Then you try to pass yourselves off as civilian patrolmen. Civilian patrolmen indeed!' he sneered.

"The commander was shaking. 'My official,' he pleaded, 'this is a misunderstanding.'

"'What do you do for a living?' demanded Ricardo.

"'I am the Pentecostal preacher in El Rosario,' replied the commander.

"'Aha!' said Ricardo. 'Now I see. You do not like him because he is a Seventh-day Adventist pastor. Fine Christian you are. Here you are a preacher trying to shoot another preacher! From now on I make you and the men under you personally responsible for the safety of my friend Rudy whenever he is in your territory. If anything ever happens to him in or near El Rosario, I will personally see to it that every one of you is shot!'

"'Oh!' clamored the civilian patrolmen, 'this is not our fault. We had nothing to do with this. It is only the commander. He is the one who wanted to kill your friend.'

"Ricardo looked around at them contemptuously. 'I hold all of you responsible for the safety of my friend, and especially you!' he said, jabbing the terrified commander of the civilian patrolmen with his gun.

"Then he turned to me. 'Do you have an *El Centinela* magazine for me before I go?'

"'Certainly,' I said. Then we talked for a few minutes.

"'My dear old friend, Rudy,' he said before he left, 'please, may I ask you for just one favor?'

"'Of course.'

"'Would you please remember to pray for me every day?'

"'Yes, Ricardo, my friend,' I said earnestly as we shook hands."

Chapter Thirty-Two

In Perils Oft

*I*f Pastor Rudy had told me that he was a modern day apostle Paul, I would have believed him.

"I pastored in Momostenango for a while," he continued, thoroughly warmed to his subject. (Momostenango is a town high up in the mountains in the department of Totonicapán.)

"Once when I went to Guatemala City to the mission, I had an unusual experience. It had gotten late, and the last bus of the day for Momostenango had already left, but I urgently needed to be there by the next morning. The guerrillas were virtually in control of the mountains, and travel at night was next to unthinkable. But by a special providence of God, I met a school teacher from Momostenango who had a car, and like myself, needed to be there by morning so much that he was willing to drive there that night if he and his wife could find someone to accompany them as a safety precaution.

"We started out from Guatemala City about seven o'clock that night. We traveled slowly in the old car, and about one o'clock in the morning we met a car coming toward us on the highway. We were signaled by the lights to stop, and we complied, knowing that to disobey could prove fatal.

"Sure enough, it was the guerrillas. They were each heavily armed with bandannas tied over their noses and mouths and caps on their heads so that only their eyes showed. The leader demanded gruffly that we tell him what we were doing in 'their territory.'

"I answered firmly, 'We are on Guatemalan soil, and Guatemala belongs to all Guatemalan citizens. We have just as much right to be here as you.'

"He was adamant. 'The mountains are free territory and belong to the guerrillas!' With that he raised his gun in a threatening gesture.

"The teacher and his wife were frightened. The other men searched them and the car, and the man continued to try to intimidate me. Presently he ordered me to step aside into the darkness with him. He prodded me along with his gun until we were out of earshot of the others. Then he stood in front of me and removed his cap and bandanna.

"'Rudy!' he said in an anguished voice. 'Rudy, what are you doing here?'

"For a moment I was shocked into silence. Then I countered, 'More appropriately, what are you doing here?' It was Samuel, a friend from academy days at ICAP. He had been the most outstanding student in my class and the spiritual leader of the boys in the dorm. The teachers and faculty loved him, and so did the students.

"'Rudy, what did you do after you graduated from ICAP?' he asked.

"'I became a pastor,' I told him. 'Right now I am pastoring in the district of Momostenango.'

"'And I am the wretched commander of the guerrilla forces of the mountain region,' Samuel said brokenly. 'I am in too deep. I cannot get out.'

"After we had talked for a few moments, he said in a desperate voice, 'Rudy, please pray for me!' We bowed our heads, and I prayed earnestly for my old friend. Then he said, 'Rudy, on my life I promise that no harm will come to you or your traveling companions tonight.'

Hope That Springs Eternal

He looked at his watch. 'It is time for me to go. Exactly ten minutes after my men and I drive away, you are to leave. We will be ten minutes ahead of you, and another car with some of my men will be exactly ten minutes behind you. We will guard you until you turn off on the dirt road that goes to Momostenango.'

"Walking back to the others, he said gruffly to his men, 'Let's go. These people are to be protected. Understand?'

"We obeyed Samuel's instructions to the letter, but if we had encountered the army that night when we were being 'protected' by two carloads of guerrillas, that would have been the end of us.

"And now, have you ever wondered what it would be like to be kidnapped by the guerrillas?" Rudy asked.

We all had to admit that such thoughts had occupied our minds at one time or another.

"While I was in Momostenango, one night I was seized and dragged away to the forest by the guerrillas. They handled me roughly and left me tied in a painful position for eight hours. When they finally untied me, my wrists and other parts of my body were bruised and bloody.

"'What do you want of me?' I demanded of them in a military tone of voice. 'Stop this nonsense of trying to terrorize me. Talk to me like men!'

"'We want you to deliver a message for us,' they told me. 'We know you are a good friend of the *alcalde* (mayor and judge) and the official down at the military zone. These men are both guilty of committing injustice against the peasants. Therefore, we, the real authorities in this region, order them to resign and leave the area immediately. Otherwise, if they do not, we will kill you! But we know they will resign for your sake because they highly respect you. If you cooperate with us, we will have, er, a certain regard for you ourselves.'

"They gave me letters to deliver to these two particular men, containing essentially the same message they had just given me.

"'I will deliver your message,' I told them, 'but as to whether or not they will resign, I cannot say. I do not believe in coaxing or coercing anyone to do something in order to serve my own interest.'

"'Just remember,' the guerrilla men said menacingly, 'if they do not resign, it will be your life, and you will not have an easy death.'

"Early in the morning I walked into the *alcalde's* office.

"'*Buenos días*, Pastor Rudy,' he said cordially. 'What can I do for you, my friend?'

"'You won't believe this'—Rudy's smile grew mischievous as he repeated the conversation to us—'but I have come this morning as a representative of the guerrilla forces. I bring you a letter and message to resign, or they will kill me.'

"He thought I was joking until I showed him my swollen, bloody wrists. Then he became very serious.

"'My friend, Rudy,' he said, 'I will resign this very day. Your noble life if worth more than my job. I resign for you, not for the guerrillas.'

"Next, I visited the official at the military zone. A similar conversation passed between us, and he too resigned that very day. In a few days I received a letter from the guerrillas which read like this: 'Respectable Señor Rudy Garcia: Congratulations for a job well done. You are a man of your word.'

"You have been to Ixtahuacán my friends?" queried Pastor Rudy. We all nodded our heads.

"As you know, Ixtahuacán is a mining town on the road to Cuilco. Many of the people who live there make their living working in the silver mine. You probably know also that the majority of the population there are in favor of the guerrilla warfare. The civilian patrolmen hardly check you when you go there, because they don't care how many guerrillas get past their checkpoints.

"Well, the Seventh-day Adventist Church members there once said to me when I was visiting them, 'Pastor, we should support the guerrilla warfare.' I didn't say anything because to object could mean death. Not that I am afraid to stand for the truth, but Christians should be 'wise as serpents, and harmless as doves.' We are to champion God's cause, not a political cause.

"However, the people of the Central American church did not like my visits to the town, and thought up a way to get rid of me, or so they thought. Although in all likelihood they are guerrilla supporters themselves, they told the military personnel in the town that I was a guerrilla.

"I was detained by the soldiers on my way out of town one day, and they threatened me with torture if I did not reveal all of the secrets of the guerrilla forces.

"'I will tell you nothing!' I declared. They were livid with anger at my lack of submission.

"They continued to threaten me. 'I will not talk to little guys in the army,' I said authoritatively. 'I want to talk to the big guys. Take me to the military zone in Huehuetenango.'

"'That we will do,' they informed me. I overheard them talking among themselves. 'He is the commander of all the guerrilla forces in Guatemala. We will be rewarded and promoted for capturing him!'

"Accordingly, I was taken to the military zone in Huehuetenango. The official in charge there and his men threatened me and tried to start the interrogation process, but again I said, 'I will tell you nothing. I will not talk to little men in the army.' Then I told them the name of one of the generals in Guatemala City, and I said that I would talk to him only.

"The official was jubilant. 'We have caught a really big guy,' he

In Perils Oft

said. He immediately radioed to Guatemala City, and the general I had asked to speak with was flown to Huehuetenango right away. When he walked into the room where I was being held, accompanied by the official that had me in custody, his face turned livid.

"'Rudy!' he exclaimed. 'What are you doing here locked up in a cage like a guerrilla?' The face of the official went white.

"I will not tell you the name of my friend, the general, but he turned to the official and berated him for 'capturing patriotic military men like a two-faced cowering guerrilla.' Then he ordered three weeks of military discipline for the official.

"Military discipline is no laughing matter, believe me," Pastor Rudy assured us. "The general and I had a nice visit. Then I was released, and he flew back to Guatemala City."

Time had flown by. It was almost sundown, and Tomás suggested that we go into the bedroom where we could all sit on the beds and sing and pray for sundown worship.

When we got into the bedroom, I had a strange feeling like I had walked into some kind of fairytale dollhouse. There were three of the shortest beds I had ever seen. They must not have been five feet long. Of course, Tomás was hardly five feet tall himself, and Marta was even shorter. The beds were made of boards with no mattresses. They each had one or two thin blankets spread over them, and that was all.

I'm glad I don't have to sleep on one of these beds tonight, I thought to myself as I sat down. *I wouldn't mind the hardness. I've slept on cement with nothing but a piece of thin plastic under me, and that is even harder, although it's not bad if you sleep flat on your back or on your stomach. But it would be miserable if I could not stretch my legs out full length.*

At five feet, three inches tall, I felt like a giant among midgets.

Chapter Thirty-Three

Led by the Spirit

*T*here was hardly two feet of space between the beds, and our knees were all crammed together as we sat facing one another. But that didn't matter. Never have I felt more unity of spirit with a group of God's children than I did that beautiful Friday evening as another blessed Sabbath began.

"My friends, I want you to meet the first fruit of our labors in Soloma," Pastor Rudy announced as Tomás ushered in a young man who introduced himself as Antonio. Short as the others, Antonio had a plain, honest looking face.

"Tomás has been studying with this young man for several months," Pastor Rudy told us. "And tomorrow our evangelistic campaign will come to a beautiful close when he is baptized in the river after church."

After the young man was seated, Pastor Rudy said, "For worship tonight I want Antonio to tell us about how the Lord led him to the Adventist truth."

We sang a song and prayed, and then Antonio began his story. "I was taken to the army when I was eighteen. During the time I served my country, I knew that I could die at any time in an encounter with the guerrillas. I began to feel a need deep within me to have a personal acquaintance with God, whoever He was, and the assurance that such

Led by the Spirit

an acquaintance must surely bring. I did not really know how to pray, but I cried out to God from my heart in the best way that I could to spare my life until the end of my three years of army service. I promised to become a Christian if He allowed me to live to do so, and I begged Him to lead me to the true church.

"He did spare my life, and just as soon as I was released from the army and returned home to Soloma, I began looking for a church. That was several months ago. I found a Pentecostal church on the outskirts of town," he said, gesturing, "and I began to go to all of the meetings. In no time I was a regular member, and I spoke in tongues with the rest of them. But I felt that something in my religious experience was missing. I had not found what I somehow knew I needed during my army service. I felt a deep soul craving to study God's Word.

"'God,' I prayed, 'please lead me to someone who can open Your Word to me. I cannot understand it on my own.' Then I met Tomás, and his knowledge of the Bible was the answer to my prayers. We studied much together."

Antonio turned to Tomás. "Thank you for your patience with me in answering all of my questions, and the many hours you have spent studying the Bible with me." Tomás' face glowed.

Then Antonio continued. "After a time I began to suspect that I did not belong in the church that I was attending, but I was not quite sure. My Pentecostal brethren assured me that the day of rest had been changed to Sunday, and they urged me to listen to the Spirit. Finally, I decided to ask the Holy Spirit directly which was the right church. Accordingly, I went the next Wednesday night to the meeting, and I knelt at the front with those who were praising God and speaking in tongues.

"'Lord,' I prayed silently, 'I am going to ask you some questions, and please let the Holy Spirit move my head yes or no in answer.'

"Then I asked silently, 'Is the seventh-day Sabbath really the scriptural day of rest?'

"My head moved up and down involuntarily. I put my hands up and tried to hold my head still, but I could not. *This is really supernatural*, I thought.

"Then I asked, 'Lord, is it Your will for me to observe the seventh-day Sabbath like the *Adventistas* do?'

"Again my head moved up and down several times.

"'Lord, is the Seventh-day Adventist Church the true church?'

"My head moved up and down.

"'Do you want me to be an *Adventista*?'

"Again my head moved up and down.

"'Is everything that Tomás taught me from the Bible true?'

"My head moved up and down again.

"'Did the Holy Spirit lead me to Tomás and the Adventist church?'

"Again my head moved up and down affirmatively.

"Convinced of the truth, I stood up and told the Pentecostal congregation about my experience. I was interrupted with 'Silence the false prophet! Cast the demons out of him!'

"I made my way to the door of the church, but they dragged me back to the front, and pushing me to my knees, they began to pray loudly all at once for the Holy Spirit to enter me and force the demons out. They had their hands on my head.

"Amid the noise I prayed silently, 'Lord, please show me and them that they are wrong by elevating me into the air on my knees.' Suddenly I was raised into the air, still in a kneeling position with my head bowed and my hands folded. I was one meter above the floor. They all tried with all of their strength to push me back down to the floor, but they could not alter my position up there in mid-air by even one centimeter. Finally, one by one, they gave up, baffled, and slipped out the door.

"When I was completely alone, I was gently lowered to the floor, and I got up and walked slowly out, determined to become a Seventh-day Adventist. My heart was full of a peaceful kind of joy," Antonio concluded.

Sabbath morning dawned clear and beautiful like a perfect spring day. The sun shone brightly, and the sky was a brilliant blue.

After church we all walked about one half of a kilometer out of Soloma to a crystal clear creek that ran about three feet deep, and twenty feet wide. I wondered if this perfectly clear water came from the magnificent waterfalls that could be seen from the road a few kilometers up, but I didn't have time to ask.

Antonio was stepping into the water now. Some naked children who had been splashing around in the creek moved a few meters downstream. They watched, fascinated. Pastor Rudy baptized Antonio, and as he stepped out of the water, we all sang a hymn. Then Rudy stretched his hands toward the people standing on the banks and path and extended an invitation to anyone who might desire to receive baptism in the future to raise their hands.

Pedro's hand went up, then some of the other people on the banks raised their hands, too. Tomás would be busy during the next few weeks. So would Antonio, who would assist Tomás in giving Bible studies. It was a beautiful ending to a wonderful evangelistic campaign.

My parents-in-law had come that morning in their Toyota station wagon, bringing a number of people along. Mamá Tona always carried a load of firewood and a *comal* tied up on the luggage rack so they could stop anywhere along the road, light a fire, and warm up her delicious food and tortillas to eat.

A young man from Ixtahuacán, whom I will call Santos, had ridden with my in-laws to Soloma that morning. Now he was anxious to get back to his hometown, so he asked Benedicto if he could go with us and drive the jeep. Benedicto obliged, and when we left Soloma, I found myself seated in the front next to the window with Benedicto beside me straddling the gearshift, and Santos driving. The young man gunned the motor and drove as fast as he possibly could over the dirt road, bouncing us hard over the potholes.

When we came to the first checkpoint, he nearly passed the civilian patrolmen who signaled for us to stop, then skidded to a sudden halt in the gravel, making us feel as though we had come close to turning over.

The civilian patrolmen eyed us suspiciously, and not without fear. If we were guerrillas, we could surely throw some kind of sophisticated explosive that would blow them all up. They peered into the jeep, and one of them demanded nervously that we tell them what the black case was.

"That is a musical instrument," Ishmael explained. He was holding it on his knees in the back. "If you want, my wife will play it for you." With that he began to open the case.

"No, no!" exclaimed the patrolmen, quickly pushing it back shut again.

A young man who could not have been more than eighteen years old put his head through the open window on my side. I tried to smile at him, but he was in no mood to be friendly with white strangers who could be Cuban terrorists for all he knew.

"Where do you live?" he asked me sharply.

"I live in El Chalum, La Libertad, in this same department of Huehuetenango," I said.

"I want to see your identification."

I handed him my passport. My mother also handed him hers from the backseat.

"If you live in Guatemala, then why do you have a passport?"

"I have a passport so that I can live in Guatemala," I explained.

He did not understand. He read the exit and entry stamps.

"Why do you go out of Guatemala every three months and then come back in?"

"In order to renew my permit to be in Guatemala," I said.

Mamma snatched her passport from his hand and turned the page to an expired residence that had been stamped there years before.

"Look, she said.

"Oh, you must be residents," the young man said, and he handed our passports back to us. He did not think to look for a residence in mine, and I didn't have one.

He had just raised his hand to wave us on when Santos snapped impatiently, "Don't waste our time. We have important things to do. Inspect our companions that are coming in the car behind us."

"Companions!" exclaimed the young patrolman in alarm. "That is a guerrilla term!"

"Oops, brethren then," said Santos carelessly.

"That is also a guerrilla term! Look, just get out of here," he said sharply. "Move it!"

With that, Santos sped off. Pretty soon Benedicto said that he wanted to drive. He asked Santos to stop, but the impetuous young man refused. "I want to get home!" he exclaimed.

"So do the rest of us," I said with a touch of grim humor.

We came to another checkpoint, and he sped past it, spraying gravel on the patrolman that was on duty there. I looked warily over my shoulder.

"He's aimed his rifle at us!" I cried out.

Santos put his foot hard on the brake, jerking us to another violent stop. The patrolman came over to his window. "I did not see the checkpoint, and I am in a hurry. I am rushing someone who is gravely ill to the hospital in Huehuetenango," Santos lied.

I grimaced. "Soon we all may be gravely ill or shot," I said under my breath. But I don't think anyone heard me.

"You had better stop at those checkpoints," I cautioned Santos a few minutes later. "The first one they would shoot is the driver for not stopping," I added dramatically.

After that he did better about stopping at the checkpoints, and Benedicto advised him to speak courteously and respectfully to the patrolmen. "If you don't, you may not get home at all," he said. After that Santos was slightly more courteous to the civilian patrolmen at the rest of the checkpoints.

At the junction where the road turned off the main highway to go to the towns of Colotenango, Ixtahuacán, and Cuilco, Santos spied a truck climbing the steep road far up on the mountainside. He was supposed to get out there at the junction and wait for a bus to take him to Ixtahuacán, but he turned onto the dirt road and went chasing wildly after the truck. We didn't catch up to it until we nearly reached the top of the mountain past Colotenango. There he got out and caught a ride to Ixtahuacán on the truck.

By this time some unpleasant fumes were emanating from under the hood of the old jeep, so we waited until it had cooled down a bit before starting back. We were all happy to get home that night.

Chapter Thirty-Four

Limestone Oven[1]

It was time for Pastor Rudy to visit the group of believers in the village of White Earth again. Carrying a small bag over his shoulder with a change of clothes and some magazines, he left the small house that he rented in Huehuetenango and set off down the street to a place where the bus to Cuilco would go by. The hustle and bustle of the little town was the same as usual. Women carried large baskets of fruit on their heads, people hurried to and from the market, a lame man begged in a sing-song voice on the corner. A drunk man with filthy hair and clothes lay on the sidewalk.

Presently an old bus came lumbering down the narrow, one-way street. Clouds of black diesel smoke emanated from the exhaust pipe, and the crowds of people scrambled to the sidewalks as the bus approached. A young man hung halfway out the door shouting, "Colotenango, Ixtahuacán, Cuilco!" Pastor Rudy signaled, the bus stopped, and he climbed aboard.

After driving around the town square, they turned down another street, then another and another, until they were on the road going out to the highway. The Cuilco junction was about forty kilometers from Huehuetenango. The bus made slow progress, stopping frequently to drop off and pick up passengers.

---

[1] Some of the names have been changed in this chapter

Pastor Rudy settled down the best he could in his crowded seat. He knew that it would take the bus three hours to get to Cuilco, even though it was only thirty kilometers from where the dirt road turned off the paved highway.

Pastor Rudy prayed, meditated, and dozed a little. Finally, the bus turned onto the dirt road. From there on, the ride was rough and bumpy. They bounced through the Indian town of Colotenango, and on toward Ixtahuacán, the mining town where he had been falsely accused of being a communist guerrilla and turned over to the military. From Ixtahuacán, the road began to descend slowly toward the lowlands where Cuilco is.

Finally, the long, hot, dusty ride was over. Now Pastor Rudy had to hike for several hours to get to the village of White Earth. Not daunted, he started out at a good pace. Rudy was a good hiker. He knew how to keep up an even pace, and he did not tire easily. An athlete would have had a hard time keeping up with him.

The sun beat down from a clear sky, but Rudy scarcely noticed it. He had many things on his mind, what with the responsibilities of all the churches and branch Sabbath Schools groups of the Huehuetenango district combined. His schedule was crowded, yet he always had time for those who needed him.

A few hours later he arrived in White Earth and went first to the house of the head elder of the little church. He was given a hearty welcome and a good supper. Afterwards, the believers congregated in the small meetinghouse. A little candle burned at the front on a table that served as pulpit, and the dim light revealed the eagerness in every face. Pastor Rudy's preaching more than met their expectations that evening, and he told the delighted group of believers that he was to remain with them for two days.

Rudy spent the next day visiting and encouraging the members

Limestone Oven

and organizing them for evangelistic outreach. He also visited some non-members, but during the whole day he kept feeling bothered by a strange impression that there was an emergency of some kind at a township called Limestone Oven, and that his presence was urgently needed.

Limestone Oven was another eight hours hike into the foothills of the volcano of Tacaná. It was a very isolated township out of Pastor Rudy's district in the department of San Marcos. But Rudy liked to visit the people occasionally when the opportunity presented itself, in order to offer some added encouragement and help.

The urgency continued until it was almost a physical pain in his heart. That evening at the meeting he told the church folks of White Earth that God was impelling him to go to Limestone Oven.

"I don't know why," Rudy told them, "but I must go tomorrow. I apologize because you were expecting me to stay with you for another day, but I know that you will understand that God is calling me."

"If God is calling, you must obey," was the general consensus of the congregation, and one of the members volunteered to accompany the pastor on his venture for God the next day.

The two men set out before daylight the next morning. The church ladies had packed a generous lunch for them to eat on the way. The air was pleasantly cool, and the two men walked fast. They talked as they walked, and the time passed quickly. Before they knew it, the sun had climbed high into the sky, and its rays beat down upon them.

"Why don't we stop and eat our lunch," suggested Pastor Rudy. "That way we won't have as much to carry in our shoulder bags."

The two men sat down beside the trail and ate, conversing pleasantly about many things. Neither one attempted to speculate as to what task awaited Pastor Rudy at Limestone Oven.

Once their lunch was finished, the two men hiked on. The trail was uphill all the way, and they were reaching the higher altitude now. Later in the afternoon, Pastor Rudy paused and took his handkerchief from his pocket to wipe the sweat from his forehead.

"The air is more pleasant up here," he commented with a smile to his traveling companion. "We should be there in about an hour and a half," he added, looking at his watch. His friend agreed, and they hiked on.

It was getting close to five o'clock when the two men arrived at the township of Limestone Oven. They still had a few more minutes of walking ahead of them before they would arrive at the head elder's house. There were some big rocks sticking out of the ground beside the trail, and Rudy and his friend sat on them to rest for a few moments. The air was chilly up here in the mountains, and the late afternoon sunshine felt good.

Rudy looked around and noticed something strange—a new plantation. Every nook and cranny of ground was cultivated, and a kind of plant grew in abundance. Pastor Rudy's friend did not appear to be aware of anything strange. *He must not know what marijuana plants look like*, thought Rudy. A young man was walking down the trail toward them.

"*Buenas tardes,*" he greeted the two strangers politely.

"*Buenas tardes,*" replied Pastor Rudy and his traveling companion almost in unison.

"Excuse me, young man," said Rudy, "could you tell me who all of this flourishing plantation in your township of Limestone Oven belongs to?"

The young man brightened. "Why yes," he replied. "All of this plantation belongs to the *Adventistas*."

Pastor Rudy gulped, but succeeded in hiding his surprise from the barefooted young man standing before him. "We must hurry to the house of the head elder," he said to his friend from White Earth.

Turning to the young man he said pleasantly, "Good day to you."

"Good day," replied the young man, and he walked on down the trail.

I wonder what I am getting into this evening by showing up here, Pastor Rudy mused to himself as they walked on toward the house of the head elder. *Perhaps I will not be received kindly this time.* He remembered his experience at Ixtahuacán when he had been falsely accused of being a communist guerrilla and turned over to the military.

Lord, he prayed silently, *You have never let me down before. Please lead me and put Your words in my mouth tonight.*

The family of the head elder welcomed Pastor Rudy and his friend with their usual enthusiasm. "Oh, pastor, how kind of you to remember us and go to the trouble of coming way out here to visit us in this far away, isolated township," said the elder's wife, nearly weeping for happiness. "Come to the kitchen! Supper is just ready!" she exclaimed.

All of the church members in the township were soon notified of Pastor Rudy's arrival, and in a little while an eager, expectant congregation sat on the backless benches in the meetinghouse, waiting to hear the message that he would bring them that night.

Soon Pastor Rudy stood before them. After the songs and prayer, he said, "My brothers and sisters, I see that you have a new plantation."

"Oh yes!" was the reply. "God has blessed us so these last few months." Several members began to talk at once, then one man stood to his feet. After clearing his throat, he began his story.

"Several months ago a man walked here from Mexico through the mountains. He carried a bag of seed with him, and said that if we would grow it, he would pay us well. As you know Pastor Rudy, up here in these mountains where the climate is cool, nothing grows that can be sold for very much money, such as coffee, for example, that grows in the lower elevations, or rubber, that grows on the coast. We have always been poor people, but now we are prospering. This new kind of plant that we are growing requires no watering or weeding, and we don't even have to buy fertilizer to put on it. All we do is plant it, harvest it two months later, and plant some more. It grows all year around. It does not have a season like other crops that are harvested once a year. We harvest this every two months. People come over here from Mexico to get it, and pay us three hundred *quetzales* a mule load!"

The people of Limestone Oven used a local name for it, no doubt derived from an Indian dialect. They had no idea what it really was. They sat and listened in shocked silence as Pastor Rudy explained to them what marijuana is, and why Seventh-day Adventist Christians should neither grow it nor sell it.

The same urgency that Rudy had felt the day before at White Earth continued to fuel him now. "We must go out at once, my brothers and sisters," he declared, "and pull it all up tonight and burn it!"

The church members bowed their heads in submission. "God has sent you to us pastor, and we must obey," they said. "We will not wait until tomorrow to destroy our plantation."

Everyone agreed except for two men who were sullenly defiant. "Who is this outsider that thinks he can come up here and tell us what to do?" they said. "We will not destroy our plantation."

Pastor Rudy did not attempt to coerce them. The two men went to their homes. That night Rudy and the rest of the congregation pulled up all of the marijuana except for the part that belonged to the two angry men, and they burned it in a big bonfire. As the fire burned, they all stood in a circle around it, singing and praying, and re-dedicating

Limestone Oven

their lives to God. It was a beautiful season of fellowship, and at two o'clock in the morning, their job finished, everyone went home to get a few hours of sleep before daylight.

The two disgruntled church members not only refused to pull up their part of the marijuana plantation, but they plotted together how to get rid of Pastor Rudy as well. It was about eight o'clock in the morning when the two men were at the house of the commander of the civilian patrolmen.

"This stranger, this Adventist pastor," they told the commander, "is a dangerous fellow. He is a communist guerrilla and is trying to use the members of his congregation to stir up trouble in this township. If he is allowed to continue unchecked, the army will come and blow us off the map."

The commander of the civilian patrolmen agreed. "He can just 'disappear' like so many other people have, and no one will ever investigate. Even if it became known, we would not get into any trouble for dealing in the ways of the army with a guerrilla. It is our duty and responsibility to guard our township and not allow the guerrilla warfare to enter here."

While the angry church members and the civilian patrolman were thus plotting, the rumble of a helicopter was heard. Helicopters and airplanes were virtually unknown to the citizens of this isolated township, and the villagers ran from their houses to see what was going on. The open-mouthed villagers stared as an army helicopter landed right in the plantation of marijuana that the two disgruntled church members had refused to pull up the night before.

Soon two army officials climbed out of the helicopter and looked around. "Who does this marijuana belong to?" one of them asked the crowd that had gathered.

Someone said the names of the two men, and the officials ordered the villagers to bring them at once. When the two men were brought, the officials handcuffed them and put them inside the helicopter. Looking around, it was plain to see that the greater part the plantation had been freshly pulled up.

"Who told the rest of you to destroy your plantation?" demanded the officials.

"The Adventist pastor," someone said.

"Bring him here at once!"

When Pastor Rudy had arrived, they demanded of him, "How did you know we were coming?"

"I did not know you were coming," Rudy told them.

"Then why did you tell your members to pull up their marijuana?"

"Because Christians should not grow marijuana," Pastor Rudy explained.

"Our visit to this township today was a top-secret mission of the military," declared the officials. Then, in a softer tone they explained to Pastor Rudy that although they had not known that marijuana was being grown in the village, they had come to catch some cocaine smugglers who were to make a connection there that day.

Because it was a top-secret mission, they insisted that Pastor Rudy must be a spy, and for a little while it looked as though he would be put into the helicopter along with the two owners of the remaining marijuana plantation.

"You must tell us how you knew that we were coming here today," they continued to demand of Pastor Rudy.

"I did not know you were coming, but God did," explained Rudy. As he witnessed to them, they softened and were visibly impressed by his words. Finally, they shook hands with him and said, "Keep up the good work." Then they climbed into the helicopter and flew away. The two men they took with them were never heard of again.

Chapter Thirty-Five

Guerrilla Invasion

*G*randma, would you please sell us some apples?"

An old lady of eighty years who had stepped out of the church into the yard for a moment turned to see who was speaking to her. Standing on the narrow cobblestone street a few meters away were four young men. One of them had spoken, and they were waiting for her answer.

"I am sorry," said the old grandmother, looking at them with a kind smile. "This apple tree belongs to the church, and the apples are not mine to sell. Besides, today is God's holy day, and we do not engage in secular business such as buying or selling on this day. But if you like, you may come to my house this afternoon, and I will give you all of the grapes you want to eat from my vines."

Cavlicán is a small town high up in the mountains of Quetzaltenango. The climate is cool, and apples and other cold weather fruits grow there. The little Seventh-day Adventist Church in this town was one of the many in Pastor Rudy's district. And today was a special Sabbath, because Pastor Rudy was there, preaching one of his powerful sermons.

Now the elderly lady was thoughtful for a moment. Then, turning back to the young men, she asked, "What do you think of Justo Rufino Barrios?"

"He was a fanatical tyrant and a dictator!" the young men answered in a chorus of voices.

"Well, no matter what you think, I believe my grandfather was a good president and a great reformer," she said, holding her head a little higher. "I am proud that the picture of my grandpa, Justo Rufino Barrios, is printed on the five *quetzal* bill."

"We did not mean to insult your ancestral heritage," the young men answered, "but our opinion of his political image remains the same."

The old lady, whom the young men called "Grandma," wasn't feeling well, and she decided to go home and rest. Walking along the cobblestone streets toward her house, she noticed that there were young men lying in the ditches holding machine guns at every corner. Taking a closer look, she noticed that they were unkempt, their clothes were soiled and full of holes, and they wore old, muddy sandals.

"Oh no," the old grandmother groaned to herself. "The guerrillas have come to town. Oh God, help us!" She had a heart problem, and suddenly she felt like she could not walk any further. Coming to a decorative water fountain, she leaned on it.

Meanwhile, back at the church the morning meeting had come to an end, and Pastor Rudy greeted the people one by one as they filed out the door. Presently the four young men who had spoken with the grandmother stepped up to him.

"We would be pleased to have you join us at a meeting we will be holding at the town square at three o'clock this afternoon," one of them said, shaking the pastor's hand.

"Are you boys university students?" Pastor Rudy asked the young man.

"We were university students, but now we are professionals," he answered evasively.

Guerrilla Invasion

Thinking they were government workers who planned to give the village people a talk on hygiene or family planning, Rudy agreed to be at the town square at three o'clock.

A few minutes later the four young men decided to take a stroll through the little town. Near the center of the village they found the grandmother who was still leaning over the fountain, frightened and feeling very faint.

"Are you tired, Grandma?" one of them asked in a cheerful voice. "We will help you home, and you can give us the grapes that you promised us."

Startled, the old lady looked up into the faces of the four young men that she had talked to a little while before. She groaned inwardly as she realized that she had invited four guerrilla terrorists to her home. It could get her into a lot of trouble.

"I don't want to go home now," she said to the young men. "I will stay here for a while."

"Oh Grandmother," they said, "we always keep our promises, and we hold others to their promises too. You will give us the grapes that you promised."

With that, two of the young men took each of her arms and started off toward her house. She knew it could cost her her life to refuse to tell them where she lived, so she complied with their wishes.

Arriving at her house, she opened the door to go in and said goodbye, hoping they would leave. But the young men insisted on going in and having their grapes. Reluctantly she led them to the enclosed garden area directly behind her house.

After they had eaten their fill of grapes, the young men went out, and the grandmother closed the door that opened onto the street behind them. Then she dropped onto a couch, faint from fright and shock.

Presently her husband came in. "Do you need some heart medicine?" he asked. "I will get some out of our little pharmacy."

"Just sit down and be quiet," she said. "The guerrillas are outside."

"The guerrillas!" exclaimed the old grandfather with glee. "I have never seen them. I will open the door and take a little peek out onto the street. I just want to look at them."

"Oh no, please don't," she begged. "Please sit down, and don't make any noise. Maybe they will forget that we are here and go away."

But the old grandfather was determined to see the guerrillas, so he opened the door out onto the street. The four young men were standing flat against the wall. They were hidden by the open door from the view of the old man who craned his neck in every direction, trying to get a glimpse of the famous guerrillas.

Suddenly the young men stepped out in front of him, and one of them said, "Grandpa, you look like you are feeling sociable and want to take a walk. Come with us."

"Oh no!" cried the old man. "I don't want to go for a walk. I want to stay home and rest!"

"Rest you shall if you don't come with us," they said. Taking the grandfather's arms, the same as they had taken the grandmother's, they started off toward the town square.

In the meantime, Pastor Rudy, true to his word, went to the town square at three o'clock. There, to his dismay, he found over one hundred guerrillas armed with machine guns and a large number of people who had been forcibly brought together to witness the events of the afternoon.

The four young men who had invited him to come to the meeting earlier that day were there, and greeting him enthusiastically, they led him up to the platform. "We want you to sit up here with the important people of the town," they told him.

Sitting on a bench up on the platform was the old grandfather, the town mayor, the Presbyterian minister, and an American-Catholic priest. Pastor Rudy was told to sit by the priest, and he obeyed.

Soon the spokesman for the guerrillas stood up and made a speech: "Ladies and gentlemen, we have come as friends to help you throw off the yoke of tyranny and restore to you what is rightfully yours. Do not be afraid of us! The reports that you hear of us killing people are not true! See, even the old grandfather here was not afraid to come out and enjoy a sociable afternoon."

Then he repeated everything he had said in the local Indian dialect. After that he turned to the old grandfather and said, "Please stand up. I want all the people to see the grandfather who came out to enjoy the afternoon."

The old grandfather wasn't anxious to stand up because if he were recognized later by army personnel, he could be shot, or worse. But the spokesman took him firmly by the arm and stood him up.

"Let's cheer for the old grandfather!" He shouted, and all the guerrillas fired their machine guns into the air with a deafening roar.

Then he told the old grandfather to sit down, and he ordered the mayor to stand up. "The mayors of our towns are guilty of much evil, injustice, and exploiting of the people!" he said. "Now, *Señor* Alcalde, what do you have to say for yourself?"

The mayor was an Adventist, and he took the opportunity to preach a powerful sermon, realizing that it might be his last. When he was through, the guerrilla spokesman said, "Would to God all of our mayors in Guatemala were like this good man!" And the guerrillas all fired their guns again.

Then the spokesman ordered the Presbyterian minister to stand up. "Who are you?" he demanded.

"I am the minister of the local Presbyterian church," he said in a small voice.

"Aha!" shouted the spokesman. "These are the men who fatten themselves on the offerings of the poor people! Where do you live?"

The minister pointed to a two-story house not far away.

"Aha!" shouted the spokesman again. "Those of you who are members of his congregation live in poor houses or even little huts, don't you? And this rich man lives from the offerings you poor people give. He is a parasite, a detriment to society!"

Then he ordered the guerrillas to ransack the minister's house and distribute everything he owned among the people who were present. When the guerrillas had finished ransacking his house, not a thing was left of his possessions except the bare walls.

Next the Catholic priest was ordered to stand up, but he indicated that he could not understand Spanish. "This man is an American and knows virtually nothing of what goes on in our country anyway, so we won't concern ourselves with him," the spokesman said.

Then Pastor Rudy began to explain what was being said to the priest in the best English that he could muster, but the guerrilla spokesman interrupted him, carrying on a conversation with the American in perfect English for a few moments.

Then Pastor Rudy was told to stand up.

"Who are you?" demanded the spokesman.

"I am a Seventh-day Adventist pastor," replied Rudy.

"Another pastor!" sneered the terrorist. "Where is your house?"

"I don't have a home," said Pastor Rudy. "I rent."

"Now that's a little bit better," said the guerrilla spokesman in a slightly softer tone of voice. Turning to the audience he said, "You people heard how the mayor spoke. He is only a lay member of the Adventist church. Imagine what this pastor here would preach like if we allowed him to speak! We have already heard enough out of these Adventists for one day."

With that, he turned to Pastor Rudy and told him to sit down.

Soon the rumble of an approaching helicopter was heard. "Some long-tongue has called the murderous army!" shouted the spokesman. "We are good people and don't want you civilians to be killed on our account, so we will leave now. Good day!"

With that, the guerrillas left the town, disappearing quickly into the jungle. The army helicopter flew overhead, but nothing unusual could be seen. The little mountain town appeared normal from the air.

A few minutes later, out on the bumpy dirt road leading to a village eight kilometers from Cavlicán, a rickety old truck rumbled along. Beside the road, a man who looked like a poor peasant signaled the driver to stop. As the truck pulled over, the man ran up close beside it and, calling to the driver, said, "Will you give me a ride to the next village?"

The trucker replied, shouting above the noise of the motor, "It will cost you one *quetzal*."

"One *quetzal*!" the man exclaimed. "I don't have one *quetzal*, but I need a ride!"

"That's too bad," the trucker shouted back. "You'll have to walk."

As the truck pulled away, the man mumbled something into a small radio. Around the next bend the guerrillas were waiting. As the truck came into view, they aimed their guns and signaled the driver to stop, which he did quickly.

"Now we know how you treat the poor peasants around here!" the guerrillas said angrily. "You charge the exorbitant price of one *quetzal* for a ride from here to the next village! Poor peasants!"

The trucker was ordered to get out of the truck. After he had obeyed, the guerrillas surrounded him, looking him up and down. "What nice boots!" one of them exclaimed. Then he ordered the trucker to take them off. One of the others called a peasant who was working in a field nearby to come. He obeyed fearfully, and was ordered to remove his sandals. He complied, looking questioningly at the guerrillas. Then he was given the trucker's boots and ordered to put them on. Again he obeyed, and the trucker was ordered to put the peasant's sandals on.

Next, one of the guerrillas said, "What a nice shirt!"

And the trucker and the peasant were ordered to trade shirts. Next they were told to trade trousers, and then the peasant was sent on his way. "Good day to you," the guerrillas said cheerily. "We are here to help people like you."

Then they turned to the trucker and said, "We want a ride to the next village." The trucker was on his way home from delivering a load, and the truck was empty.

Although deathly afraid, he had no other choice but to comply with the wishes of the angry guerrillas. If they encountered the army along the way, he would be killed along with the guerrillas. But to refuse to take them in his truck would mean death as well.

The guerrillas quickly dragged loads of clay pots tied together in nets made of rope that they had hidden in the nearby jungle and loaded them onto the back of the open truck, concealing their guns underneath. Then they all piled on, approximately one hundred of them. To any onlooker, it looked like a truckload of Indian workers, moving from one job to another.

A little ways down the road, a young Adventist man hailed the truck down and asked for a ride to the next village. The men in the back said in a chorus that he could ride with them, and they helped him climb up. But once he was up there, he saw the guns under the clay pots, and he realized that he had hitched a ride with a truckload of guerrillas. He tried to climb back down, but the guerrillas insisted that he "be a man" and ride with them like he had started out to do.

The young man prayed silently. The guerrillas might decide to recruit him and take him to live in their jungle hideouts with them, where he would have to train to be a terrorist.

About forty minutes later as they approached the next village, the guerrillas banged on the sides of the truck, thus signaling the driver to stop. "This is where we get off," they told him. They quickly unloaded their guns and clay pots and then presented the trucker with one hundred *quetzals*, which he tried to refuse.

"Oh, but you have to take it," they exclaimed. "We always pay our way."

With that, they gave him the money, then taking their guns and clay pots, disappeared quickly into the jungle. The rumble of an army helicopter was heard as the young Adventist man rode with the trucker in silence on into the village. The guerrillas had not decided to "recruit" him.

Would the guerrillas be spotted by the army men in the helicopter? Would there be an encounter between the army and the guerrillas this afternoon? And if so, how many innocent civilians who were in the wrong place at the wrong time would be killed and their bodies counted by the army as dead guerrillas? These questions and many more were whispered by fearful citizens, not only in the town square that Sabbath afternoon, but in the villages and cities throughout Guatemala nearly every day during the unforgettable 80s.

It was hard to be a Guatemalan peasant then, knowing that at any time someone in your family might disappear or you might be accused of being a guerrilla and caught and tortured by the army to extract information. Or you might be accused by the guerrillas of being a spy for the army and suffer a similar fate at their hands. If you had money, you or your children were a target for kidnapping. Or your car might be burned or your home ransacked. But I think the hardest thing of all was to be a pastor. God bless our dear, courageous, hard-working, self-sacrificing pastors! God's hand was over his people during that time. Oh yes, there were tragedies, but there were also miracles, stories of courage and of God's protection!

Chapter Thirty-Six

Where Vengeance is a Way of Life[1]

*I*t was a hot, humid day in the lowlands of one of the departments in the eastern part of Guatemala. Javier walked along the dusty trail with his neighbor Juan. Javier was tall for a Guatemalan, of a sturdy build, and light complexion. He had wavy brown hair and light brown eyes. So light in fact, that they were almost yellow. Juan was a bit shorter, although also of a sturdy build, and slightly darker complexion. They had many things in common. They were both in their mid-thirties, they were both married, and each had several children. They each owned a parcel of land, and each had several hundred heads of humpbacked cattle. One would think that as rich as they were, they would build better homes to live in. But they were contented with their country life and their humble adobe houses.

The day was hot, and as the two men walked along, conversation lagged. The trail led them through a wooded area. Suddenly Javier looked up. Stopping dead in his tracks, he pointed toward the dense foliage overhead and said, "I'll bet there's a parrot's nest up there."

"Let's climb up and have a look," Juan said enthusiastically, forgetting the hot day and the dusty trail. The two men climbed easily over the tangled vines into a large tree and soon located the nest. It was nesting season for the parrots, and they usually laid three to five

---

[1] Some of the names have been changed in this chapter.

eggs in the nest. This nest had three eggs in it, and Juan said to Javier, "Let's come back in May when the parrots are nearly old enough to leave the nest and get them. I will take one home to my family, you can take one home to your family, and we will sell the other one and split the money between us."

The weeks flew quickly by, and by the time the month of May came, both men had forgotten the parrot's nest. Until one evening Juan's wife said, "It is time for the baby parrots to leave their nests. I wonder if there might be a nest nearby somewhere."

Juan's face brightened. "I had forgotten until now," he said, "but since you mention it, I remember that Javier and I found a nest in the grove a couple of kilometers down the trail going toward the village of Bartolomé. I will go in the morning and get the parrots."

The next day Juan went to check the parrot's nest, but upon climbing the tree, he found only one baby parrot. The other two had already flown away. "Oh well," he said to himself, "I will take this one home and make it right with Javier later."

The next day Javier was walking along the trail toward Bartolomé. As he passed the tree of the parrots' nest, he suddenly remembered his bargain with Juan. "I will check the nest now," he said to himself, "and take the parrots to Juan. Then we will decide which one to sell and which ones to keep."

With that, Javier climbed the tree, only to find the nest empty. "I see Juan has already been here," he said to himself. "I will visit him this afternoon and see to it that he keeps his part of the bargain like a good *orientano* (easterner)."

Later that day, Javier stopped by Juan's house. "Where are the parrots?" he demanded.

"I only found one in the nest," Juan replied. "But you can take it home with you if you want it." Juan's wife had wrapped the baby

Where Vengeance is a Way of Life

parrot in a cloth and placed it in a small basket near the fire. It was raining, and she wanted to make sure the little parrot didn't get chilled. Juan pointed to the parrot. "Take it home with you," he urged Javier.

But the quick-tempered Javier flew into a rage. "You double-tongued woman!" he shouted at Juan. "You sold the other two parrots! No one fools Javier. I will get even with you for this!" With that, he turned and stalked out.

Juan was silent and tight lipped. His sensitive pride was thoroughly wounded. "No one shall get away with calling Don Juan a double-tongued woman!" he brooded to himself

Nearly a year passed. The two men avoided each other. When they met on the trail, each looked the other way. Then one day Juan heard that Javier was thinking of buying some cattle that belonged to a man whose parcel of land was over on the other side of the river. Juan didn't reveal his inner thoughts by the slightest twitch of his heavy mustache, and only for a split second did his eyes glitter maliciously.

By a bit of clever inquiry, he soon learned just which day and at what hour Javier would go to see the cows over on the other side of the river. Juan knew where Javier would cross. He would walk over the big log that served as a bridge. Juan planned it well. He knew just where he would hide. It was during the time of the terrible guerrilla uprisings under the administration of President Lucas. No investigation would be made. It would be counted as another mysterious killing. The guerrillas would be blamed, no doubt. Or perhaps the army. It really didn't matter.

"Every good *orientano* defends his own rights and executes the law with his own hands," Juan reasoned to himself. "To think that Javier had the nerve to call me—I who am a true, pure-blooded, courageous *orientano*—a double-tongued woman! Now he will pay for it; he will. A man who doesn't abide by the rules of the people of the orient doesn't deserve to live anyway."

The morning that Javier was to cross the river dawned bright and clear. Juan was hidden at a certain vantage point among the bushes and tangled vines along the river. Javier would walk straight toward him over the log from the opposite side of the river.

"I will shoot until he falls into the river," Juan breathed to himself. "If he does not die from the bullets, he will drown in the river. That will be the end of the fool who called me a double-tongued woman."

Suddenly Juan tensed. Javier was stepping onto the log at the opposite side of the river. Juan aimed his gun and fired. Javier kept walking. Juan fired again. And again. And again. Javier faltered, but he still kept walking. Desperately Juan continued to shoot. "I can't stop now," he said to himself between clenched teeth. "If he doesn't die, he will kill me."

Presently Javier came to the end of the log on the same side of the river where Juan was hidden. As he stepped off the end of the log, he fell face down on the ground.

Juan quickly fled the scene of the crime.

At a short distance from the river, five men, all of whom were friends with Javier, were caring for the cattle that he had been going to see that morning. Upon hearing the shooting, they all hurried down to the river's edge where they found Javier, lying face down. The blood was pouring from his chest, and not knowing what else to do, they tried to turn him over on his back.

But Javier said thickly, "Leave me on my face. I would rather die like this than to drown in my own blood."

Two of the men went to get a stretcher while the other men stood guard over him. Who could tell whether or not the would-be murderer might decide to come back and make sure his victim was really dead?

When the two men returned with the stretcher, Javier was carefully laid on it face down, and they carried him to the first-aid station in Bartolomé. From there he was sent to a hospital in Guatemala City, where he remained for nearly a year. He had eighteen bullets in his chest! It was reported that one bullet was only a hair's breadth away from his heart.

Javier determined that if he ever recovered, he would kill Juan, the prime suspect in his mind. But during his stay in the hospital, some evangelical Christians visited Javier, and he decided to accept Jesus Christ as his Savior.

"I will have to give up my plan to kill Juan," he decided. Nearly a year later, at the end of his convalescence, he returned home. Juan had fled to El Salvador for a few months, and he had returned home a few days before Javier did.

One day Javier went to see Juan. "I am not going to kill you, even though justice demands that I do after what you did to me. I have become a Christian, which prevents me from killing you, like any good *orientano* would do under my circumstances. But neighbor, you had better sell your cattle, your home, and your parcel of land and go live some place far away. Because who knows whether or not I might backslide from the Christian faith someday, and then I would kill you."

Juan was sullen. I am an *orientano*," he said. "I am not a coward. I will not sell my property, and I will not leave my home. I am not afraid of you."

Javier shrugged his shoulders. "I have warned you," he stated matter-of-factly. With that he turned on his heal and left.

One day a few weeks later, Javier was visiting his mother. "Juan must die!" she stated emphatically.

"I am a Christian and cannot kill anyone now," Javier replied.

"You do not need to kill anyone or concern yourself with it," his mother said. "Leave it all up to my *compadre* and me. We will take care of him. My *compadre's* brothers are both military officials. He can kill anyone he wants to, and no questions will be asked."

Javier shrugged his shoulders. "Mother, please do not mention it to me further," he said.

Unruffled by her son's reply, she continued, "As you know, my *compadre* will not do the killing himself. He has *pistoleros* who do his jobs for him."

"Please mother! Don't ever mention it to me again."

His mother smiled. "I won't," she said.

About one year later, three men who appeared to be buyers of cattle made their way over the muddy trail across Juan's parcel of land to his house. Juan's wife came out and stood in the doorway of the kitchen.

"*Buenas tardes*," the men greeted her politely.

"*Buenas tardes*," she answered, "what can I do for you men?"

"We would like to talk to your husband about buying some cows from him, and see if he would take us to look at them," they said to her.

"My husband is out working, but he will be in about one o'clock for lunch," Juan's wife said pleasantly. "Would you men like to wait for him? I will serve you refreshments, and when my husband returns, you can eat lunch with him."

The men smiled. "We would appreciate that. We have walked a long way today."

About one o'clock Juan walked up the trail to the house. He had been out tending the cattle and was all muddy. Stepping up to the three men, he shook hands with each of them. "In what way can I serve you gentlemen today?" he asked.

"We heard you had some cattle for sale and came to see if we

Where Vengeance is a Way of Life

might make a deal with you," one of the men explained.

Juan was puzzled. "That is a strange thing you heard," he said, "because I haven't said anything to anyone about selling any of my cattle, and frankly, I had not planned to sell any now."

The three men looked at each other as if a bit surprised. One of them spoke, "Perhaps we misunderstood the directions and came to your parcel of land when we were really supposed to go somewhere else. But now we have walked so far to come out here, and we have gotten ourselves all muddy. Please at least let us look at your cattle," they urged him.

"OK," Juan said at last. "Come and eat lunch, then I will take you on a tour of my parcel of land and show you my cattle."

"*Muchas gracias*," they said politely to Juan's wife. "Lunch was excellent. *Muchas gracias*, Don Juan. Now, if you will please show us your cattle."

Juan and the three visitors had not walked far down the trail when one of them turned and said gruffly, "We have not come to buy cattle. Our *patrón* sent us to kill you! You owe for your deeds."

The pleasant stillness of the afternoon was rudely shattered by three pistol shots. Juan's wife rushed outside down the trail to where her husband's still form lay on the ground. The three men quickly disappeared in the distance. The little terrified woman bent over her husband's body. He was dead, that was plain to see. One more man had been mysteriously murdered. But this man was her husband. That made it so much different.

"So you see, son, justice never fails here in the east," gloated Javier's mother. "No one will ever 'know' except the *compadre* and me and the three—"

"Mother," interrupted Javier, "please don't ever mention it to me again!"

"I won't," she smiled.

Javier walked away, his hands in his pockets, and his eyes on the ground.

Don Ricardo Quintana was a personal acquaintance and neighbor of both Juan and Javier, and he told me this story. He was also a neighbor and friend of my father-in-law, who bought a parcel of land over in that part of the country and raised cattle for a few years.

The guerrillas tried to recruit Ricardo Quintana into their forces, and he knew that if he did not join them, they would kill him. Managing to stall for a little time, he went to see my father-in-law and told him of his predicament. Papá Eustaquio gave him directions to the township of Chalum way over in the department of Huehuetenango almost on the Mexican border. "You will be safe there," he told Ricardo. "The guerrillas will never find you in that place."

He has been living in Chalum for nearly four years now. Eventually he will be able to return to his home. My brother-in-law, Julio, kindly invited him to live in his home and hired him to work on his coffee farm.

Don Ricardo Quintana married a lady in Chalum, and they now have two children, a boy and a girl. He attends church regularly with the rest of the Matías community. Perhaps he will someday give his heart to Jesus Christ. He is somewhat rough and crude, but the Lord surely had a reason for bringing him here to our community.

Chapter Thirty-Seven

Elena

The lady sitting next to me looked vaguely familiar. She turned to me and spoke. "Do you remember me? I am Elena. I have a cousin whose name is Kelva. We went to Dr. Graves' school years ago when we were just girls. You were small, maybe five years old. We used to play with you, and everyone called you 'Pumpy.'"

I remembered all right. Elena and Kelva were both about twelve years old when they were in Graves' school, and they had always taken time to play with me. I had liked them very much.

Today Elena and I were both waiting to see a doctor. There Were about ten people ahead of us. We would have to wait for a while yet, so we relaxed on the wooden bench where we were sitting side by side and talked.

"How many children do you have?" I asked Elena.

"Two beautiful daughters," she said with a note of sadness. "My husband is dead."

"Oh, I am so sorry. What happened?"

"Well, it was almost three years ago now. It was just getting dark, and my husband was supposed to come home any minute. The girls and I were in the house when we heard the footsteps of many people outside and a loud knocking on the door."

"I went to see what was going on, knowing that to refuse to open the door would only bring trouble. 'Lord, help us,' I prayed as I opened the door and stepped outside, closing it behind me. There was a crowd of twenty armed men.

"'Surrender your husband's guns to us immediately!' they ordered.

"'But my husband does not have any guns,' I said.

"'We want the grenades as well,' they demanded.

"'You must be confusing my husband with somebody else,' I said to the men. 'He does not have a gun of any kind at all, much less grenades.'

"Then they began to beat me and threaten to break into the house and rape my little girls if I did not turn the guns and grenades that they insisted my husband had hidden somewhere in the house over to them.

"'Oh God, save my little girls,' I prayed as the men beat me.

"Then my husband drove up in the car. As he got out, they aimed their guns at him and said fiendishly, 'Today you must die, *Don* Antonio.'

"My husband put his hands up and said, 'Sirs, I have done no one any wrong, and if it is my time to die, may God's will be done.'

"Then they fired their guns, and my dear husband fell to the ground. The men quickly left, and I ran to my husband's side. He was dead.

"Later, I received a note of apology from the guerrillas, saying that they had mistaken my husband for an army commissioner who had the same name. My daughters were ten and eleven years old when that happened. How I pray that God will protect other women and not permit them to suffer as I have."

"God bless you, Elena," I said as she got up and went in to see the doctor.

Many Guatemalan women have similar stories of sadness and loss at the hands of the guerillas. May God bless and keep them and heal their wounded hearts.

Chapter Thirty-Eight

Some More Miracles

*D*addy died of throat cancer on March 9, 1986, at eight o'clock in the morning. We were in Georgia, and he was buried there. Daddy left a legacy of faith and courage that I will never forget. I will be so happy to see him again at Christ's Second Coming. I will be so excited to introduce Daddy to my son who was born one year and five months after my father passed away.

Ismaías Lemuel Recinos was born August 25, 1987, in Bonner County Hospital, in Sandpoint, Idaho. He was small, six pounds, four ounces, with black hair, inky black eyes, and brown skin. In time his hair turned reddish-blond like mine, and his skin became a ruddy, in-between color, but his eyes stayed the same. Eventually his hair turned brown.

About two months after the birth of our son, we found out that on the evening of September 30, 1987, Ishmael's brothers and brothers-in-law had a sort of committee meeting in the home church in Chalum. The topic under discussion was how to evangelize the township of El Injerto most successfully.

Don Gilberto was a big landowner in El Injerto, and he was the one that had sold the land in Chalum to Papá Eustaquio many years before. For years now, the Matías brothers had been praying and searching for the right way to reach *Don* Gilberto with the message of God's love.

Hope That Springs Eternal

They had tried to talk to him on various occasions, but he had always been indifferent if not antagonistic to anything of a religious nature. At last, however, *Don* Gilberto had consented for the Matías brothers to hold evangelistic meetings for his peons right on the big cement area near his house, which he used for drying coffee in the dry season close to the banks of the little river.

Don Miguel was *Don* Gilberto's steward, and he was bitterly opposed to any kind of meetings being held for the peons. Years before, *Don* Gilberto's brother, *Don* Rogelio, would not even allow anyone to teach his peons how to read and write. Although he would not come out and say it, the reason was because people who become educated also become unwilling to work hard for starvation wages. But *Don* Miguel simply liked to party and have a good time, and he did not want to have his conscience disturbed by the evangelistic meetings.

El Injerto is in a canyon several kilometers above Valparaíso in the mountains. The same river that runs through the canyon of El Injerto runs through Valparaíso right where my family lived when I was a child.

On this particular evening the Matías brothers were to have held a meeting in El Injerto, but *Don* Gilberto was called away suddenly, and Ishmael's brothers decided to postpone the meetings until he should return, so that he would not miss any of them. Even if he did not attend the meetings, he would hear the preaching from his house.

As the committee meeting in the Chalum church progressed, it began to rain and rain and rain. The torrential rain was so loud on the tin roof of the church that a man could not hear himself shout. The brothers and brothers-in-law sat patiently and waited for the rain to stop. Usually such a heavy rain as this did not last longer than twenty minutes. But this rain did not stop for a long time.

In the meantime, *Don* Miguel was having a party in his house in El Injerto to celebrate his birthday. There was going to be dancing and

Some More Miracles

drinking. His daughters were putting on their makeup and painting their long, well-manicured fingernails a bright red. Outside the sky was turning angry and black. There was a deathly stillness. The only thing that could be heard was the little river a few meters away, singing merrily on its way.

Some of *Don* Miguel's friends had already arrived for the party. The tamales were ready, and *Don* Miguel had bought plenty of liquor for himself and his friends to drink that night.

Then it began to rain very hard. Undaunted, the people inside of the house went ahead with the party. Suddenly an Indian peon burst through the door. "*Patrón*," he said breathlessly to *Don* Miguel, "the river is going to flood. You must get out now! Run for your lives!"

Don Miguel laughed uproariously. "The river has more sense than you do!" he said to the peon. "It knows where to go, and it will not come up here into my house and interrupt my party!"

The peon left, but he returned shortly. "Get out!" he implored. "Get your family out!" But *Don* Miguel ignored him. So did his wife and daughters. Then the peon ran for his own life, barely escaping the great wall of water that came rushing down the canyon. It was pitch dark, and the raging torrent relentlessly did its work of destruction. Houses, huge trees, and boulders were all swept away, disappearing together.

In another house a man was visiting a friend and neighbor, and they were reading the Bible and earnestly discussing the things that they had learned from the Matías brothers.

As the rain grew louder, one man said to the other, "You must hurry home to your family. No good is going to come of this rain." The man rushed out into the blackness and ran into his house just as the water began to crumble the adobe walls. "Son!" he heard his mother call out into the darkness. "I am gone. Just try to save your children.

Hope That Springs Eternal

Good-bye."

The man grabbed his two children and held them up over his head. The water was rising fast. "Lord," he prayed, "please forgive my sins. You know that had I had the opportunity, I would have been baptized into the Adventist church. Please save my children if it is Thy will."

As he prayed, he felt the water rising over his chest, up to his chin. Now it was choking him, but he tenaciously hung onto his precious children. As he said "amen," he suddenly felt the water recede. It went down, down, down, and was gone! His house was gone; it had been washed away. But he and his two little ones were safe. A miracle!

"Lord, I will serve you with all my strength for the rest of my life," he whispered reverently.

An Indian peon later said that he had found himself being carried downstream on a log. He was way out in midstream, in fact. His chance of survival was practically nil. Then he noticed a mysterious stranger riding on the log with him. About one half kilometer downstream the stranger said to him, "Here, my friend, is where I am going to let you off."

He woke up the next day about noon. He was lying in the mud at the edge of where the flood had swept through. His family had found him and was cleaning the mud out of his nose, out of his mouth, out of his ears, and out of his eyes. His head began to clear, and he started coughing.

"He's alive! He's alive!" His relatives chattered excitedly in Mam, the Indian dialect of the area.

In *Don* Gilberto's house there was only one person at home that night—the maid. She was a young girl about sixteen. She had gone to bed early and fallen asleep immediately, but the sudden roar of the river alerted her. It was dark. She knew she did not have time to run. Quickly she climbed into the rafters of the adobe house and hung on.

Some More Miracles

She did not dare to come down. The hours passed slowly. She was small but sturdy, and she continued to hang on.

Morning dawned at last. She looked out from her perch in the rafters on a strange, new world of debris left by the flood. Only the piece of adobe wall supporting the rafters where she was had been left standing. The rest of the landowner's grand house had melted away like a sandcastle in the flood. Huge, massive trees had been uprooted and carried away like toothpicks, without a trace of them ever being found again. Yet this little piece of adobe wall where this young girl hung in the rafters withstood the tremendous force of the water. This was just another miracle in the mountains of Guatemala.

One of the few recognizable things that were found after the flood was an arm and a hand with bright red fingernails. No one doubted that it belonged to one of *Don* Miguel's daughters who died because of their father's carelessness and love of partying.

In El Injerto, all of the people who most bitterly opposed the Adventist evangelists died in the flood. But none of the people who were favorable to the preaching died or suffered injury. The Indian peons said that it was a sign that God was with the *"Adventistas"*; and in the next few months, a great number of them were baptized.

Up in the canyon the river cut a deep path. In Valparaíso, the riverbed was filled in with huge boulders even higher than where the banks of the river had been before. The houses where we lived when I was a child, even the huge sabino trees growing along the river's edge, were all gone. There was not even a trace of what had been before. But the saddest thing of all was that the babysitter and the children of the caretakers who had been living there died in the flood. The parents happened to be gone that night.

Several kilometers above El Injerto in the mountains, the greater part of a township had been swept away. It is estimated that several hundred people from that township died in the flood.

About a twenty-minutes hike above El Injerto, a road turns off to the right and threads its way up another canyon to the township of El Paraíso (paradise). A small river runs along the bottom of that canyon and joins the river that did all the damage right there at the little junction.

Catalina, the wife of my brother-in-law, Julio, is originally from the township of El Paraíso. Her family is of Irish descent. Her father had blue eyes and white hair when I knew him, and some of the others have red hair and freckles with the typical fair, sun-sensitive complexion of the Irish.

Ishmael's cousin, Rebeca, married Catalina's brother, Adelino. They had two boys. At the time of the flood, they were there living with his folks in El Paraíso. Catalina was also there at the time because their father, *Don* Angel, was dying of cancer. He had a tracheotomy, just like my dad had before he died. *Don* Angel told his wife, children, and grandchildren not to mourn for him when he died, because he was ready to go, and he had the blessed hope of the resurrection.

The night of the flood, *Don* Angel stood in the corridor of the house looking out at the storm. "This rain may wash us away tonight," he said.

The family congregated in the kitchen by the fire. It was raining hard, and the air was damp and chilly. Also, they thought the kitchen was a safer place to be than the bedrooms. The bedrooms were built back against the mountainside, but the kitchen was out away from it a little.

"I am going to bed now," announced *Don* Angel at last. "Have a good night, and may God watch over you all."

Pretty soon Rebeca's younger boy said, "Mommy, I want to go to bed now."

Some More Miracles

"But son, you will be alone in there, and besides, it is safer out here. Why don't you wait with the rest of us until the rain stops, darling?"

"No, *Mamá*. I want to go to bed now. I am not afraid."

At her son's insistence, Rebeca took him to the bedroom and tucked him into bed. Then she knelt and prayed with him. "Sleep well, son," she said as she kissed him good night.

"Good night, Mamá. I love you," he said.

"I love you, too, said Rebeca. "Do you want me to leave the candle burning?"

"No, *Mamá*, take it with you," he said.

Rebeca walked to the door. Her hand was on the knob when there was a deafening roar. Her candle went out. She turned to run to her son, but in the darkness she could only feel a wall of mud in front of her. She called frantically to her little boy, but there was no answer. A landslide from the mountainside had buried the part of the house where *Don* Angel and her youngest boy were in bed.

Rebeca turned the knob and ran through the corridor toward the kitchen, stumbling along the way in the dark. She called to her older son, but there was no answer. The candles in the kitchen had gone out, and all was dark. She groped around. Apparently her older son and his cousins were pinned under the kitchen cabinets and other debris.

"Where are you? Where are you?" she called.

Finally she heard the voice of one of the girls speaking faintly. "We are buried."

At the sound of the landslide, Catalina's mother ran out into the darkness. Catalina ran after her. "Mother, Mother, where are you going? Come back!" she called. She could hear her mother calling out. She ran, stumbling over rocks and debris toward the sound of her voice. They did not know that they were running toward the mountainside, right into the worst of the landslide in the darkness.

Suddenly there was another landslide, and Catalina found herself buried to her waist. She called out to her mother, "Where are you?"

"I am buried to my armpits. Come help me!"

But Catalina could not move. The rain continued, and they screamed for help, but no one could hear them. Hours passed. The rain finally stopped, and they called out again for help. This time Santiago, another one of Catalina's brothers, heard them and came from his house. It was nearly morning now.

"Wait," he told them. "I am going to find some men to help me dig you out."

In a little while he returned with several neighbor men, and they carefully dug the two women out, so as to not further dislodge the landslide. Catalina's mother had a broken hip, but Catalina had suffered no serious injury.

Digging the children out of the kitchen was tedious and difficult. It took several hours. At first they could not decide where to start, for fear of further injuring the children, because no one could tell just where they were, except for the girl whom they could faintly hear, trying to call to them. They began to move rocks and debris, and pretty soon they saw some tufts of bright red hair. Amazingly enough, the girl had no serious injuries when they got her out. Even more amazingly, neither did any of the other children. But *Don* Angel and Rebeca's younger son were dead.

Aid was sent in from other countries after the flood for the people who had been left homeless. There were truckloads of clothes and blankets. But some of the well-to-do folks who were put in charge of the distribution coveted the things and kept them for themselves or gave them to their own relatives and friends who did not really need them.

Some More Miracles

Catalina's mother hobbled on crutches down to the gas station where the road turned off the highway into the mountains. She was a tough little lady, but she was a widow, and her house had been destroyed by the landslide. Booths had been set up there at the gas station where the homeless could go to sign up for assistance. But at every booth they turned her away. At last she went to the booth that belonged to the SAWS and they gave her fifty dollars.

In spite of the mismanagement by the local people who had been left in charge of the distribution of supplies, eventually about two hundred small block houses were built for some of the homeless families. For those who had previously lived in thatched-roof huts, it was an improvement. And for those who had lived in better houses, at least the little block ones provided shelter and a place to call home.

Up in Chalum, the mountain surrounded swale is made up of funnel-shaped craters with underground passages where the rainwater runs through and out into the river in the canyon below. Every rainy season a stream of water would run down from the township of El Chicharro above us in the mountains, into a crater and disappear. But the night of the flood the torrent of water carried rocks and logs, and the crater it ran into got plugged up way down inside.

The heavy rains of the next rainy season filled that crater clear up, destroying several *cuerdas* of the flourishing coffee plantation that belonged to Ishmael's aunt. After that, the water ran into the next crater. But eventually it got stopped up with rocks and mud, too. Now the water runs into the crater behind our house. If it ever gets plugged up, we will be in trouble.

Because of these underground craters and passages, from time to time the ground has sunk away in different places of the coffee plantation, leaving round, deep holes.

Once a young man named Salvador was in the coffee plantation on a steep slope in one of the craters when he noticed the coffee bushes near him shaking. "It must be a tremor," he thought. But then the ground under his feet began to crack and sink away. He grabbed for the coffee bushes above him, but they too began to slide down. Somehow, he managed to scramble out of the way just in time to avoid falling into the deep hole that was formed in just a few seconds time. The coffee ground and coffee bushes with it just sunk away before his eyes.

The first crater that got stopped up eventually filled in with dirt, rocks, and sand. It is now a flat piece of ground. The people think it is solid enough to plant coffee, but no one would ever venture to build a house there.

The Lord is coming soon. I pray that God will keep our house and those of the rest of the family standing until we do not need them anymore.

Chapter Thirty-Nine

To Raise a Child

*M*y sister suggested that we call our little one "Lemmy" for short. Lemmy is easy to say in both English and Spanish, so we followed her suggestion.

When our beautiful son was eight months old, we went back to Guatemala. My mother accompanied us, and how I appreciated her help and encouragement! It was April, the hottest part of the dry season. I call April and May the dysentery months. And it wasn't long before little Lemmy came down with vomiting and diarrhea. Soon he began to show signs of dehydration. I have seen babies and small children come down with dysentery, become dehydrated, and die in a matter of a few hours. So when my baby vomited and fainted, I immediately sent one of our nieces to the coffee plantation to call Ishmael.

We quickly piled into our new four-door double-cab Toyota pickup and headed down the mountain as fast as we could to the nearest doctor. A crowd of concerned in-laws waved to us as we drove away. We took little Lemmy to Dr. Quiñones in La Mesilla. There were several patients in the waiting room, all sick with the violent diarrhea and vomiting.

"Congratulations for bringing your child in time," the doctor said to us. "He is very sick, but he has a strong constitution. Therefore he does not appear to be as sick as he really is."

The doctor continued talking, "The twelve year old boy in the waiting room is going to die. His parents waited until he had been sick three days before carrying him down from the mountains to get treatment. Now it is too late for him. But your baby will live."

A flood of relief washed over me. I had held my baby close and cried all the way to the doctor's office. But thanks to modern antibiotics, it was no longer necessary for anyone to die of the dysentery if treated in time. Once the crisis was passed, my little Lemmy struggled for several weeks with the dysentery, then became immune and grew out of it.

It wasn't long before we received an invitation to go to the wedding of a relative of Anastacio and Rosaura's over in the village of Tablón. We were to take the marimba, and a number of the Matías family besides the ones who would play the marimba wanted to go along, so we set out caravan style with several pickups.

At Camojá the dirt road turned off to go to Nenton where the guerrilla warfare had been strong for several years. Another road turned off of that one to go to El Tablón—that whole area had been the "hot spot" of Central America for a time when the guerrilla warfare was centered there.

At one place our whole caravan was stopped by three policemen for a routine check. We were heading into the lowlands along the Mexican border where a lot of contraband smuggling takes place. That was why the policemen were there.

"Some more thieving policemen to hassle us along the way," I sighed to myself. But these men were different. When they came up to our pickup, one of them leaned into the window on the driver's side. He was about twenty years old, and he had an angelic smile.

"You people are Christians, aren't you?" he asked me.

"Yes," I answered.

To Raise a Child

"God bless you, and may you have a good meeting," he said. "I am a Christian, and so are my companions here," he continued, pointing toward the other two policemen. "It makes us happy to meet other Christians. We would love to go to your meeting with you, but we have to work here. No matter. We are serving our country. Perhaps another time we can go to one of your meetings."

As our little caravan drove away, they waved and said, "God go with you."

From El Tablón we drove four kilometers further to the town of San Antonio Huista, the municipality, or county seat of the area. The bride was dressed in an elaborate wedding gown and veil with a long train. We all crowded into the office of the *alcalde*, who performed the civil marriage ceremony. It was already hot, and the crowd made the heat stifling in the little room. But the wedding ceremony only took a few minutes. Then we all followed the bride and groom in a procession along the dirt streets across town to the groom's parents' house. Several hundred guests assembled in the open area of the house, and a preaching service was held. The groom's family were Pentecostals and had graciously invited us—the Adventists—to participate in the religious service to be held after the wedding ceremony.

Several hymns were played on the marimba. Everyone listened in fascinated silence as the sounds swelled majestically and enveloped the crowd in a world of music. Afterwards I was called upon to play my autoharp and sing a wedding song. Then the Pentecostals preached. Meanwhile, the bride and groom sat stiffly side by side, in all their gala attire. How they could stand it in the stifling heat was more than I could fathom.

I sat with little Lemmy on my lap. During the long service, he began to cry, then writhe in agony and scream. He had trouble with colic up until he was nearly a year old, and his little tummy had chosen this time to ache. I took him to the *pila* and gave him a cool bath to soothe him. The old ladies were all over us, chattering and clicking their tongues. "He will get pneumonia and die," they told me. I assured them that he would not, that a cool bath was the best thing for him in all this heat. I smiled and tried hard to be patient with the old ladies.

The bath completed, I ran out to the pickup and climbed in with Lemmy in my arms. So did Mamma, and we rolled up the windows and locked the doors to keep the people from leaning in all over us. Lemmy was a nervous baby, and when he was sick, he wanted no one but me. I was thankful for the protection of the atrociously hot pickup where I could try to soothe my little one to sleep. Mamma and I talked to him quietly and kept moistening a washcloth from a jug of water that we carried in the truck and washing the sweat off him. He finally relaxed and went to sleep.

It took a long time for the guests to eat. There were a lot of them, and they ate by relays at a long table. I hoped I could get away without eating, but there was no chance that the kind lady of the house would overlook the Americans. I would not offend this dear lady for anything, so when I was called to the table, I went. Lemmy had slept for a while and was feeling better now. The afternoon shadows were getting longer, and it wasn't quite so hot anymore.

That evening I came down with amoebic dysentery. At home I always kept medicine on hand for such ailments, but I had forgotten to bring any along. Traveling in the backwoods of Guatemala was not easy for a nursing mother, nor for the baby either. "I will be so glad to get home tomorrow," I thought wearily. "And I will stay home until Lemmy gets older."

That night the whole bunch of us from Chalum stayed with Anastacio and Rosaura. They insisted that my mother, Ishmael, and I sleep in the beds, and the rest of the people slept on the floor, spread out from wall to wall. But before we retired for the night, the husband of one of Rosaura's sisters stopped by and talked to Mamma and me for a while. He told us that the three policemen we had seen on our way to Tablón had been killed by a grenade just a little while after we talked to them that morning. A car had gone by with several people in it, and instead of stopping for the inspection, one of the passengers threw a grenade out the window at the policemen, and then the car sped away as fast as possible over the dirt road.

The next day on our way home we saw the black place in the road where the grenade had exploded. Also, to one side of the road we saw what remained of a black jeep that the three policemen had had with them.

For a while I retreated into the solitude of my own thoughts. I remembered the angelic smile of the youngest of the three policemen and the kind friendliness of all three of them. "We are Christians," they had said.

Surely I will meet those policemen again someday, I thought.

Chapter Forty

The Young Plantation Owner

*L*and erosion was making our church in Chalum sink around the platform, and the adobe wall was cracking. For a long time no one did anything about it, and sometimes I wondered if the church might fall on us someday while we were meeting. Then Antonio, the husband of Ishmael's younger sister, started a successful campaign to raise funds for a new church. In a few weeks the old church was torn down, and the pulpit and church benches were neatly arranged in the corridor of Benedicto's house right next door to us, where we held all of our meetings for about three months.

There was a group of about fifty Indians who lived in El Chicharro, the next township in the mountains directly above us. These people had all been baptized, and they walked about two hours to come to church every Sabbath morning. Most Sabbaths each family in the church invited several of them home for lunch, but occasionally we all put our food together and had a fellowship dinner in the corridors of the houses that were built close together.

One Sabbath we had a fellowship dinner, and everyone ate quickly and the Indians from Chicharro said good-bye and hurried up the path toward home. It was early rainy season, and it looked like there would be a heavy cloudburst that afternoon. Just enough time had passed for the folks from Chicharro to get home, when it began to rain. It was a

The Young Plantation Owner

real cloudburst all right. The rain came down in sheets for about forty minutes. I wondered if a person would be able to breathe out in that rain, or if one would drown. I was not curious enough to experiment, though.

By the next morning news had gotten around that the rain had caused a mammoth size landslide. At Sarral, the whole mountainside had slid into the river, destroying over half a kilometer of road. No one would be able to go anywhere for a long time unless they walked across the landslide. It just so happened that the yellow truck was in Chalum, and the four-door double-cab pickup was in Valparaíso that day.

So when we needed to go to town, we rode in the yellow pickup down as far as the landslide, then walked across it and took the other pickup from there. Walking across the landslide was muddy and slippery. Ishmael carried baby Lemmy, and Mamma and I carried little backpacks.

One day we had gone to Huehuetenango, and when we were returning home in the afternoon, it began to rain. It didn't come down in sheets, but it was a heavy rain nevertheless. By the time we got to the landslide, the rain had tapered off to a drizzle, but it was precarious walking in the mud. Especially in one place where there was an eighteen-inch ledge that one had to walk across the chasm on. There was the steep mountainside wall on one side, and a yawning chasm on the other. The river was at the bottom far below us. Not only was the ledge narrow, but it slanted down toward the river.

On this particular afternoon, Ishmael walked ahead with the baby, and Mamma and I followed with our backpacks. My mother was walking ahead of me. We were crossing on the ledge, when suddenly her foot slipped. For a split second my heart stood still. I just knew it was the end for her. I didn't even have time to pray, but the prayer I didn't say was answered. It looked impossible, but she regained her

To someone unused to "our" road, meeting and getting around an oncoming vehicle was an unforgettable experience.

footing and went on. Pretty good for a seventy-year-old woman! After that I decided that we ladies would stay home until a safer way was made to cross the landslide.

The men of the Chalum township filed a request for the highway department to come and make a new stretch of road with their machinery, but after three months of waiting, the entire community came out with picks, shovels, and hoes, and made a road by hand. From the looks of things, one would have thought that more of the mountainside would slide away into the river the next rainy season, but during the five years that have passed since then, there have been no more major landslides. The worst parts of the road to Chalum have even been cemented, so that chains are seldom necessary any more. Now we only have to use our four-wheel drive.

It was almost August 25, the date of Lemmy's first birthday. He was a favorite with all the aunties, uncles, and cousins, and they hoped that we would have some kind of a fitting celebration.

"A celebration would give us a chance to hold an evangelistic type of meeting," Ishmael said one day. "Just like when an Adventist dies, the family of the deceased hold an all-night 'wake' kind of like other people do here in Guatemala, but the purpose is to use the opportunity to preach to the neighbors who will surely come about the blessed hope of the resurrection.

"And you know how we also have 'coming out' parties for Adventist girls on their fifteenth birthdays in order to invite the neighbors over," Ishmael continued, "but instead of dancing and drinking like others do, we have an evangelistic meeting with lots of music, and of course we give everyone tamales and sweet bread to eat, and the party lasts until midnight, in keeping with the traditional custom.

"So we could celebrate Lemmy's first birthday and invite lots of people over according to custom, then have a preaching service with lots of special music and singing. And after that we can pass out the tamales and hot chocolate with sweet bread to everybody."

"I guess we'll have to figure out how much it will cost to make five hundred tamales and hot chocolate and sweet bread for five hundred people," I said.

Ishmael went outside and called to some of his brothers and their wives in their nearby houses. A group of relatives soon congregated in our kitchen, and with great enthusiasm we all began to plan the party.

The day before the party I made fifty pounds of flour into gluten to put in the tamales in place of meat. Rosaura had come all the way from Tablón to stay with us and help with the birthday celebration. Together we cooked the gluten in a tin tub over a fire on the ground outside a little ways from the house.

Hope That Springs Eternal

Ismaias Lemuel Recinos (Lemmy) having a bath in the pila. He would play in the water until he turned blue, and still not want to get out.

Lemmy's birthday celebration began at two o'clock in the morning. A couple of young men came with their guitars and serenaded us outside our bedroom door. They sang the traditional *Mañanitas*," then some Christian birthday songs. Lemmy slept soundly through it all, of course, but I had a surprise for the boys. They thought I was sleeping, but Ishmael and I had been waiting for them, and when we heard them tiptoeing up the stairs, I tiptoed over to the door and turned on the tape recorder that I had set up the night before to record the serenade.

When the serenade was over, the boys came into the bedroom and in the customary way, wished Lemmy a happy birthday and a long, happy life, patting and hugging him where he lay sleeping in his little bed. He didn't wake up, but his proud parents were pleased.

After the serenade I served hot chocolate and sweet bread to the boys, and played back the recording of the lovely songs they had sung.

The Young Plantation Owner

We all had a jolly good time while the object of our celebration slept soundly upstairs.

In a few minutes the neighbor ladies began to gather, and fires were lit outside to cook the tin tubs of *masa* for the tamales. The wood stove in the kitchen was also used to cook large tubs of *masa* made of rice.

When Lemmy got up, I brought him downstairs, and he had a grand time walking up and down the corridor, showing off for all of the cheering aunties, uncles, and cousins. He had taken his first steps alone just ten days before. His older cousins were determined that he must walk before his first birthday, and they had worked with him for weeks until they achieved their goal.

No one needed to teach him how to talk, though. By his first birthday, he could talk fluently in English and Spanish. He would excitedly rattle off whole paragraphs in Spanish to his cousins, then turn and repeat it all in English to me.

He was showered with attention, so much so that sometimes he would just push his doting relatives away and bury his face in my shoulder. They nicknamed him "*El Patroncito*," meaning "The Young Plantation Owner." I don't think a crown prince was ever more pampered than Lemmy.

Ishmael helped some of the girls wilt big banana leaves over the fires, then they cut them into sections and laid them out on a large table that had been set up in the carport. I snapped pictures of them spooning cooked *masa* out of one of the tubs that was set in the middle of the wooden table. Some was spooned onto each section of leaf, then in the middle of that they put a couple of spoonfuls of a kind of red sauce made from ancho berries and native grown spices, with ground squash and sesame seeds.

Chayotes, carrots, and potatoes were cut into long, diagonal pieces, fried raw, and mixed through the sauce in generous amounts. Then a couple of pieces of the gluten that Rosaura and I had made were put in the middle of each one, and the tamales were folded into secure "packages" and tied with *cheche*, a stringy sort of stuff that grows in the trunk of the banana stock, kind of like bark. Then the tamales were cooked over the fires in the tin tubs. By late afternoon all five hundred tamales were done and ready to be served. Tin tubs of chocolate drink were now being heated over the fires and on my woodstove. Mamma and I set about getting Lemmy dressed for the evangelistic service. People were gathering, and the music had started outside. Friends and church members hiked all the way from other townships to grace us with their presence, to wish our son much happiness, and to eat tamales.

The old church had been torn down by this time, and the new one was under construction, so we met each Sabbath and three times during the week in Benedicto's corridor. The pulpit, church benches, and a blackboard had been set up there. (The benches in our church had backs on them.)

Today the meeting place had been adorned for the gala occasion with flowers and greenery. In addition, green, fragrant pine needles were spread on the floor like a thick carpet. The people crowded onto the benches until they were full to overflowing, and the rest stood. Singing groups of young men had come from churches in other townships, bringing their guitars with them, and the air regaled with their music, the melodious notes echoing from the mountainsides all around us.

Herculano preached a lovely sermon, prayers were offered for the prosperity, happiness, and future usefulness to humanity of the birthday boy, and then the tamales, hot chocolate, and sweet bread were served. It was the rainy season, but fortunately it did not rain on this

The Young Plantation Owner

memorable day.

After a while, most of the people left to hike back to their townships, and only our many relatives remained. As many as could had brought presents, and since there were too many people to fit inside the house, we set up a table in the corridor, put all of the presents on it, and sat Lemmy in the middle. He rose to the occasion, grandly showing off while opening his presents amid the cheers of a hundred or so relatives. He held the contents of each package up for all to see, exclaiming, "*Camisa! Pantalón! Juguete!*" (Shirt! Pants! Toy!)

Suddenly Oziel, Lemmy's favorite cousin, pressed his way through the crowd. (He had married Gilda, a teacher who had come to teach our church school, and they now had a baby girl. He was "Negro," the same boy who had put the *chiquirín* fly on me in Ixcán years before.) He was carrying a colorful present in his hands.

"I'm sorry I couldn't bring this present before," he said with mock remorse. Oziel was a clown by nature, and Lemmy loved him. Lemmy took the present eagerly and tore it open. Out tumbled old broken parts from the machinery used to process the coffee. Lemmy squealed with delight, and pushing all of his other things to one side, hugged the old broken pieces to his heart. They were his favorite playthings for the next whole year until we left for the States, leaving them put away in our house.

Lucy, Lemmy's favorite playmate, joined in the celebration. She was the soon-to-be-one-year-old blond-headed daughter of Lemmy's cousin, Hortencia, and Paco. Grandmother Catalina set her on the table beside Lemmy, and they played together serenely, hugging and kissing each other frequently, and never quarreling. Lucy would be one year old in three weeks. She was a special little girl, and a celebration similar to ours was in the making for her.

What beautiful children, I thought as I surveyed the scene. I looked out over the sea of faces. The lamp flickered a little, and the shadows danced around the many doting relatives.

Such loving people with hearts of gold, I thought to myself. *What a happy life I have, and how blessed I am.*

Suddenly Lucy leaned over and kissed "Emmy" on the cheek. Then she reached out her little arms and called "Mamma, Mamma." Someone swooped her up, everyone said good night, and the *fiesta* was over.

Here is a poem, dedicated to Lemmy by me with love:

THAT BABY ANGEL DOLL
The day was long. "Let's rest," I said,
and then I put the babe to bed.
But when I went to lay him down,
just then the babe began to frown.

And when I sang the lullaby,
the little guy began to cry.
"I want to play," the baby wept,
"I do believe I've overslept!"

But pretty soon he got so still,
I said, "I'll go to bed, I will!"
But when I'd closed my weary eyes,
just then I heard my baby's cries.

And when I thought I'd get some sleep,
the little guy began to weep!
"Now baby go to sleep," I said,
"and stay there in your little bed."

The Young Plantation Owner

So then I thought I heard him snore,
and laid me down a little more.
But soon he raised his little head,
and said he needed to be fed.

Then next he said, "I'll go to sleep,
and you'll not hear another peep."
But soon his promise all forgot,
up bounced the playful little tot!

I said, "You've cut my night in half,"
and then my babe began to laugh.
And then his feet began to walk,
his little tongue began to talk;
and soon my baby grew so tall,
where is that baby angel doll?

Chapter Forty-One

A Few Questions

*I*t was September 15, independence day in Guatemala. Everyone had gone out to the ballfield for the celebration. The school children from our church school and the ones from the public school would put on programs for the adults of the township, and then there would be soccer games. Booths would be set up where sweets and other delicacies would be sold, and there would be a parade. Yes, a parade up and down the rough little roads around the township. The school children would march, and there would be floats, too.

The old yellow truck along with some of the other farm trucks would be decorated elaborately with flowers, greenery, and crepe paper, and the queen of independence day of our township, the queen of Colegio Sinaí, and the queen of the public school would ride on the floats, dressed in their gala attire. The trucks would drive around the rough, muddy roads for a while, bouncing and sliding around with the pretty girls riding on them, dressed in prom-type dresses complete with crowns and scepters.

The army had imposed this custom on us several years ago in an effort to inspire patriotism and loyalty to the government. That way the people would not be as susceptible to the lies of the guerrillas, or so was the thinking of the army officials. It was OK. The folks of our township liked to have a bit of wholesome recreation.

A Few Questions

Due to the influence of the Adventists, the Central American church, and the Pentecostal church in our township, the Catholics forbade their members to dance. So the celebration consisted of singing, speeches, and the reciting of patriotic poetry.

A few of the old fellows who liked to drink would get some jungle brew from somewhere, and by night they would be drunk. Some of them would be found lying in the ditches along the trails and others would be seen staggering around talking nonsensically.

Mamma and I had decided to stay home with Lemmy. It was sure to rain in the afternoon, and we didn't relish walking the one half kilometer back home from the ballfield in the mud. We were sitting in the kitchen at the table. Lemmy had snuggled down into my arms for a good meal.

Suddenly I looked up and saw two Indian men standing outside the window. They were dressed in brand new costumes with a new *moral* each slung over their shoulders, and new machetes. This was very unusual because the Indian people who came looking for work on the coffee plantations were always dressed in old, ragged clothes.

Mamma went outside to see what they wanted, and they said that they were looking for work. She didn't know what to tell them, so I got up and went out, carrying Lemmy in my arms. I noted that one fellow was about thirty, the other about eighteen. These men looked bright-eyed and alert, not dull-eyed like most of the plantation workers. In fact, they looked shrewd. I felt apprehensive.

"*Buenas tardes,*" I said, forcing my most beguiling smile.

"*Buenas tardes,*" they answered, wooden faced.

"What can I do for you?" I asked.

"We are looking for work, but we want to know for sure whether or not someone will hire us before we go get our packs."

"Where are your packs?" I asked them.

"In San Pedro, Necta."

This aroused my suspicions even more because San Pedro, Necta, was rather notorious for its support of the guerrilla warfare. In fact, it had been Indian guerrillas from that town who had blown up all of the bridges from La Democracia to Huehuetenango. The United States had sent temporary wooden bridges to replace the ones that had been destroyed, and these were still being used. It was years before new bridges were built. The destruction of bridges had stopped only when President Lucas threatened to send in the army to blow San Pedro, Necta, off the map if one more bridge was destroyed.

"Why are your packs in San Pedro, Necta?" I asked them. "Do you live there?"

"No," replied the older man, who apparently was the spokesman for the two. "We were working there, but we are from Colotenago." (Another town populated with Indians.)

The younger of the two men listened intently. I noticed that he was very alert and was scrutinizing me and especially little Lemmy very carefully. Something that had happened about two years before flashed into my mind.

I had been in the Chalum church with a group of young people one afternoon. We were practicing singing some songs for a program we were planning, and I was playing my keyboard. A couple from Valparaíso were in Chalum working at the time, and they were singing with us, too. They had four small children who sat quietly while we practiced.

Suddenly "Tonito," as everyone called Antonio and Melca's third son, burst through the door of the church. He was about twelve years old at the time. "There are about thirty men trying to take *Doña* Juanita's little two-year-old girl away from her!" he exclaimed, panting heavily after running to tell us the news.

A Few Questions

Doña Juanita lived in a little hut high up on the mountainside. Her home was more isolated than anyone else's in the whole township. "Get your children home!" Tonito said to the couple from Valparaíso. "They are out kidnapping children."

"God will care for our children," said the father calmly, and the mother agreed. But since the flimsy church doors could not be locked, we all decided that it might be wiser to go home.

We were all filing out of the church door, calmly but as quickly as possible, when suddenly we could feel a vibration in the ground through our feet, and we could hear the tread of many people running.

"The civilian patrolmen have heard *Doña* Juanita's screams and are all running toward her hut from all over the township," Tonito said.

The couple from Valparaíso herded their children toward the house where they were staying, and the rest of the young people went home with me, since my house was the closest one to the church. Tonito ran on down the trail to find out what was going on.

In a few minutes he was back. "It's over now," he said. "When the kidnappers heard everyone running toward the hut, they ran away into the coffee plantation. Now the civilian patrolmen are chasing them out of the township toward Palmira. That is where they sneaked into the township from, through the coffee plantations. They didn't use the road. No one knows who they are, because they all have bandannas tied over their faces, and they are armed with machetes.

"They entered *Doña* Juanita's hut and tried to grab her little girl right out of her arms. But she hung on and screamed. Then the men threatened to break her arms and kill her if she did not let go of her child, but she continued to hang on tenaciously and scream. Then they heard everyone running up the mountainside toward the hut, and that was when they turned and fled. They didn't get the little girl."

Around that same time some men, perhaps the same ones, entered the house of an army commissioner one night in Valparaíso and tried to take two of his children. In a flash the man pulled out his pistol and shot and wounded one of them. With that the men fled.

The next day a prominent member of the community had an unaccounted-for bullet wound. He was arrested and taken to court, and to the surprise of everyone, he produced a license signed by President Vinicio Cerezo giving him permission to engage in secret activities. Whether it was forged or genuine, no one ever knew. But there were a number of small children kidnapped from their parents in various places around that time. Also, it was rumored that someone had seen a plane loaded with small children taking off from one of the airports one night in Guatemala City, allegedly on a secret flight to Cuba.

It was not hard to assume that the children who were abducted were being sent to Cuba to be brainwashed and trained as terrorists.

As I thought of this, my grip on Lemmy tightened. "None of the men are here right now," I told them. "You could go to the ballfield where the fiesta is, and someone there might hire you."

A look of ill-disguised fear crossed both of their faces. This confirmed my suspicions that they were guerrillas. Why else would they be afraid to face a whole township of civilian patrolmen who were peace-loving and friendly, but who would not be afraid to fight to defend their families and township or capture a couple of guerrilla spies and haul them down to the army base in Valparaíso where they would receive "strict military justice"?

The older man abruptly changed the subject. "How much did you people in this township pay your laborers per box of picked coffee during coffee harvest?" This was a strange question for them to ask during the rainy season.

Many people had saved themselves from being shot, or worse, by gaping in the typical Guatemalan way and saying, "I don't know what you're talking about. I know nothing of politics." I decided to use the same trick.

"I was not here during coffee harvest," I said truthfully. "I cannot tell you how much was being paid at that time." I continued to act pleasant, but I kept my white-knuckled grip on Lemmy. Fortunately, he didn't protest. I was thankful that none of the pickups that were usually parked in our yard were here today. (A favorite pastime of the guerrillas is to steal and burn cars and pickups along with the people who own them, or at least who the guerrillas think might own them!)

"How big are the plantations here?" The older man was asking me now. (It was a well-known fact that the guerrillas would send spies to new areas to find out who owned automobiles, who owned land, and how much property each landowner had. Those who the guerrillas deemed too rich were automatic targets for terrorism.)

"No one in this township owns a large amount of land," I told them. They looked incredulously at the coffee-plantation-covered mountainsides.

"Do the people here own *cuerdas* or *caballerías* of land?"

"Only *cuerdas*. No one in this township owns as much as one *caballería* of land," I told them.

Suddenly I had an idea. I would send them to *Don* Adrián, the commander in chief of the civilian patrolmen of the township. Maybe he would figure out that they were guerrillas and arrest them.

"Do you see that house up there?" I asked, pointing to a blockhouse that was half hidden by coffee bushes and Chalum trees up above us on the mountainside. *Don* Adrián lives there, and he is one of the larger plantation owners here in the township. He just might hire you."

I had given them what they wanted—some information about someone in the township, or so they thought. They started off toward

Don Adrián's house, and I went back inside.

Several weeks later I was visiting with Ester, a cousin of Ishmael's who is about the same age as I am. She used to live next door to us with her husband and two children until an incident occurred that was the final "blow" that ended their marriage.

While we were visiting this particular day, I told her about the two men who had questioned me on independence day. I was describing the two men and our conversation when Araceli, Ester's daughter, said, "Those same two men stopped at our house and questioned us, too. They asked us all of the same questions they asked you, and Mamma gave them all of the exact same answers that you did."

"I wonder if they found *Don* Adrián's house," I mused.

"They sure did," said Ester, "and he hired them, too."

"He didn't suspect that they might be guerrillas?"

"Apparently not. They are still working for him. They may have been afraid to ask him the typical 'guerrilla questions' like they asked us women."

"Well," I said, "I guess we have a couple of guerrillas in the township now."

"Yes," said Ester. "But they will never be able to generate any support to speak of for the guerrilla cause around here. But they could make bad trouble in other ways."

"I know."

"Say!" piped up Araceli. "Guess what I saw the other day!"

"A long-haired, ragged guerrilla hiding in the coffee plantation somewhere I suppose," I joked.

"That is exactly right," said Araceli soberly. "I was walkig home from school a few days ago when I had to move off of the road because *Don* Adrian's pickup was coming. I was right on that narrow switch back up there, so I had to move clear over into the coffee bushes a little ways."

"There to my surprise I saw a man with long, dirty hair. He was barefooted, and his clothes were dirty. He was sitting on a rock among the coffee bushes, whittling on a stick with a pocketknife."

"When he saw me, he said, 'Don't be afraid; I won't hurt you.' Then he said, 'Whose pickup is that going by?'"

"I just said, 'It belongs to a *señor*, and I took off running for home. As soon as I got home I told my mother, and together we went outside to a place where we could look right down and see him sitting there among the coffee bushes."

"Suddenly he looked up and saw us watching him. Then he jumped up and ran away through the coffee plantation with huge, long strides."

"You had better keep a close watch on Lemmy," Ester warned me seriously.

I couldn't have agreed more. Ever since independence day, I had not let him go outside alone. A few days later we were in Huehuetenango. Araceli and I were sitting in the cab of the four-door pickup. We were parked on the edge of the narrow street. Suddenly Araceli looked up and said, "There comes the man I saw in the coffee plantation!"

I looked at the man. He fit the description she had given me. At first glance he would appear to be no different from the ragged beggars and drunken street bums. But looking closer, I could see that he was sober, and his eyes had that same shrewd look that the two Indian men who questioned me on independence day had. I was holding Lemmy, and I noticed that he scrutinized us closely.

Not long after that, when we went to Huehuetenango again one day, a military truck was blown up on the highway by the guerrillas just a few minutes after we drove by that particular place. That same afternoon Mamma, Lemmy, and I happened to ride home in someone else's pickup. Oziel drove, and Lemmy rode proudly next to his favorite cousin. He would put his little hands on the wheel and pretend to help Oziel drive.

Presently we saw about fifteen soldiers on the highway ahead of us. They motioned for us to stop, then they "asked" for a ride. (To refuse them a ride would be unthinkable.) With the back of the pickup full of military soldiers, we would be a prime target for the guerrillas to fire down on from the mountainsides on either side of the highway.

As we drove along, I glanced back over my shoulder at the soldier boys. Their faces had green stuff smudged all over them to better camouflage them in the jungle. Obviously they were on a *rastreo* looking for the guerrillas who had blown up the military truck that morning. They looked relaxed and happy, so I decided that there was not really any imminent danger.

After a few kilometers, they signaled for Oziel to stop. Then they all jumped down and filed quickly away into the jungle. That was near the place where we saw the black spot in the road where the military truck had been blown up that morning. The presence of the guerrilla warfare was still real.

On another occasion, I was walking toward the marketplace in La Democracia, carrying Lemmy in my arms. There was a *fiesta* in town, and I was hoping to get some bargains. There was a man walking toward us, coming from the marketplace. He was carrying a turkey and some produce in a pack on his back. Just as we were passing each other on the little street, another man ran up behind him with a knife and stabbed him to death in the back right before my eyes. Shuddering, I quickly stepped around the corner of a building, and keeping Lemmy quiet, stayed there until the dead man had been carried away.

As I stood there shaking, I remembered the words of Josefina

A Few Questions

many years before when I was a little girl and the woman was shot in the lobby of the hotel where we were staying: "It is not good to go to the theater. It is better to go to church."

Today I decided that perhaps that could apply to going to the *fiestas* as well. I was thankful that no one noticed that I was there or that I had witnessed the incident. That could have caused me a few problems. I was also glad that the attacker had not decided to make Lemmy and me his target.

Chapter Forty-Two

The Move Home

*P*apá Eustaquio, always full of the spirit of adventure, had bought a parcel of land that was offered for sale at a very low price several kilometers from Frai Bartolomé de las Casas, hometown of President Lucas, in the department of Alta Verapaz, way over on the other side of Guatemala, next to Petén.

A number of businessmen took advantage of the opportunity and bought large tracts of land that were being offered for sale by the government under President Lucas. During his presidential campaign, he had offered houses and lands to the poor people of Guatemala. Perhaps this was his way of trying to at least appear to be keeping his promises. Meanwhile, under his administration thousands of people were being ruthlessly slaughtered by the army.

Frai Bartolomé de las Casas was about a three-hour drive over "washboard" roads from the nearest paved highway. Driving over its dirt streets, one would get the impression that this town was just a little bit of civilization that had been imported into the jungle. The mansions of President Lucas and his brother were there, complete with an airstrip and private airplanes. There was also a military base.

A few kilometers away, the crude oil resources of Guatemala were being "exploited" by the Americans. These oil wells had provided the

The Move Home

area with just enough civilization and activity from the outside world to interest the guerrillas, and the nearby jungles provided the kind of hideouts they liked for their camps.

Papá Eustaquio started a cattle farm in the little, virtually unpopulated township of Cebol, about four kilometers from "Frai," as everyone called Frai Bartolomé de las Casas.

Papá Eustaquio raised the large humpbacked cattle and gloried in his quiet life out in the hot, muggy, and sometimes extremely swampy lowlands. He tried for years without success to persuade his sons and daughters to sell their coffee farms in the mountains and come live near him in the poisonous snake and malaria-infested country that he had come to love so well.

We all took our turns and dutifully visited the "old folks," only I was dutiful just twice during the years my parents-in-law lived at Cebol. During my first visit, I was nearly devoured skin and bone by mosquitoes and gnats. It was the rainy season, and the mud was knee deep as I trudged (or rather floundered) around Papá Eustaquio's farm.

The water sources in the lowlands are contaminated, and after my second visit there, I came down with a life-threatening kidney infection. Ishmael was stung by a scorpion once when he visited his folks in Cebol, and another time he contracted malaria while staying there for a few weeks. All of the family wanted the folks to move back to their home in Valparaíso, but Papá Eustaquio would not hear of it.

The old folks occasionally came to see us, and on his trips back and forth, Papá Eustaquio always preferred to take the shorter back road through the mountains of the department of El Quiché. But those mountains were hot with the guerrilla warfare, and it was very risky to travel there, especially at night. His hired chauffeur told us that he was stopped on various occasions by the guerrillas and had to turn a lot of money over to them, but no one knows how much. Papá Eustaquio will not talk about it.

One year when Ishmael went to see the folks, during the time he was there, a note was found in the corridor of the house which stated that Papá Eustaquio had to turn over two thousand *quetzals* to the guerrillas whose particular clandestine group went by the initials E. G. P. (standing for Guerrilla Army of the Poor). If he did not comply, the note said that one of two things would happen to him: either he would be killed or his automobile would be burned. He was to wrap the money neatly into a package, place it on the ground next to a certain fencepost, and attach a small board to the top of the fencepost to indicate that the money was there.

Ishmael and Papá Eustaquio, always adventuresome and daring and never afraid, cut a whole bunch of newspapers into strips the size of *quetzal* bills. Then they wrapped them up in a neat package and placed them next to the fencepost indicated in the note, with a small board nailed to the top of the fencepost kind of like a cross.

They also called all of the civilian patrolmen of the neighborhood to come and watch from the bushes, to see who would come out of the jungle to collect the package of "money." There was the possibility of a shoot-out with the guerrillas, and one by one, each of the civilian patrolmen thought of urgent reasons why they needed to go home. At last, only two people were left: a seventeen-year-old boy, and Roger, Ishmael's eleven-year-old nephew. (Ishmael had to leave the day before the date specified in the note when they were to turn over the money to the guerrillas.)

The two boys waited breathlessly in the bushes near the fencepost. The older boy had been given a pistol to use on the guerrillas. The headman at the military base had given the civilian patrolmen the order to shoot to kill at whoever appeared to pick up the "money."

The older neighbor had grown up in the lowlands, and his frail,

The Move Home

malaria-ridden body succumbed to the oppressive heat and the fatigue that clung to him constantly, and he fell asleep as the two boys watched from their concealed vantage point in the bushes. Roger had not been in the lowlands long, and he had the robust health and alertness of the folks from the mountains. He watched with wide-eyed excitement, never for an instant taking his eyes from the fencepost with the cross on it beside the package of "funny money."

Suddenly he saw a man emerge from the nearby jungle and approach the fencepost. "Quick!" he hissed, poking the other boy in the ribs. "They're coming!"

The older boy, unnerved at waking from a sound sleep, fired a pistol shot which missed the man who was now stuffing the package into his ragged, dirty shirt.

If the boy had been more alert, he no doubt would have fired another shot and possibly killed the man before he sprinted back into the jungle. But the civilian patrolmen, upon hearing the shot, bolted from their homes or the fields where they were working in hot pursuit of whoever the thief or thieves would turn out to be.

They ran for about one kilometer through the jungle, following the trail left by the robbers who were obviously retreating as hastily as possible with the coveted package of what they thought was money.

Suddenly they saw a clearing up ahead. Two men were squatting on the ground over the contents of the package. When they heard the footsteps of the rapidly approaching civilian patrolmen, they jumped up and ran, leaving the spilled contents of the package on the ground. They got away, but not before one of the younger men who was running ahead of the others was able to recognize one of them as a neighbor from the township of Cebol.

The man was later arrested, but since he was only a neighbor and not really a guerrilla, the military sent him to the local police authorities. Evidently the military official who was stationed in Frai at that time had a sense of justice. Otherwise the would-be-terrorist-thief would have been a dead man. He was referred by the authorities of Frai Bartolomé de las Casas to a higher court in the department capital of the town of Cobán several hours away, where he had to appear repeatedly to pay "fines" in order to keep himself from being jailed.

Papá Eustaquio decided that the man must have gotten angry once when he asked him for a ride to Frai. But the Toyota station wagon was already crowded to overflowing, and it was just not possible to crowd in one more passenger. So Papá Eustaquio told the man that he was sorry, but he could not give him a ride that day. Maybe some other time.

In other parts of the country, the guerrillas tortured and killed common criminals who masqueraded as communist guerrillas. I don't know whether or not that man ever realized how lucky he was to have gotten off so easily.

The very next year the guerrillas decided to take up their abode on Papá Eustaquio's land. They came to his house often to talk with him, thus putting him in a very precarious situation. At night after dark, whenever he heard pebbles falling on his tin roof, he knew the guerrillas were outside and wanted him to come out and talk with them.

The group that camped on Papá Eustaquio's land had some well-educated people among them, including a medical doctor.

"If you ever need any help, just let us know," they would say solicitously to my father-in-law, then proceed to ask him to bring supplies out to them from Frai in his station wagon. Poor Papá Eustaquio. He dared not refuse.

One time they wanted him to take them two tons of corn. "If I buy all that corn in Frai, it will make people suspicious," he told them. "The army might even come out to investigate, and I know you don't

The Move Home

want that. The most I can bring you without arousing anyone's suspicions is one quarter of a ton."

"Let the army come!" they boasted. "We will deal with them."

But they didn't try to force him to bring the whole two tons of corn that they wanted. My father-in-law was fortunate.

In time the army did find out about the presence of the guerrillas on Papá Eustaquio's land. "Why are the guerrillas camped on your land?" the official demanded of my father-in-law.

Papá Eustaquio answered with dignity. "As you know, I am an ex-military man myself. The guerrillas could kill me for that. Also, I did not ask them to come and camp on my land. They take up their abode wherever they please, without inquiring first as to whether or not they are welcome. You know also that I am a Christian, and I do not take sides in matters pertaining to politics."

"Yes, I know, I know," muttered the official.

One day there was a big shoot-out between the guerrillas and the army on Papá Eustaquio's land, and the official demanded that my father-in-law use his Toyota station wagon as an ambulance to transport the wounded soldiers to the nearest medical facility. This of course would mean that the guerrillas might kill him, but no one dared to refuse to comply with the wishes or demands of anyone pertaining to the army.

Papá Eustaquio spoke to the official like a wise old chief. "My hired chauffeur is not here. You may use the vehicle, but you will have to provide a driver." The official scratched his head. "I need to stay with my men and oversee the shooting, but I must also drive the wounded soldiers into town to the clinic."

Papá Eustaquio cleared his throat. "My wife, my son, and I will accompany you." (Irene, the spastic one, had never married, and he still lived with his folks. He was their errand boy and right-hand man.)

The official looked sharply at my father-in-law. "Why do you want to go with me? You must stay here."

Papá Eustaquio held his ground with a kind of fatherly sternness. "Since you are availing yourself of the use of my vehicle, the least you can do in return is to protect me and my family. If we remain here while you are using my station wagon, in all likelihood the guerrillas will kill us before you return."

"OK, OK. Call your family and come get in, but hurry!" On the way to Frai the official said to Papá Eustaquio, "I hear you have been carrying supplies to the guerrillas in this rig. What do you have to say for yourself?"

"You know that I too am a military man. You also know that one does not refuse to comply with the wishes of the guerrillas and live. Also, as a Christian, it is my duty to help all people who need my help without regards to their political bias."

"Now if you want to kill me, go ahead. I am not afraid to die. You might as well do it right now and get it over with."

"No, no," said the official. "I would not kill a man like you. You have the heroic spirit of a true son of our beloved country. Guatemala needs more people like you."

When he had returned home and the shoot-out was over and the army had taken their leave, the guerrillas soon visited Papá Eustaquio. "Why did you let the army use your vehicle during the shoot-out? Don't you know that when you help the army, you are betraying your country?"

"As you know," my wise old father-in-law told them, "to have refused my vehicle to the army official would have meant death to me and my family. But that is not the reason why I complied with his wishes. I am a Christian, and as such, I consider it my duty to help all people who come to me in need, without regards to their political bias.

The Move Home

But if you want to kill me, I am not afraid to die. Go ahead and get it over with now!"

But the guerrillas had come to respect Papá Eustaquio. "We would not kill you," they told him. "Guatemala needs more people just like you. And in order not to cause you further trouble, we are going to move off of your land tonight. Also, we have seventy-thousand fine guerrilla soldiers stationed in the jungles all over Guatemala. We are going to send word to protect you wherever you may travel."

Unimpressed by the generous promise of protection from the guerrillas, Papá Eustaquio decided at last to sell his farm and return to his home in Valparaíso soon after that. (The man who bought Papá Eustaquio's parcel of land was very fortunate. There is now an oil well right behind where the little house was.)

The family were delighted that Papá Eustaquio and Mamá Tona were moving home, and they set about helping the folks get back home as soon as possible.

The district of Huehueteriango had grown so much that not long before it had been divided into two districts. So now there was a new pastor and his wife who needed a place to live. Papá Eustaquio and Mamá Tona rented half of the house to the young pastoral couple, living in the other half of the house themselves.

It was a nice arrangement and all went well until one day when Irene was working hard at cleaning out the old warehouse that had served to store coffee before the move to Cebol.

Irene noticed a strange object and picked it up and looked at it carefully, turning it over in his hand. It was not uncommon to dig up ancient artifacts from the Mayan Indians when planting coffee, corn, or beans. Assuming that this strange object must be something like that, Irene set about cleaning and scraping off the rust and mud that was caked onto it.

Hope That Springs Eternal

After about forty minutes Irene decided that the strange object was now clean enough to take into the house to show to the pastor's wife. When he got inside, he found her visiting with Marta, a cousin who lived nearby, and her little three-year-old daughter. The small girl's thick, long hair was braided into two very heavy french braids. Her eyes danced with excitement.

"What is that thing in your hand, Uncle Irene?" she asked in a high-pitched voice.

"I don't know, but I think it must be an ancient Indian artifact," Irene answered, trying hard to contain his own excitement. He held it out to the pastor's wife. "I spent a long time cleaning it up so you could look at it" he added.

The pastor's wife paled when she saw it. "My dear brother, you must get that out of here quickly!" she exclaimed. "It is a bomb of some kind."

Irene had not known it, but he was handling a grenade. Obediently, he turned to carry it outside and lay it down carefully someplace far away from the house. The small girl pattered along right behind him. They had not gotten any farther than the front step of the house when the grenade went off right in Irene's hand.

Upon hearing the terrifying explosion, Mamá Tona rushed from the kitchen to see what had happened. The other two ladies hurried from the room where they had been visiting. They found that Irene had been blown to bits; the little girl was still in one piece, but she was also dead.

Everyone was shocked and grief stricken, but no one could possibly be as heartbroken as the two bereaved mothers. In spite of their grief, Papá Eustaquio and Mamá Tona decided to have a large, conventional funeral so that the pastor could preach an evangelistic sermon to the people of the neighborhood who would come to eat and offer their sympathy.

The Move Home

All of the relatives from Chalum came down, everyone bringing something to contribute, and they wept as they prepared the great amount of food.

The pastor said he felt too overwhelmed to be able to preach a sermon that night, but at last he was able to control his sorrow enough to stand before the people and tell them about the blessed hope of the resurrection of all those who die in the Lord.

At first the official at the nearby military base refused permission to have the funeral because he thought the guerrillas might come and attack during the service. But upon examining the grenade, it was discovered that it belonged to the army, and therefore had not been tossed into the warehouse by the guerrillas.

After a little investigation, it was discovered that the grenade had been thrown into the warehouse by some drunken soldiers who had fought each other a few feet away on the highway several months before. There was a country saloon nearby that sold liquor and other pleasures to the young soldier boys from the military base. All of the other grenades that had been thrown around in the ditches were picked up, but no one had known about the one that landed inside of Papá Eustaquio'a warehouse.

All of the personnel from the military base attended the all-night funeral service to show their respect for the relatives of the deceased. After that, even though the soldier boys who were stationed at the base at this time were not the same ones who had thrown the grenades around months before, they were put on "military discipline" to show the people the army's disapproval of such behavior. Sometimes I am tempted to think that it might have been more effective if they had just blown up the saloon instead.

Irene and the little girl died in May 1992. Time passes by quickly and no one can tell what the future may bring. But I am sure of this: the coming of our Lord is not far off, and we will be seeing some amazing things happen before our very eyes in the future. May the Lord give each of his people faith and courage to cope with whatever may come.

Ellen G. White wrote, "We have nothing to fear for the future, except as we shall forget the way the Lord had led us, and his teaching in our past history" (*Life Sketches*, p.196).

My friend, I hope you have found these stories encouraging and uplifting. But this brief sketch that I have written of events in my life and in the lives of some of my friends is only "part of the story." We will hear "the rest of the story" when we walk and talk with Jesus beside the river of life. In the meantime, let me say that God is no respecter of persons. He will perform miracles for you and for me if we let Him.

In closing, I want to share a poem with you that I wrote. May we all stay faithful to God and meet one day in heaven.

COME UP HIGHER
The great angelic anthems,
so full of melody and praise,
perhaps could not express
the way a sinner prays,
whose sins have been erased-forgiven,
for he is God's own child!

We smile into the sunshine,
and sing our songs of love and praise;
but angels stoop to listen
to a sinner when he prays.
For though he's been redeemed-forgiven,
God chastens his dear child.

The Move Home

"My children, come up higher,
come higher, higher, higher!
You'll sing of Moses and the Lamb,
my precious, blood-bought choir!"

The servant is not greater
than Jesus Christ who walked the way
of sacrifice and pain.
Our sins upon Him weighed;
He was shut out from God and heaven,
God's own begotten child!

His children must be baptized,
and drink the cup and walk the way
of sacrifice and pain;
and angels come to weigh
out teardrops in the scales of heaven,
for we are each God's child!

"My children, come up higher,
come higher, higher, higher!
You'll sing of Moses and the Lamb,
my precious, blood-bought choir!"

Epilogue

*Q*uite a few years have passed since the last words of this book were penned, and we've all changed in one way or another, although I'm sure I'd still enjoy playing with some old machine parts now and then! Papá Eustaquio and Grandma Iris passed away at the ripe ages of ninety-nine and ninety, respectively, and I am anxiously awaiting the day when the trumpet sounds and I get to see them again.

Immediately after the events of this book, my parents continued life as normal, but they slowly drifted toward spending more time in the States. During my childhood, we traveled back and forth from Guatemala to the States quite often, and I have very fond memories of the many years I had growing up there, although my own adventures were nowhere near as exciting as the ones told in this book!

We settled quasi-permanently in Georgia the year I started academy so I could have a place to come home to when I was on vacations and also because my mother's immune system had taken its toll serving in the jungles of Guatemala and it finally refused to fight back anymore.

Although my dad still travels back to Guatemala regularly to keep tabs on the coffee farm and visit relatives, school and such have kept me from visiting for more than a week or two. However, even on my short trips home, I can tell that Guatemala is drastically changing. It is no longer the Guatemala of my childhood and even less that of the stories of this book. The twenty-first century has reached even the most remote parts of Guatemala, and I must confess that the influences it has brought have not been good ones. Cell phones, television, and access to the "outside" world—although good things in and of themselves—have opened large windows of opportunity for the enemy to corrupt those who are willing to give him a foothold. Now more than ever, the secular, materialistic lifestyle of America is envied and emulated by the Guatemalan people, making the spread of God's wonderfully good news all the more difficult.

My mother once had a dream in which the whole stretch of highway between Camojallito and La Mesilla—a good 14 miles—was completely built up with businesses and houses. This idea seemed preposterous at the time given that both "towns" were nothing more than a small collection of ramshackle houses with one or two small house-stores. However, on my last visit to Guatemala, I marveled at how even since my previous trip the numbers of houses, buildings, and such along the road had doubled and even tripled in some places. It is now just as my mother dreamed, and it is growing every day. Urbanization has brought its woes, and where as before people had to brave the perils of living amidst a civil war, now they face the dangers of rampant drug-related crime and a government that for the most part stands by, doing nothing.

Although I lament the perils that have befallen Guatemala and would love nothing more than to go back to the Guatemala of my childhood and of these stories, I know it is just one more sign that this world is suffering greatly and that Jesus' return is nearer than ever. Many of the evangelists and preachers in this book have grown old, but the seeds they planted have flourished and grown amazingly, and the beautiful message of God's love is still being spread. Even I haven't been able to escape God's calling, and I am hoping that soon after I graduate with my bachelor's degree in civil engineering I will be able to do my part in hastening His coming. My prayer is that these stories have been as much of a blessing to you as they were to me during my childhood. I also pray that one day we may all gather together under the tree of life and meet many of the extraordinary characters from this book. Until then, may God bless you abundantly as you continue to grow in His love and truth.

Ismaias Lemuel "Lemmy" Recinos

"Then He said to them, 'The harvest truly *is* great, but the laborers *are* few; therefore pray the Lord of the harvest to send out laborers into His harvest" (Luke 10:2, NKJV).

We invite you to view the complete
selection of titles we publish at:

www.LNFBooks.com

or write or email us your praises,
reactions, or thoughts about this
or any other book we publish at:

TEACH Services, Inc.
P.O. Box 954
Ringgold, GA 30736

info@TEACHServices.com

www.ingramcontent.com/pod-product-compliance
Lightning Source LLC
Chambersburg PA
CBHW071605170426
43196CB00033B/1786